Advances in Pattern Recognition

Advances in Pattern Recognition is a series of books which brings together current developments in all areas of this multi-disciplinary topic. It covers both theoretical and applied aspects of pattern recognition, and provides texts for students and senior researchers.

Springer also publishes a related journal, **Pattern Analysis and Applications**. For more details see: http://springlink.com

The book series and journal are both edited by Professor Sameer Singh of Loughborough University, UK.

Also in this series:

Principles of Visual Information Retrieval
Michael S. Lew (Ed.)
1-85233-381-2

Statistical and Neural Classifiers: An Integrated Approach to Design
Šarūnas Raudys
1-85233-297-2

Advanced Algorithmic Approaches to Medical Image Segmentation
Jasjit Suri, Kamaledin Setarehdan and Sameer Singh (Eds)
1-85233-389-8

NETLAB: Algorithms for Pattern Recognition
Ian T. Nabney
1-85233-440-1

Object Recognition: Fundamentals and Case Studies
M. Bennamoun anf G.J. Mamic
1-85233-398-7

Computer Vision Beyond the Visible Spectrum
Bir Bhanu and Ioannis Pavlidis (Eds)
1-85233-604-8

Hexagonal Image Processing: A Practical Approach
Lee Middleton and Jayanthi Sivaswamy
1-85233-914-4

Support Vector Machines for Pattern Classification
Shigeo Abe
1-85233-929-2

Digital Document Processing
Bidyut B. Chaudhuri (Ed.)
978-1-84628-501-1

Sameer Singh • Maneesha Singh

Editors

Progress in Pattern Recognition

 Springer

Sameer Singh, PhD
Maneesha Singh, PhD
Research School of Informatics, Loughborough University, Loughborough, UK

Series editor
Professor Sameer Singh, PhD
Research School of Informatics, Loughborough University, Loughborough, UK

British Library Cataloguing in Publication Data
A catalogue record for this book is available from the British Library

Advances in Pattern Recognition Series ISSN 1617-7916
ISBN 13: 978-1-84996-683-2   e-ISBN-13: 978-1-84628-945-3

Printed on acid-free paper

9 8 7 6 5 4 3 2 1

Springer Science+Business Media
springer.com

Organisation

Executive Committee

Conference Chair

Sameer Singh
(Loughborough University, UK)

Organizing Chair

Sameer Singh
(Loughborough University, UK)

Maneesha Singh
(Loughborough University, UK)

Organizing Manager

Chatrina O'Mara
(Loughborough University, UK)

Programme Committee

Alberto Del Bimbo
University of Florence
Italy

Ana Fred
Institute of Telecommunication
Portugal

B. B. Chaudhuri
Indian Statistical Institute
India

Boaz Lerner
Ben-Gurion University
Israel

Bob Duin
Technical University Delft
Netherlands

Christophe Garcia
France Télécom R&D
France

Daniel P. Lopresti
Lehigh University
USA

Edoardo Ardizzone
University of Palermo
Italy

Fabio Roli
University of Cagliari
Italy

Filiberto Pla
Universitat Jaume I
Spain

Geoff West
Curtin University
Australia

Godfried Toussaint
McGill University
Canada

Hans Burkhardt
University of Freiberg
Germany

Heather Ruskin
Dublin City University
Ireland

Jasjit Suri
Biomedical Technologies
USA

Jean-Michel Jolion
INSA
France

Jesse Jin
University of Newcastle
Australia

John McCall
Robert Gordon University
UK

Jonathan Hull
Ricoh Innovations Inc.
USA

Louisa Lam
Hong Kong Institute of Education
China

Ludmila Kuncheva
University Wales, Bangor
UK

Luigi P. Cordella
University of Napoli
Italy

Mads Nielsen
University of Copenhagen
Denmark

Mahesan Niranjan
University of Sheffield
UK

Mario Figueiredo
Institute for Telecommunication
Portugal

Mario Vento
University of Salerno
Italy

Mark Last
Ben-Gurion University
Israel

Martin Crane
Dublin City University
Ireland

Mayer Aladjem
Ben-Gurion University
Israel

Michal Haindl
Academy of Sciences
Czech Republic

Miroslaw Pawlak
University of Manitoba
Canada

Peter Meer
Rutgers University
USA

R D Boyle
University of Leeds
UK

Daming Shi
Nanyang Techological University
Singapore

Malcolm Strens
QinetiQ
UK

Vittorio Murino
University of Verona
Italy

Witold Pedrycz
University of Alberta
Canada

Xiang "Sean" Zhou
Siemens Corporate Research Inc.
USA

Xiaoyi Jiang
University of Munster
Germany

Nicu Sebe
University of Amsterdam
Netherlands

Peter Tino
University of Birmingham
UK

Ross Beveridge
Colorado State University
USA

Steve Maybank
Birkbeck College
UK

Venu Govindaraju
State University of New York
USA

Vladimir Pavlovic
Rutgers University
USA

Wojtek Krzanowski
University of Exeter
UK

Xiao Hui Liu
Brunel University
UK

Preface

Overview and Goals

Pattern recognition has evolved as a mature field of data analysis and its practice involves decision making using a wide variety of machine learning tools. Over the last three decades, substantial advances have been made in the areas of classification, prediction, optimisation and planning algorithms. In particular, the advances made in the areas of non-linear classification, statistical pattern recognition, multi-objective optimisation, string matching and uncertainty management are notable. These advances have been triggered by the availability of cheap computing power which allows large quantities of data to be processed in a very short period of time, and therefore developed algorithms can be tested easily on real problems. The current focus of pattern recognition research and development is to take laboratory solutions to commercial applications.

The main goal of this book is to provide researchers with some of the latest novel techniques in the area of pattern recognition, and to show the potential of such techniques on real problems. The book will provide an excellent background to pattern recognition students and researchers into latest algorithms for pattern matching, and classification and their practical applications for imaging and non-imaging applications.

Organization and Features

The book is organised in two parts. The first nine chapters of the book describe novel advances in the areas of graph matching, information fusion, data clustering and classification, feature extraction and decision making under uncertainty. A wide variety of application areas are addressed within the first part including intrusion detection, protein prediction and stock market trading. The second part of the book focuses specifically on biometrics which is one of the fastest growth areas that applies pattern recognition algorithms. The chapters included cover face image analysis, human dynamics, text modelling, character and barcode recognition, iris recognition, and environment context recognition. The key feature of all chapters is the emphasis on solving real complex problems, and suggesting advanced theoretical tools that often build upon previous work as well as demonstrate lateral thinking.

Target Audience

The target audience for this book include academics, university research staff and students, and research staff in R&D companies with a research interest in pattern recognition, machine learning and data mining. It is expected that practitioners working in the areas of engineering, and IT sectors will find this book particularly interesting and useful.

Suggested Uses

The book can be used as a research reference book. Several of the algorithms mentioned in the chapters can be programmed by readers, and used in their own application area.

Acknowledgements

We owe special thanks to the contributing authors and to the reviewers of the chapters presented in this book. The content of this book was also presented at the International Workshop on Advances in Pattern Recognition (IWAPR, 2007). We would like to thank IWAPR administrator Chatrina O' Mara, and Dr. Chris Hinde for help with organising technical matter, and Springer staff for their organisation of this book. The workshop was deemed very successful by the participants, and we plan to organize future workshops of the same kind.

Prof. Sameer Singh
Dr. Maneesha Singh

Research School of Informatics
Loughborough University
Loughborough LE11 3TU
UK

Contents

Part I Pattern Matching and Classification

Part II Biometrics

Part I
Pattern Matching and Classification

1 Estimation in Feedback Loops by Stochastic Learning

Geir Horn[1] and B. John Oommen[2] * **

[1] SIMULA Research Laboratory
    P.O. Box 134
    1325 Lysaker, Norway
    Geir.Horn@simula.no
[2] School of Computer Science
    Carleton University
    Ottawa, ON K1S 5B6, Canada
    oommen@scs.carleton.ca

Abstract. There are many *black box* situations where a system has limited observability: The only observable quantity is whether the object under study reacts positively or negatively to a certain stimuli. Given that each possible stimulus posesses an unknown probability for a positive reaction, the problem is to *estimate* these probabilities from the sequence of positive or negative responses. The maximum likelihood approach would be to try each kind of stimulus a large number of times, record the number of positive responses and estimate the probability as the ratio between the number of times the action has received a positive response to the number of times the action has been tried. This is a rather slow process and is further unsuitable for unstationary settings. This paper proposes a novel estimator based on *learning* the underlying probabilities using the principles of the *linear reward penalty learning automaton*. Apart from deriving its formal properities, it is shown, by simulation, that the proposed estimator converges faster than the maximum likelihood estimator. This is a useful property for situations where the system's underlying response probabilities may abruptly change over time.

1.1 Introduction

Many cybernetic systems are impossible or too complex to model to the desired level of accuracy. They consequently remain *black box* systems. Examples are complex chemical reactions, or for instance, patients under medical treatment. There is a set of inputs or stimuli one may try, and the only observable information is whether the reaction moves in the positive direction, or whether the patients' condition seems to improve. It is often the case that the feedback is not consequent and the same stimulus may have different effects depending on other unknown states of the studied system.

---

* *Chancellor's Professor* ; *Fellow of the IEEE* and *Fellow of the IAPR*

** This author also holds an *Adjunct Professorship* with the Department of Information and Communication Technology, Agder University College, Grooseveien 36, N-4876 Grimstad, Norway.

One may think of this system as a black box reacting positively or negatively to each type of stimulus according to an unknown underlying probability distribution described by a vector s of probabilities to respond positively to a given stimuli, input or *action*. The issue of system identification, without a parametrised model of the system, then becomes the question of estimating this unknown probability vector from the sequence of observable positive or negative feedback responses to the input.

The intuitive approach of *maximum likelihood* estimation (MLE) would be to try each kind of stimuli in random order a certain number of times, record the number of positive responses and estimate the probability as the ratio between the number of times the action has received a positive response to the number of times the action has been tried. This is a rather slow process. It can also be prohibitive since it may be necessary to try an unfavourable input quite a few times in order to gather sufficient confidence in the estimated value. It will for instance be unethical to continue to randomly administer treatments to patients after a period when it is well known that no patient has ever responeded positively to a given treatment. Furthermore, in order to produce valid unbiased estimates, the action to be tried should be independent of the previous actions and hence independent of the feedback obtained from the system.

Although the MLE is well-known for having good computational and statistical properties, the fundamental premise for establishing the quality of estimates is based on the assumption that the probabilities being estimated does not change with time. In other words, the distribution s is assumed to be *stationary*. Then, as the number of samples increases, the estimate, $\hat{s}$, will converge to s with probability 1, and in a mean square sense. In a stationary situation one can not do better than the MLE.

Consider a scenario where the underlying system is known to undergo a rapid or abrupt state change as a function of the accumulated stimuli. The traditional strategy to deal with such non-stationary situations has been to use the MLE with a *sliding window* [1]. The problem with such a "sliding window" is that the width of the window is crucial. If the width is too "small", the estimates are necessarily poor. On the other hand, if the window is "large", the estimates prior to the change of the abrupt state change influence the new estimates significantly. Also, the observations during the entire sliding window must be retained: When the next sample is observed, the least recent observation must be deleted, and the current observation must take its place.

Apart from the sliding window approach, many other methods have been proposed, which deal with the problem of detecting change points during estimation [2], including the Bayesian method for point detection in stochastic processes [3], and the sequential change-point detection and estimation method (based on approximations from large samples and the null hypothesis) [4]. Another method recently proposed [5] deals with the problem of detecting the changes in the parameters of the distributions.

This paper proposes an estimator based on *learning* the underlying system probabilities within the repeated feedback loop using the techniques of *learning automata*. This means that the estimates will be updated taking the full feedback history into account, and the actions or stimuli tried will be based on the current estimates for the reward probabilities. Hence, the proposed estimator is more likely to try an action that has previously seen a positive response, than the stimuli receiving negative responses.

In all brevity, the proposed estimator is quite different from all the above mentioned alternatives. First of all, unlike the work of [3], our method does not require the assumption of any prior distributions for the underlying probabilities. It is also different from [4] because it does not infer the change in the system state by invoking a hypothesis testing strategy. Neither does the method proposed here implicitly assume the large sample approximations of the index used to infer the change, which in their case is the score vector. Finally, the proposed estimator is quite distinct from the other techniques proposed in [2] because it does not invoke any likelihood ratio tests or cumulative sum tests. An approach that is related to the present contribution is that of estimating the log-normal multivariate distribution in non-stationary environments [6].

The closest relative is, however, the recently introduced Stochastic Weak Learning Estimator (SLWE) [7]. As the present estimator, is the SLWE also based on learning. However, it only takes the positive system feedback into account and ignores the negative feedback. The estimator proposed here uses both the positive and negative feedback signals.

Furthermore, *all* of the above estimators assumes that the system stimuli or action is mutually independent, and in particular independent of the estimates. This estimator is, to the present authors' knowledge, the first estimator that allows the system stimuli to be based on the current estimates, and still succeeds in estimating the underlying system probabilities. This makes it useful for a wide range of applications where the estimator has to be used in the control loop.

The first part of this paper, Section 2 introduces the basic concepts and derives the estimator for the binomial case, i.e. with only two system probabilities. Section 3 generalises the concept to the multinomial case. Both sections contains simulation results to support the theoretical results. In the interest of brevity, no proofs will be given in this paper.

1.2 Binomial estimation

Assume that the elements $x(k) \in \{1, 2\}$ of the binary observed sequence have probability s_1 and $1 - s_1$ respectively. These are to be estimated using a linear reward-penalty automaton maintaining two probabilities p_1 and $p_2 = 1 - p_1$ for the two possible outcomes. The action chosen by the automaton at iteration k is a random variable that with probability p_1 and p_2, attains the value $\alpha(k) = 1$ or $\alpha(k) = 2$ respectively. When the action value is compared with the observed value a *reward*, $\beta(k) = 1$, is generated if the action matches the observed value, $x(k) = \alpha(k)$, and a *penalty*, $\beta(k) = 0$, otherwise. This system is depicted in Figure 1. The four different outcomes are given in Table 1 together with their probabilities.

Result 1.2.1(Binomial Probability Model) *The probability model defined by Table 1 is consistent*

$$Pr[\beta(k) = 0] + Pr[\beta(k) = 1] = 1$$

Q.E.D.

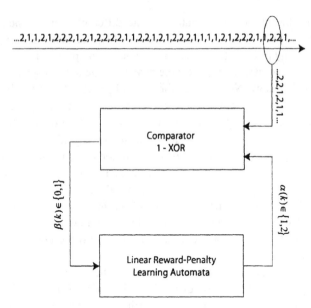

Fig. 1. The estimator system: The estimating automaton proposes an action $\alpha(k)$ that is compared with the observed observation $x(k)$. If $x(k) = \alpha(k)$ a *reward*, $\beta(k) = 1$, is returned as a feedback to the automaton, that, in turn, updates its action probabilities before chosing the next action.

Table 1 The observations $x(k)$ and the automaton action $\alpha(k)$ yields four different comparison outcomes $\beta(k)$ with their associated probabilities as below

	$x(k) = 0$	$x(k) = 1$
	$\Pr[x = 0] = s_1$	$\Pr[x = 1] = 1 - s_1$
$\alpha(k) = 0$	$\beta(k) = 1$	$\beta(k) = 0$
$\Pr[\alpha(k) = 0] = p_1(k)$	$s_1 p_1(k)$	$(1 - s_1)p_1(k)$
$\alpha(k) = 1$	$\beta(k) = 0$	$\beta(k) = 1$
$\Pr[\alpha(k) = 1] = 1 - p_1(k)$	$s_1(1 - p_1(k))$	$(1 - s_1)(1 - p_1(k))$

Table 2 The different updates possible for the automata probability based on the action chosen $\alpha(k)$ and the outcome $\beta(k)$. The event probabilities are taken from Table 2

$p_1(k + 1)$	Event		Probability	Outcome
$1 - \lambda_R p_2(k)$	$\alpha(k) = 0$ and	$x(k) = 0$	$s_1 p_1(k)$	Reward
$\lambda_P p_1(k)$	$\alpha(k) = 0$ and	$x(k) = 1$	$(1 - s_1)p_1(k)$	Penalty
$1 - \lambda_P p_2(k)$	$\alpha(k) = 1$ and	$x(k) = 0$	$s_1(1 - p_1(k))$	Penalty
$\lambda_R p_1(k)$	$\alpha(k) = 1$ and	$x(k) = 1$	$(1 - s_1)(1 - p_1(k))$	Reward

The idea behind the Linear Reward-Penalty automaton (L_{R-P}) is to increase the action probability for a chosen action if a reward is received, and to decrease the probability if a penalty is received. Let $0 < \lambda_R < 1$ be the learning constant used when the response is a reward and $0 < \lambda_P < 1$ be the learning constant used for penalties. Table 1 lists the possible events and the corresponding updated values of $p_1(k+1)$ with their associated probabilities from Table 1.

1.2.1 Convergengence and the Expected Value

Normally, in learning, one wants to be able to identify the action posessing the largest reward probability, and it is desirable that the automaton eventually selects *only* this action. By ignoring the penalties, $\lambda_P = 0$ it can be proven [8] that the resulting reward-inaction automaton is ϵ-optimal. In other words, if $s_1 > s_2$ we can make $p_1 \to 1$ and always select $\alpha = 1$. This is obviously not what is desired for an estimator trying to identify the true probability s_1, and because of the non-stationary environment an ergodic scheme is needed. Treating rewards and penalties the same, by setting $\lambda_R = \lambda_P = \lambda$ will give the desired ergodic scheme.

Theorem 1 (Expected value). *The expected value of the L_{R-P} binomial estimator at iteration k is*

$$E\left[p_1(k)\right] = \left(1 - \lambda^k\right) s_1 + \lambda^k p_1(0) \tag{1}$$

where $p_1(0)$ is the action probability initially assigned for action 1 by the automaton.
Proof: The proof is found in [9].   Q.E.D.

Taking the limit shows that the expected value of the estimator equals asymptotically the unknown system probability

$$\lim_{k \to \infty} E\left[p_1(k)\right] = s_1 + \left(p_1(0) - s_1\right) \lim_{k \to \infty} \lambda^k = s_1 \tag{2}$$

The result follows since $\lim_{k \to \infty} \lambda^k = 0$ when $0 < \lambda < 1$.

1.2.2 Variance

Theorem 2 (Binomial variance). *The variance of the estimate $p_1(k)$ of the L_{R-P} estimator is given as*

$$\mathrm{Var}\left[p_1(k)\right] = ak\lambda^{2k} + \frac{b\left(\lambda^{2k} - 1\right)}{\lambda^2 - 1} + \lambda^{2k}\mathrm{Var}\left[p_1(0)\right] \tag{3}$$

Proof: See [9].   Q.E.D.

Taking the limit of the variance as $k \to \infty$ gives

$$\lim_{k \to \infty} \mathrm{Var}\left[p_1(k)\right] = \lim_{k \to \infty} \left(ak\lambda^{2k}\right)$$
$$+ \lim_{k \to \infty} \left(\frac{b\lambda^{2k}}{\lambda^2 - 1} - \frac{b}{\lambda^2 - 1}\right)$$
$$+ \lim_{k \to \infty} \lambda^{2k}\mathrm{Var}\left[p_1(0)\right]$$
$$= a \lim_{k \to \infty} \left(k\lambda^{2k}\right) - \frac{b}{\lambda^2 - 1} \tag{4}$$

The first term will obviously go to zero with increasing k since $0 < \lambda < 1$. However, if λ is close to unity this convergence may be quite slow since the term will first increase linearly before being dominated by the term λ^{2k}. The maximum is attained for $k = k^+$ satisfying

$$a \left. \frac{d\left(k\lambda^{2k}\right)}{dk} \right|_{k=k^+} = 0$$

$$\lambda^{2k^+} + 2k^+\lambda^{2k^+} \log(\lambda) = 0$$

$$1 + 2k^+ \log(\lambda) = 0$$

$$k^+ = -\frac{1}{2\log(\lambda)}$$

This implies that the variance will increase with the number of iterations as the learning parameter λ increases. As examples, $\lambda = 0.99$ yields $k^+ = 49.7$, while $\lambda = 0.999$ results in $k^+ = 499.7$.

Corollary 1 (Asymptotic binomial variance). *The variance of the binomial estimator converges to*

$$\lim_{k\to\infty} Var\left[p_1(k)\right] = \frac{1-\lambda}{1+\lambda}\left(s_1 - s_1^2\right) \tag{5}$$

Proof: Follows from the theorem above and can be found in [9].   *Q.E.D.*

Here $s_1^2 \leq s_1$, because $0 \leq s_1 \leq 1$, with equality to be achieved only in the extreme case with the maximum difference attained for $s_1 = 1/2$. In the same way, only as $\lambda \to 1$ will the variance go to zero at the expense of a rapidly increasing k^+ slowing down the convergence as pointed out above. The good feature of this estimator is that the mean value of (1) will more rapidly converge to the true s_1 for smaller values of λ.

1.2.3 Initialisation

The true underlying probability $s_1 \in [0,1]$ is unknown. One could chose the initial probability of the automaton to any fixed value in this interval, or one could draw one value at random. The latter makes the starting point $p_1(0) \in [0,1]$ a uniform random variable with expectation and variance [10]

$$E\left[p_1(0)\right] = \frac{1}{2} \tag{6}$$

$$Var\left[p_1(0)\right] = \frac{1}{12} \tag{7}$$

1.2.4 Simulation

To investigate the ability of the estimator to follow a non-stationary underlying probability the following simulation parameters were used:

- The underlying probability s_1 is assigned a new randomly generated value after every 50 iterations.
- 500 iterations are simulated.
- The reported estimate is the *ensemble* average over 1000 simulations.
- The value of the learning parameter λ is drawn randomly in the interval $[0.9, 0.99]$ for the full ensemble, i.e. the same λ is used for all the 1000 simulations in the ensemble.
- A Maximum Likelihood Estimator (MLE) with a sliding window was used for comparison. The window size was drawn randomly over the interval $[20, 80]$. As is the case of λ, also the window size was kept fixed for all the simulation runs in the ensemble.

  A fundamental assumption for the MLE is that the observations have to be independent from the estimates. This implies that it can not be used for in loop estimation like the one studied here. To allow the comparison for this paper, the "actions" presented to the environment had to be drawn uniformly. Note that this will actually prevent its use many experimental situations.

These parameters were chosen to allow comparison with the results reported in [7, Fig. 1-4] for the SLWE estimator. The results in Figure 2 clearly shows that the value of the learning parameter, λ, is not so important for the L_{R-P} estimator's ability to follow the changing environment. However, the MLE is critically dependent on the size of the sliding window. If this happens to be larger than the stationary period of 50 samples of the underlying probabilities, the MLE may fail dramatically as can be seen in Figure 2(d).

1.3 Multinomial Estimation

1.3.1 Probability Model and Updating Rules

The binary binomial situation above can be generalised to the situation where the observations can take r different values $1, \ldots, r$ with probability distribution $\mathbf{s} = [s_1, \ldots, s_r]^T$. At the same time the automaton maintains a vector of probabilities $\mathbf{p}(k) = [p_1(k), \ldots, p_r(k)]^T$. The set up is the same as in Figure 1 with the difference that there are now r different actions and observations possible.

The probability model is $\mathbf{P}(k) = \mathbf{p}(k) \otimes \mathbf{s}$, where $\otimes$ is the tensor product or outer product. $\mathbf{P}$ is a matrix whose columns are $\mathbf{p}(k)s_1, \ldots, \mathbf{p}(k)s_r$. Thus the sum of the elements in each column is $s_1, \ldots, s_r$ respectively, and adding the column sums together gives unity proving that this is a proper probability model. Since rewards will be given whenever $x(k) = \alpha(k)$, and this occurs with probability $s_i p_i(k)$, the probability for a reward is the sum of the elements on the main diagonal of $\mathbf{P}$, i.e. $\Pr[\beta(k) = 1] = \sum_{i=1}^{r} s_i p_i(k)$.

The probabilities of the automaton will be updated according to the symmetric multiaction linear reward and penalty L_{R-P} scheme treating the penalties and rewards the same, i.e. $\lambda_R = \lambda_P = \lambda$. The different events and updates for the probability $p_i(k+1)$ of the chosen action $\alpha(k)$ are shown in Table 3. A couple of elements require

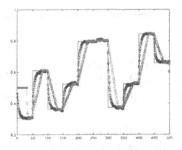 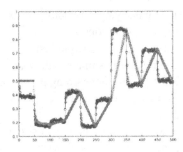

(a) $\lambda = 0.817318$ and the window size is 32

(b) $\lambda = 0.59153$ and the window size is 48

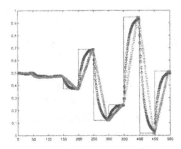 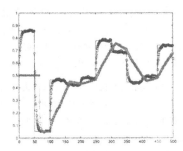

(c) $\lambda = 0.9234$ and the window size is 45

(d) $\lambda = 0.770685$ and the window size is 66

Fig. 2. The mean value of the $\hat{s}_1$ obtained from an ensemble of 1000 simulations. Both the L_{R-P} estimator (circles) and the windowed MLE (squares) are shown superinposed over the true s_1 value of the environment. Error bars are omitted for clarity

comments. First the case where $\alpha(k) = i$ and $x(k) = i$, i.e. the action chosen is based on the action probability vector and it is rewarded. Then all the other probabilities should be downscaled and so:

$$p_i(k+1) = 1 - \sum_{j \neq i} \lambda p_j(k)$$

$$= 1 - \lambda \sum_{j \neq i} p_j(k)$$

$$= 1 - \lambda \left[\left(\sum_{j=1}^{r} p_j(k) \right) - p_i(k) \right]$$

$$= 1 - \lambda \left[1 - p_i(k) \right]$$

$$= (1 - \lambda) + \lambda p_i(k)$$

Second, a normalising constant is necessary in the case of a penalty when $\alpha(k) = j$ and $x(k) \neq j$. The only information available in this case is that the action chosen

Table 3 The different updates possible for the automaton's probability $p_i(k+1)$ based on the action chosen $\alpha(k)$ and the outcome $\beta(k)$.

$p_i(k+1)$	Event			Probability	Outcome
$\lambda p_i(k)$	$\alpha(k) \neq i$	and	$x(k) = \alpha(k)$	$\sum_{j \neq i} s_j p_j(k)$	Reward
$(1 - \lambda) + \lambda p_i(k)$	$\alpha(k) = i$	and	$x(k) = i$	$s_i p_i(k)$	Reward
$\lambda p_i(k)$	$\alpha(k) = i$	and	$x(k) \neq i$	$(1 - s_i)p_i(k)$	Penalty
$\lambda p_i(k) + \frac{1-\lambda}{r-1}$	$\alpha(k) \neq i$	and	$x(k) \neq \alpha(k)$	$\sum_{j \neq i}(1 - s_j)p_j(k)$	Penalty

was wrong, but we do not know which is the right action that should see an increase in its probability. Thus, $p_j(k+1) = \lambda p_j(k)$, but how should the other probabilities $i \neq j$ be updated? Most of the probabilities should actually be downscaled since they do not correspond to the true underlying observation $x(k)$. The obvious choice is to downscale *all* the other probabilities should with λ. However, the vector $\mathbf{p}(k+1)$ should remain a probability vector and sum to unity. Hence there is a need to add a constant c to all the elements after downscaling to ensure that $\mathbf{p}(k+1)$ remains a probability vector:

$$1 = \sum_{m=1}^{r} p_m(k+1) = \lambda p_j(k) + \sum_{m \neq j}^{r} (\lambda p_m(k) + c)$$

$$1 = \left(\lambda \sum_{m=1}^{r} p_m(k) \right) + \left(\sum_{m \neq j}^{r} c \right)$$

$$1 = \lambda + (r - 1)c$$

and solving for the constant c gives

$$c = \frac{1 - \lambda}{r - 1}$$

1.3.2 Expectation

Theorem 3 (Expected probability). *The expected values of the action probabilities are*

$$\bar{p}_i = \frac{1/(1 - s_i)}{\sum_{j=1}^{r} 1/(1 - s_j)} \tag{8}$$

Proof: See [9]. Q.E.D.

The *estimator* $\hat{s}_i(k)$ for s_i has to be computed on the basis of the probabilities $\mathbf{p}(k)$ available at iteration k. Equation (8) seems to suggest that the estimator can be given by solving for s_i.

Definition 1 (Multinomial estimates). *Given the current action probabilities* $\mathbf{p}(k)$ *the estimates for the individual underlying probabilities are obtained as*

$$\hat{s}_i(k) = 1 - \frac{1}{C(\mathbf{p}(k))p_i(k)} \qquad (9)$$

where $C(\mathbf{p}(k))$ *is a normalising constant and a function of the current probabilities.*

Theorem 4 (Estimator constant). *Let the constant* $C(\mathbf{p}(k))$ *of (9) be given by*

$$C(\mathbf{p}(k)) = \frac{1}{r-1} \sum_{i=1}^{r} \frac{1}{p_i(k)} \qquad (10)$$

Then as $\mathbf{p}(k) \to \bar{\mathbf{p}}$ *the estimates* $\hat{s}_i \to s_i$. *Proof: See [9].*   Q.E.D.

1.3.3 Contraction of the probability space

The reader will observe that the transformation from $\mathbf{s}$ to $E\left[\mathbf{p}(k)\right]$ is quite direct, and that it obeys (8) . However, the irony of the computation process is that at any time instant, we do not have access to the *expected* value of $\mathbf{p}(k)$, but only to the current instantiation of $\mathbf{p}(k)$ obtained by virtue of the L_{R-P} rule. This poses an interesting dilemma. If (9) is used to get an estimate of $\hat{\mathbf{s}}(k)$ from $\mathbf{p}(k)$ (rather than from its *expected* value), it turns out that that the "learned" estimate may not be a probability vector, as some of its components may be negative. The reason for this anomaly[1] is that the full probability vector space of $\mathbf{s}$ is contracted under the transformation (8) so that only a subset of the probability vector space of the possible action probabilities $\mathbf{p}(k)$ actually corresponds to a valid underlying probability distribution $\mathbf{s}$.

This can be illustrated in the three dimensional situation. Figure 3(a) shows the probability space. Since $s_1 + s_2 + s_3 = 1$, all the valid points will lie in a single plane with base vectors

$$\mathbf{v}_1 = \begin{bmatrix} -1/\sqrt{2} \\ 1/\sqrt{2} \\ 0 \end{bmatrix} \quad \text{and} \quad \mathbf{v}_2 = \begin{bmatrix} -1/\sqrt{3} \\ -1/\sqrt{3} \\ 1/\sqrt{3} \end{bmatrix}$$

Figure 3(b) shows the s-probability space projected into this probability plane by the transformation

$$\begin{bmatrix} \xi_1 \\ \xi_2 \end{bmatrix} = \begin{bmatrix} -1/\sqrt{2} & 1/\sqrt{2} & 0 \\ -1/\sqrt{3} & -1/\sqrt{3} & 1/\sqrt{3} \end{bmatrix} \begin{bmatrix} s_1 \\ s_2 \\ s_3 \end{bmatrix} \qquad (11)$$

This shows the probability space of $\mathbf{s}$ in the form of an equilateral triangle as could be expected. Applying the mapping (8) to the s-space, the mapped points will stay in the same probability plane and the resulting space is shown in Figure 3(c) superimposed

---

[1] We are not aware of any estimation procedure which demonstrates such an anomalous phenomenon.

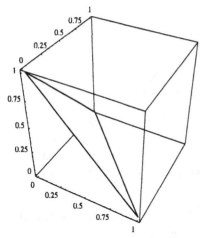

(a) The probability space for the underlying probabilities in three dimensions lies in a plane

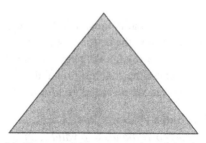

(b) The probability space viewed in the probability plane

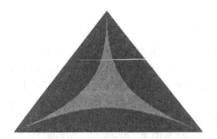

(c) The probability space contracted under the transformation (8) superimposed over the unrestricted action probability space of the automaton.

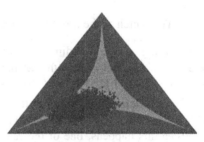

(d) A trajectory of an automaton in the action probabilities may move outside of the feasible region. The black dot indicates the expected action probability vector.

Fig. 3. The underlying probability space is contracted under the transformation to the expected value of the action probability vector. This leads to a situation where the automaton may move outside of the confined region such that the estimates no longer corresponds to a valid set of underlying probabilities.

over the unrestricted equilateral triangular space of the action probabilities **p**. This clearly illustrates that only a subset of the action probabilities will correspond to valid estimates.

In order for the estimates in (9) to be valid they have to fulfil $0 \leq \hat{s}_j(k) \leq 1$. The upper limit is obviously satisfied since both $C(\mathbf{p}(k))$ and $p_j(k)$ are positive. Thus, there is always a positive number subtracted in the last term of (9) making $\hat{s}_j(k) \leq 1$. However, can the subtracted number be so large that the estimate actually becomes negative?

In order to avoid this, it is evident that

$$\frac{1}{C(\mathbf{p}(k))p_j(k)} \leq 1$$

implies that:

$$\frac{1}{p_j(k)} \leq C(\mathbf{p}(k)) = \frac{1}{r-1}\sum_{i=1}^{r}\frac{1}{p_i(k)} \tag{12}$$

This last inequality must hold for all elements of the vector $\mathbf{p}(k)$. Thus a simple test to see if a point in the action probability space is a transformation of a set of probabilities s is to check the above inequality for the smallest action probability, $p_j = \inf \mathbf{p}(k)$. This because the smallest probability value will have the largest reciprocal value. This validity test can be stated as a formal result.

Theorem 5 (Validity test). *Let $p_{min}(k) = \inf\{\mathbf{p}(k)\}$. Then the vector of action probabilities corresponds to a valid estimate $\hat{s}(k)$ if and only if*

$$\frac{1}{p_{min}(k)} \leq \frac{1}{r-1}\sum_{i=1}^{r}\frac{1}{p_i(k)} \tag{13}$$

Proof. The sketch of the proof is given above. Q.E.D.

Returning to the three dimensional situation, Figure 3(d) shows a trace of 10000 iterations of an automaton with learning parameter $\lambda = 0.95$ starting from the initial position $\mathbf{p}(0) = [1/3, 1/3, 1/3]^T$. The underlying probabilities are $\mathbf{s} = [0.6, 0.3, 0.1]^T$ which maps close to the border of the feasible region, $\bar{\mathbf{p}} = [0.496, 0.283, 0.220]^T$. It is clearly seen that the automaton will move outside the feasible region.

When this happens, one of the estimates in $\hat{s}(k)$ will be negative. Arguably the best thing to do is then to set the negative estimate to zero and renormalise the estimate vector. This is the same as assuming that the automaton was exactly on the boundary of the feasible region. There is no need to change the automaton probabilities itself since this will create a discontinuous change of the probability vector and invalidate the above convergence analysis. It is fortunately possible to avoid this situation altogether as the following result shows.

Theorem 6 (Qualitative estimate validity). *There exist a learning parameter close to unity, $\lambda \geq 1 - \epsilon$ for $\epsilon > 0$, such that if the minimal underlying system probability is sufficiently greater than zero, the probability of obtaining illegal estimates will be arbitrarily small. Proof: See [9].*   *Q.E.D.*

1.3.4 Simulation

The simulation used the same parameters as for the binomial case in Section 2.4. The random selection of the single underlying probability was replaced with the random selection of a probability *vector* every 50 iterations. A four dimensional problem was considered to allow comparison with [7]. The Euclidean distance of the *estimates* away from the true underlying probability vector was used to quantify the a goodness of the estimation. The results are shown in Figure 4.

It is apparent that the L_{R-P} estimator converges faster than the MLE. However, it also exhibit larger stationary variance. The same parameters as in [7, Fig. 6] were used: $\lambda = 0.986232$ and the window size of the MLE was 43. The pattern seen is similar to their observation. However, if the MLE uses a window larger than the period length of the non-stationary environment, it will never have time to converge to the true values. In general it may be difficult to estimate the length of period between the changes of the underlying probability vector, and hence what window sizes can be used. With the L_{R-P} estimator proposed here, the length of the stationary period is not an issue.

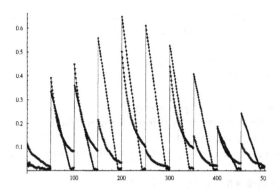

Fig. 4. The mean Euclidean distance between the underlying probability vector and the estimates for an ensemble of size 1000. The windowed MLE shows linear behaviour in its convergence, but fairly large initial errors, while the L_{R-P} estimator exhibit larger stationary variance.

1.4 Conclusion

This paper proposed a weak learning based estimator to be used in applications where it is impossible to directly observe the realisations of the underlying stochastic process. Apart from doing a formal rigorous analysis, an empirical analysis through simulations indicate that the proposed estimator converges faster than a sliding-window MLE when the underlying statistical distribution is time variate. This benefit comes at the expense of a larger stationary variance than what will eventually be achieved with the sliding-window MLE. The convergence of the proposed estimator is *weak*, i.e. it converges with regard to the first and second moments. The speed of convergence as well as the variance of the estimates decrease with the value of the learning parameter $0 < \lambda < 1$.

Acknowledgements

The authors would like to thank Dr. Dragos Calitoiu for inspiring discussions on the multinomial estimator.

References

Jang, Y.M.:

Estimation and Prediction-Based Connection Admission Control in Broadband Satellite Systems.

ETRI Journal **22**(4) (2000) 40–50

Krishnaiah, P., Miao, B.:

Review about estimation of change points.

In: Handook of Statistics. Volume 7., Amsterdan, Elsevier (1988) 375–402

Ray, B., Tsay, R.:

Bayesian Methods for Change-point Detection in Long-range Dependent Processes.

Journal of Time Series Analysis **23**(6) (2002) 687–705

Gombay, E.:

Sequential Change-point Detection and Estimation.

Sequential Analysis **22** (2003) 203–222

Baron, M., Grannot, N.:

Consistent estimation of early and frequent change points.

In: Foundation of Statistical Inference, Heidelberg, Springer (2003)

Ho, T., Stapleton, R., Subrahmanyam, M.:

Multivariate binomial approximation for asset prices with non-stationary variance and covariance characteristics.

Review of Financial Studies **8**(4) (1995) 1125–1152

Oommen, B.J., Rueda, L.:

Stochastic learning-based weak estimation of multinomial random variables and its applications to pattern recognition in non-stationary environments.

Pattern Recognition **39** (2006) 328–341

Narendra, K.S., Thathachar, M.A.L.:

Learning Automata.

Prentice-Hall (1989)

Horn, G., Oomen, B.J.:

Estimation in feedback loops by stochastic learning.

Systems, Man and Cybernetics (Submitted 2007)

Larsen, R.J., Marx, M.L.:

An Introduction to Mathematical Statistics and its Applications.

Prentice-Hall International (1986) ISBN 0-13-487166-9.

2 Combining Exhaustive and Approximate Methods for Improved Sub-Graph Matching

Thomas Bärecke and Marcin Detyniecki

Université Pierre et Marie Curie - Paris6 UMR 7606, DAPA, LIP6, Paris, France,
thomas.baerecke@lip6.fr

Abstract. Reams of different methods have been applied on the inexact graph matching problem in the last decades. In fact, there are two disjoint groups of approaches, exhaustive search and approximate methods. The first ones guarantee that the best solution is always found while the last ones generally have a significantly reduced time complexity at the expense of accepting sub-optimal solutions. This article aims, first, at comparing the two complementary approaches. Secondly, we show that one can bridge the gap between them and that their combination can lead to improved performance, i.e. maintains the guarantee for the best solution while reducing the convergence time.

Key words: Evolutionary Computation, Graph Matching, Structural Pattern Re-cognition, Graphical Models

2.1 Introduction

Despite the exact graph isomorphism problem, which has not yet be shown to be in P nor in NP [1, 2], all other instances of the graph matching problem, of practical importance, are NP-complete [3]. Attributed relational graphs (ARGs) are universal graphical models that occur frequently in structural pattern recognition. For example, content-based image retrieval can rely on graphs modeling the spatial entities and their mutual relationships in a segmented image. The nodes and edges are attributed with feature vectors. The retrieval process in such systems requires efficient methods to compare ARGs. In fact, the computation of the distance between two ARGs implies the resolution of an inexact (also referred to as error-correcting) (sub-)graph isomorphism problem. Even if filtering techniques (e.g., [4]) can reduce the number of matchings for the identification of the best-matching ARG for a given query, there will always remain numerous graph isomorphisms to compute.

Graph matching already has a long tradition in the domain of pattern recognition [5]. In general, it can be divided into exact and inexact matching. Exact matching requires two graphs to be exactly equal whereas inexact matching allows certain structural differences between them. Both sub-problems have been addressed by a wide range of methods. These can be classified either as explicit tree search approaches

[6, 7, 8], which always find the optimal solution, or as optimization methods which reduce the complexity at the cost of accepting sub-optimal solutions. Recent approaches tackling inexact graph matching include spectral [9, 10], least-squares [11], bayesian [12], and genetic [13, 14] methods.

Comparison between these algorithms as in [15] is usually restricted to algorithms of the same class, i.e. search methods or optimization techniques. This paper focuses on the comparison of the two general approaches. We select one representative of each class and evaluate its performance against one algorithm of the other class. We aim at pointing out general advantages and restrictions and a possible combination of the two complementary methods in the domain of pattern recognition. We choose a state-of-the-art exhaustive tree search method [8] and compare it to two new genetic matching algorithms. These are universally applicable methods since they do not impose any constraints on the ARGs.

The remainder of the paper is organized as follows: We formally define the problem in the next section. In Sect. 3, the A*-based [6] method is briefly reviewed. The genetic approaches are detailed in Sect. 4. Sect. 5 outlines how to combine the methods. In Sect. 6, we present experimental results on artificially created data. Finally, conclusions are drawn in Sect. 7.

2.2 Problem definition

Let us consider two attributed relational graphs $S = (V_S, E_S)$ and $G = (V_G, E_G)$. We suppose, without loss of generality, that S is not larger than G, which means $|V_S| \leq |V_G|$. The exact (sub-)graph isomorphism problem consists in finding an injective function $m : V_S \rightarrow V_G$ mapping each vertice of S to a distinct vertice of G such that the resulting node-induced subgraph G' of G is isomorph to S. That means, related nodes, and edges respectively, have the same attributes.

The inexact version of the problem arises when the graphs contain slightly different attributes. Thus, the inexact (sub-)graph isomorphism problem can be stated as the problem of finding a mapping that minimizes some kind of graph distance (e.g., the graph edit distance [16]).

In ARGs, nodes and edges are labeled with application-dependent values. We need to assume that distance metrics for both vertices (δ_V) and edges (δ_E) are provided. The attribute distance is defined by the sum of all edge distances [8]:

$$\mu_a^m(S, G) = \sum_{v \in V_S} \delta_V(v, m(v)) \tag{1}$$

Likewise, the total edge distance defines the relationship distance:

$$\mu_r^m(S, G) = \sum_{v, w \in V_S | v \neq w} \delta_E((v, w), (m(v), m(w))) \tag{2}$$

The overall distance is then defined as a convex combination of these two distances. A context-dependent coefficient usually controls the relative importance of vertice vs.

edge distance. For the purpose of this article we suppose that both distances are equally influential which leads to the following equation:

$$\mu_m(S, G) = \mu_a^m(S, G) + \mu_r^m(S, G) \tag{3}$$

2.3 Exhaustive graph matching using an A^* like approach

Exhaustive graph matching is based on explicitly searching the space of all possible assignments between the nodes of the graphs [17]. A solution is obtained incrementally by growing a partial assignment of the vertices of one (sub-)graph S to the vertices of the other graph G. The solution space is organized as a tree, where the kth level contains all partial assignments of the first k entities of S [16, 17]. The evaluation of a partial assignment is based on Eqs. 1 and 2 restricted to the vertices already included in the mapping. Since the distance of two graphs under any partial mapping is monotonically non-decreasing with the tree level for any branch, partial assignments scoring a distance over a predefined threshold of maximum acceptable dissimilarity μ_{max} can be safely discarded without risk of false dismissal. The A^* algorithm [6] performs a depth-first search, which always extends the partial mapping toward the local optimum, and which backtracks when the scored distance of the current assignment runs over a maximum acceptable threshold. When the inspection reaches a complete mapping, a match under the threshold is found. At this point, the global optimum is not guaranteed, but the obtained scored distance implies a stricter threshold for acceptable distance that is then used to efficiently extend the search until the global optimum is found.

Several approaches extend the A^* scheme using an admissible heuristic to increase the cost of the current partial assignment with a lower boundary of the future cost. In Berretti's [8] case, the extension cost estimate is obtained using the solution of a bipartite matching problem with a discrete relaxation algorithm. This requires only polynomial time. Based on this value, partial assignments that can not lead to a final match with acceptable similarity can be discarded earlier, thus accelerating the convergence of the algorithm while preserving result's optimality.

2.4 Genetic approaches

Genetic algorithms [18] are optimization methods inspired by the natural evolution process. They operate on a set (population) of solution candidates, the chromosomes. These are randomly initialized and undergo genetic operators such as selection, recombination, and mutation. This creates very good approximations after several iterations.

GAs provide decent solutions in a very short time. Moreover, they can return a complete candidate solution *at any time*, its quality increasing with the time (i.e. number of generations). The user is able to balance the trade-off between accuracy and run-time directly by choosing an appropriate stop criteria.

GAs explore large heterogeneous search spaces very fast at the expense of a non-exhaustive exploitation. This means that not all possible solutions are evaluated. In particular, it can occur that the standard GA finds a good region and the search does not continue into the direction of the optimal solution. Genetic local search (GLS) algorithms are GAs which are combined with local search strategies as for instance 2-opt. We implemented both, a standard GA and a GLS. The difference between them is that the GLS does not apply mutation at all, but performs a 2-opt local search on each crossover offspring.

2.4.1 Encoding and selection

A permutation is the most efficient way to encode a particular mapping between the nodes of two graphs of the same size. In this case, the application of the corresponding recombination operators is straightforward. In order to avoid repair mechanisms in the case of subgraph matching (due to operators capable of creating illegal solutions) and to generally prevent the operators from becoming too complex, we use the larger graph size as chromosome length. During the fitness evaluation, we do only take into account the portion of the chromosomes that actually corresponds to an existing node of the subgraph.

The selection of individuals for reproduction is based on the accumulated distances of nodes and edges (see Eq. 3), and follows a tournament strategy. A set of tournament size individuals is chosen randomly and the best individual produces offspring. This strategy is very efficient since it neither requires normalization nor ordering of the individuals by their fitness and decreasing fitness (error) functions can be directly incorporated.

2.4.2 Recombination and mutation

Although varied recombination operators for permutation encodings are available, none was specially developed for graph matching. Since the influence of any node pair, and thus of a specific allele in the gene, depends equally on all other alleles, it is reasonable to apply an unbiased strict position-based crossover operator. Thus, we combine the idea of position-based crossover [19] with the idea of uniform crossover. This differs from the original position-based crossover in the point that the order from the second parent is not imposed onto the child, but as many alleles as possible are placed on the same locus as of the parents. The average number of mappings inherited from the two parents is approximately equal. An allele that has the same position in both parents always keeps this position.

A swap operator is used for the mutation in the GA. It simply exchanges the loci of two alleles.

2.4.3 Local search strategy

The local search strategy of the GLS replaces each offspring by the dominating gene of its neighborhood. We use the 2-opt algorithm in which the set of chromosomes emerging from a given chromosome by exchanging two values is considered. This space is exhaustively searched for the locally optimal individual which replaces the

```
     Input: S = (V_S, E_S) and G = (V_G, E_G), |V_S| ≤ |V_G| ;        /* Two Graphs */
     /* First step: genetic algorithm with elite replacement    */
 1   Initialize Population p randomly ;
 2   repeat
 3       Tournament Selection ;
 4       for i ← 0 to crossover.probability * size(p) do
 5           (p[i],p[i+1]) ← Crossover (p[i],p[i+1]) ;
 6           i ← i+2 ;
 7       forall Gene g ∈ p do
 8           if Algorithm.type=GLS then
 9               Local Search;
10           else
11               Mutate with mutation.probability ;
12   until fitness(best individual) has not decreased during last n generations ;
13   f = fitness (best individual);
     /* Second step: Berretti's algorithm                        */
14   acct ← f ;                          /* Use f as acceptance threshold */
15   m ← ∅ ;                             /* Start with empty mapping */
16   repeat
17       Evaluate partial mapping m by δ_m(S, G) ;
18       Estimate future extension cost c_m(S, G) ;          /* Lower boundary */
19       Add best matching node pair (v_S, v_G) to m ;
20       if δ_m(S, G) + c_m(S, G) > acct then
21           Backtrack ;
22   until m is complete or no valid extension is possible ;
23   if m is complete then
24       acct ← δ_m(S, G) ;
25       Continue Search ;
26   else
27       return last complete mapping ;
```

Algorithm 1: Simplified pseudo-code of the combined algorithm

initial chromosome. The evaluation of a 2-opt-switch is computationally less expensive ($\mathcal{O}(n)$) than the evaluation ($\mathcal{O}(n^2)$) of entire chromosomes, since only the nodes and edges whose mappings changed are considered.

2.5 Combined algorithms

We combine the Berretti's algorithm[8] with both versions of our genetic approach. A simplified pseudo-code is given in Alg. 1 to illustrate the approach. We first perform a genetic search. The scored distance of the best individual in the final generation is obviously an upper bound for the globally minimal distance. Thus, we perform Berretti's matching algorithm with this value as initial maximal acceptance threshold. This ensures that the optimal solution is always found. The advantage over the original form of Berretti's algorithm is that several non-promising branches of the search tree can be discarded earlier. In the following, the combined approaches will be referred to as CGA, and CGLS respectively.

2.6 Experimental results

We compare the algorithms using a set of randomly attributed complete graphs. A graph G of size n is complete when it consists of n vertices and any node pair is connected by an edge. During graph generation, both edge and node attributes are uniformly chosen random values from the unit interval.

A node-induced subgraph S is extracted from each graph G. Technically, we create a (uniform) random permutation of the nodes of G and select its first $o : o \leq n$ nodes in order to establish S. In our tests, o is either n (graph isomorphism) or $n - 5$ (subgraph isomorphism).

We perform the matching of every subgraph S against all original graphs. We consider two test cases: a *positive* case for isomorph graphs and a *negative* one that aims at finding the optimal (distance-minimizing) mapping between non-corresponding graphs. We compare the execution time and accuracy of all algorithms. The results of the exhaustive approach serve as benchmarks for the genetic approaches. Since, in the negative test case, the exhaustive search becomes intractable with increasing graph sizes, this type of test is only performed for small graphs. Since, in the positive case, the time complexity of Berretti's algorithm does not climb that fast, we evaluate the behavior for larger graph sizes by focusing only on isomorph graph pairs, i.e. we ensure that an optimal solution with zero distance exists.

2.6.1 Solution quality for pure genetic approaches

The relative distance of the solutions obtained by the pure genetic approaches with respect to the optimal solution for small graph sizes is illustrated in Tab. 1. For the negative case, let m' be the globally optimal mapping. Then, for any mapping m, the term $(\mu_m(S, G)/\mu'_m(S, G)) - 1$ describes the gap to m'. In the positive case, we cannot use this measure for the assessment of the solution quality since $\mu'_m(S, G) = 0$. Thus, we use the distance imposed by m itself (i.e., $\mu_m(S, G)$) and the absolute number of mismatches (denoted as Errors).

We observe that the GLS obtains nearly perfect results and always finds the optimal solution in the positive case. The solutions of the standard GA are of lower quality. Our tests on increased graph sizes showed that the quality of the solution decreases with the graph size. This effect is especially strong for the standard GA whereas the error of the GLS does only increase marginally.

2.6.2 Time complexity

As shown in Tab. 2 the execution time of the GA is lower than for the GLS. However, this is inversed when we observe the combined versions, since the better quality solution provide lower maximum acceptance thresholds for Berretti's algorithm. An

Table 1. Error of the pure genetic approaches

Algorithm	Graph Size		Positive case		Negative case	
	S	G	Errors	Mean distance	Mean	Maximum
GLS	10	10	0	0	0.74 %	10.33 %
GA	10	10	1	0.4788	6.93 %	20.48 %
GLS	10	15	0	0	2.21 %	13.83 %
GA	10	15	3	2.0456	13.86 %	39.21 %

Table 2. Time for graph matching. On the left graph matching between graphs of size 10 is performed. On the right subgraphs of size 10 are matched against graphs of size 15

	Graph isomorphism			Subgraph isomorphism		
	Positive	Negative	Mean	Positive	Negative	Mean
A* Ref. Time	31.3 ms	12683 ms	11418 ms	76.6 ms	286930 ms	258250 ms
A* Rel. Time	100.00 %	100.00 %	100.00 %	100.00 %	100.00 %	100.00 %
GLS	208.95 %	1.40 %	1.46 %	191.64 %	0.13 %	0.14 %
GA	35.46 %	0.34 %	0.35 %	38.64 %	0.02 %	0.02 %
CGLS	233.87 %	86.04 %	86.08 %	201.70 %	83.38 %	83.38 %
CGA	54.95 %	93.36 %	93.35 %	71.41 %	97.43 %	97.43 %

interesting result is that the combined algorithms outperform the exhaustive search although it is included in them. In the case of exact matching Berretti's algorithm outperforms the GLS. However, due to the huge difference of the absolute execution times this has nearly no influence on the mean values.

Figures 1 and 2 show the effect of increasing graph sizes on the performance of the algorithms for the case of exact graph matching, both for the graph isomorphism and subgraph isomorphism problem. The execution time is normalized by the execution time of Berretti's algorithm. In other words, the relative execution time t is obtained by dividing the absolute execution time of a given algorithm by the absolute execution time of Berretti's approach for the each graph size. This allows to compare the evaluation of execution times vs. the exhaustive reference algorithm on a linear scale.

We observe, that the execution time of the genetic approaches grows much slower than that of the exhaustive one. Additionally, the combined versions compare favorably to the A*-like approach. The difference between pure GA and and its corresponding combined versions depends on the quality of the intermediate solutions. We also observe that the better the solution, the lower the time spent for its verification.

2.7 Conclusions

The implementation of local search into the genetic approach enhances the solution quality significantly. Indeed, the GLS found every exact matching until the size of 35. The pure GA obtains only very poor approximations for increasing graph sizes.

We combine two complementary types of algorithms. We observe, that this combination can obtain better results than with either of them in general. We keep the

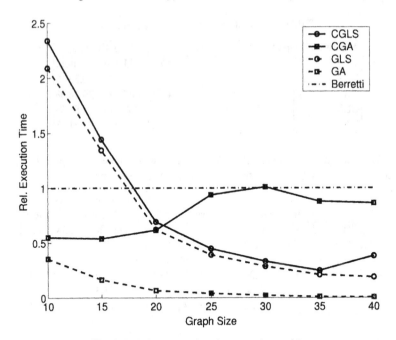

Fig. 1. Relative execution time, graph matching

best-solution guarantee from Berretti's algorithm and reduce its execution time by supplying it with an approximate solution from the GA. A decreased starting value of the acceptable threshold speeds it up significantly. Therefore, in applications, where the maximal acceptable error is a priori known and sufficiently small, the exhaustive algorithm is preferable. For the general case one should prefer combined genetic approaches. In fact, if the GA provides high quality solution the combination does not influence the time complexity very much. However, we did not compare the algorithms on real-world data so far and we expect that this would favor the GLS more than its corresponding combined approach.

We are planning to apply them to content-based image retrieval in the near future, in particular we are going to address the problem of identifying a person based on a two-dimensional image using a database of three-dimensional face models.

Acknowledgements

The authors thank Stefano Berretti for his support and for providing the source code of his algorithm. We also acknowledge the valuable comments of the reviewers.

References

Köbler, J., Schöning, U., Torán, J.:

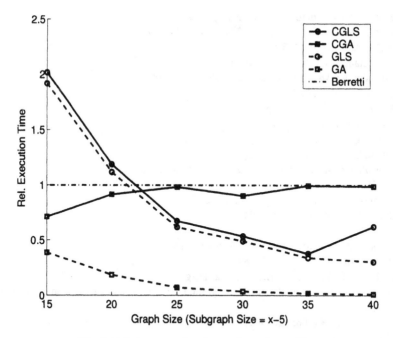

Fig. 2. Relative execution time, subgraph matching

The Graph Isomorphism Problem: Its Structural Complexity.
Birkhäuser, Boston (1993)
Arvind, V., Kurur, P.P.:
Graph isomorphism is in SPP.
Information and Computation **204** (2006) 835–852
Garey, M., Johnson, D.:
Computers and Intractability - A Guide to the Theory of NP-Completeness.
Freeman and Company (1979)
Irniger, C., Bunke, H.:
Decision trees for error-tolerant graph database filtering.
In: Graph-Based Representations in Pattern Recognition. Volume 3434 of LNCS.
(2005) 301–311
Conte, D., Foggia, P., Sansone, C., Vento, M.:
Thirty years of graph matching in pattern recognition.
Int. Journal of Pattern Recognition and Artificial Intelligence **18** (2004) 265–298
Ullmann, J.R.:
An algorithm for subgraph isomorphism.
J. ACM **23** (1976) 31–42
Cordella, L.P., Foggia, P., Sansone, C., Vento, M.:
A (sub)graph isomorphism algorithm for matching large graphs.
IEEE Trans. Pattern Anal. Mach. Intell. **26** (2004) 1367–1372
Berretti, S., Del Bimbo, A., Vicario, E.:
Efficient matching and indexing of graph models in content-based retrieval.
IEEE Trans. Pattern Anal. Mach. Intell. **23** (2001) 1089–1105
Shokoufandeh, A., Maçrini, D., Dickinson, S.J., Siddiqi, K., Zucker, S.W.:

Indexing hierarchical structures using graph spectra.
IEEE Trans. Pattern Anal. Mach. Intell. **27** (2005) 1125–1140
Robles-Kelly, A., Hancock, E.R.:
Graph edit distance from spectral seriation.
IEEE Trans. Pattern Anal. Mach. Intell. **27** (2005) 365–378
van Wyk, B.J., van Wyk, M.A.:
Kronecker product graph matching.
Pattern Recognition **36** (2003) 2019–2030
Caetano, T.S., Caelli, T., Schuurmans, D., Barone, D.A.C.:
Graphical models and point pattern matching.
IEEE Trans. Pattern Anal. Mach. Intell. **28** (2006) 1646–1663
Myers, R., Hancock, E.:
Least-commitment graph matching with genetic algorithms.
Pattern Recognition **34** (2001) 375–394
Suganthan, P.N.:
Structural pattern recognition using genetic algorithms.
Pattern Recognition **35** (2002) 1883–1893
Cesar, Jr., R.M., Bengoetxea, E., Bloch, I., Larrañaga, P.:
Inexact graph matching for model-based recognition: Evaluation and comparison of optimiza-
    tion algorithms.
Pattern Recognition **38** (2005) 2099–2113
Eshera, M., Fu, K.S.:
A graph distance measure for image analysis.
IEEE Trans. Syst. Man, Cybern. **14** (1984) 398–407
Tsai, W., Fu, K.S.:
Error-correcting isomorphism of attributed relational graphs for pattern analysis.
IEEE Trans. Syst. Man Cybern. **9** (1979) 757–768
Mitchell, M.:
An introduction to genetic algorithms.
MIT Press, Cambridge (1996)
Syswerda, G.:
Schedule optimization using genetic algorithms.
In Davis, L., ed.: Handbook of Genetic Algorithms, New York, Van Nostrand Reinhold (1991)
    332–349

3 Information Fusion Techniques for Reliably Training Intrusion Detection Systems*

Francesco Gargiulo, Claudio Mazzariello, and Carlo Sansone

Università di Napoli Federico II
Dipartimento di Informatica e Sistemistica
via Claudio 21 — 80125 Napoli (Italy)
{francesco.grg,cmazzari,carlosan}@unina.it

Abstract. Many approaches have been proposed to tackle network security; among them, many exploit machine learning and pattern recognition techniques, by regarding malicious behavior detection as a classification problem. Supervised and unsupervised techniques are used, each with its own benefits and shortcomings. When using supervised techniques, a suitably representative training set is required, which reliably indicates what a human expert wants the system to learn and recognize. To this aim, we present an approach based on the Dempster-Shafer theory, which exploits the Dempster-Shafer combination rule for automatically building a database of labeled network traffic from raw tcpdump packet captures. We also show that systems trained on such a database perform approximatively as well as the same systems trained on correctly labeled data.

3.1 Introduction

As attack strategies become more and more sophisticated, the task of detecting attacks or malicious activities in network traffic becomes harder and harder. The first class of systems which can be used for detecting network intrusions (Network Intrusion Detection Systems - N-IDS) relies on the exact knowledge of any malicious activity to detect. Many researchers claim that attacks carry the burden of a well recognizable *signature*, which is easily related to their presence, and allows an accurate detection. The practice of searching for well-known attack signatures in network traffic, is commonly known as *signature detection* [1, 16]. Signature-based detection is characterized by a very low rate of false alarms, as it searches for precise and well defined symptoms of malicious activities. The counterpart, though, is a very low sensibility to detect novel attacks (the so-called *zero-day attacks*). Signatures, in fact, are usually hand-coded by a human expert, and are not easily kept up to date.

*This work has been partially supported by the Ministero dell'Università e della Ricerca (MiUR) in the framework of the PRIN Project "Robust and Efficient traffic Classification in IP nEtworks" (RECIPE), and by the Regione Campania, in the framework of the "Soft Computing for Internet Traffic Anomaly Detection" (SCI-TrADe) Project.

While signature-based detection explicitly states what the single attacks to be detected look like, other techniques might give a high level description of the problem. Techniques explicitly modeling malicious behavior realize the principle at the basis of *misuse detection* [8, 14]. In general, when using misuse-based detection techniques, a model of malicious behavior is given, and what falls within such model is reported as anomalous. If the model is accurate enough, it can give raise to a very low false alarm rate. Anyway, as they are particularly good at describing the known anomalous behaviors searched for, they might fail in detecting zero-day attacks, too. Note that the above discussed signature-based techniques can be regarded as an implementation of a misuse-based detection strategy.

On the opposite, it is also possible to model the expected normal behavior of the system. In this case, whatever falls outside such model gives raise to an alert. Such techniques, referred to as *Anomaly-based*, suffer from a quite high false alarm rate, at least higher than misuse-based techniques. Yet, as mutation of known attacks might still be significantly deviating from the expected normal behavior of the average users, anomaly-based techniques are in some cases able to detect novel or modified attacks.

According to the relative importance of each type of error, be it a missed detection or a false alarm, it is possible to choose the most suitable detection technique. What is common to all of them, indeed, is the difficulty in defining a suitable model of normal or malicious behavior. To this extent, *Pattern Recognition* (PR) and *Data Mining* techniques are widely used. By analyzing features extracted from network traffic, such techniques are able to effectively build models which describe the analyzed scenario. In [6] it is shown how the network intrusion detection problem can be easily formulated as a typical classification problem: given information about network connections between pairs of hosts, the task is to assign each connection to one out of two classes, respectively representing normal traffic conditions or the attack category. Here the term *connection* refers to a sequence of data packets related to a particular service, such as a file transfer via the ftp protocol. Since an IDS must detect connections related to malicious activities, each network connection can be viewed as a *pattern* to be classified. Since the classifiers considered in [6] need to be trained in a *supervised* way, the above cited formulation implies the use of an IDS based on a misuse detection approach. The main advantage of a PR approach is the ability to generalize which is peculiar to PR systems. They are able to detect some novel attacks, without the need of a complete description of all the possible attack signatures, thus overtaking one of the main drawbacks of misuse detection approaches, especially those implemented by means of signature detection techniques. Indeed, anomaly-based systems have been considered in the PR field [19] as well. They can be ascribed to the more general category of *unsupervised* systems based on the novelty detection approach [15]. Anyway, it is worth noting that an IDS realized by means of a PR approach based on supervised learning techniques typically performs better than those based on unsupervised learning techniques [10].

One of the main drawbacks occurring when using PR-based system in real environments is the difficulty in collecting a representative labeled set of data for training them. This aspect is often disregarded in papers proposing PR approaches for coping with the intrusion detection problem, where usually standard labeled databases, such as the well-known [4] *KDD 99*, are used for testing [12, 20]. This choice is no longer accepted in the IDS community, since network traffic is now significantly changed and some papers (see for example [13]) highlighted many flaws in the construction of such database.

Hence, in this paper we propose a general methodology for automatically obtaining a dataset of labeled packets starting from raw tcpdump traces. Such dataset can be then used for the training phase of supervised PR algorithms. In particular, we present an architecture for automatically building up a network traffic database made up of packets, each labeled either as *normal* or as an *attack*. As we propose to use multiple detection techniques, it is necessary to employ some information fusion strategy in order to combine them. As we have no prior knowledge about traffic characteristics, we use the Dempster-Shafer [7] theory, which completely disregards any prior knowledge about the data to be classified. Note that, though some works already propose to exploit the results of such a theory for intrusion detection (see for example [18]), its use for labeling network traffic is novel. We will also evaluate to which extent a dataset labeled by using our approach can effectively be used to train a PR-based IDS. In order to do that, we trained such system by using both the real labels of the traffic and those calculated in the previously cited step, and compared the obtained results.

By using the Dempster-Shafer theory we also define a suitable *index* that is used for denoting the reliability of the packet labeling. In this way, unreliably labeled packets can be discarded from the database. We evaluate how this choice can affect the training and generalization performance of the considered IDS.

The paper is organized as follows: in section 2 we will present the architecture aimed at allowing the automated labeling of raw packets from tcpdump traces. In section 3 we will describe our tests. In particular, we first show how it is possible to obtain a reliably labeled traffic dataset. Then, we will show that systems trained on such dataset perform approximatively as well as the same systems trained on correctly labeled data. Finally, in section 4 some conclusions are drawn.

3.2 An Architecture for Building a Training Dataset

In network security, there are not too many issues in collecting large amounts of traffic which might be used to train a supervised classifier. Unfortunately, such traffic often lacks a reliable labeling. This gives raise to a paradox: if we want to properly train a classifier, we need to have correctly labeled network traffic; but, if we have such labeled traffic, maybe we already know how to exactly discriminate between normal and malicious behavior. Hence, we already know how to tell attack packets apart from normal ones, thus we don't need a classifier.

In order to overcome such a paradox, we propose an architecture for automatically building up a traffic database, containing packets each labeled either as *normal* or as an *attack*. The proposed architecture (see figure 1) consists of several base classifiers, called Base IDS (B-IDS in the following). According to the definition of our framework, B-IDS must not require to be trained on labeled data. Typical examples are signature-based IDS (such as Snort[TM2]) or, more in general, any IDS based on unsupervised techniques. The bank of B-IDS starts analyzing offline the packets contained in a dumped traffic database. As we propose to use multiple detection techniques, it

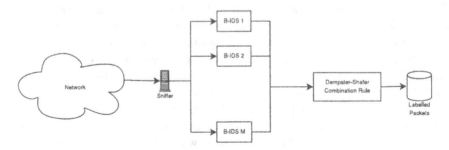

Fig. 1. B-IDS and the D-S combination rule

is necessary to employ some fusion strategy in order to combine their outputs. As we have no prior knowledge of the traffic characteristics, we use the Dempster and Shafer [7] combination rule, which completely disregards any prior knowledge about the data to be classified. According to the theory of Dempster and Shafer (D-S theory), a Basic Probability Assignment (BPA) can be associated to each base classifier, which describes the subjective degree of confidence attributed to it. What is modeled, then, is not the analyzed phenomenon, but the belief in what the base classifiers report about it.

The D-S theory has been frequently applied to deal with uncertainty management and incomplete reasoning. Differently from the classical Bayesian theory, D-S theory can explicitly model the absence of information, while in case of absence of information a Bayesian approach attributes the same probability to all the possible events. The above described characteristics can be very attractive for managing the uncertainties of the network security domain, due, for example, to the presence of the zero-day attacks.

When assigning a BPA, there are some requirements which have to be met. They descend from the fact that the BPA is still a probability function, hence has to respect the constraints for mass probability functions. Each BPA is such that $m : 2^\theta \rightarrow [0,1]$, where θ indicates the so called *frame of discernment*. Usually, the frame of discernment θ consists of N mutually exclusive and exhaustive hypotheses A_i, $i = 1, \ldots, N$. A subset $\{A_i, \ldots, A_j\} \subseteq \theta$ represents a new hypothesis. As the number of possible subsets of θ is 2^θ, the generic hypothesis is an element of 2^θ. In our case, we only consider two hypotheses (classes), namely *Normal* and *Attack*; hence, the frame of discernment is $\theta = \{\{Normal\}, \{Attack\}\}$ and $2^\theta = \{\{Normal\}, \{Attack\}, \{Normal, Attack\}\}$, whereas in the Bayesian case only the events $\{\{Normal\}, \{Attack\}\}$ would be considered. $\{Normal\}$ and $\{Attack\}$ are referred to as *simple events* or *singletons*, while $\{Normal, Attack\}$ as *composite event*. Furthermore, also the following properties have to hold:

---

[2]http://www.snort.org

$$m(\emptyset) = 0 \qquad\qquad \sum_{A \subseteq 2^\theta} m(A) = 1$$

The aim of assigning a BPA is to describe the reliability of a particular classifier in reporting a specific event. Such a representation is suitable for combination, but as we want to deal with combined results in the same way, we also impose the constraint that the combination of several BPA by means of the D-S rule still has to be a BPA. The uncertainty in the final decision will be inversely proportional to the extent to which the base classifiers agree. If we have n base classifiers, the combination rule is such that:

$$m(A) = K \sum_{\bigcap_{i=1}^{n} A_i = A} \prod_{i=1}^{n} m_i(A_i) \tag{1}$$

where:

$$K^{-1} = 1 - \sum_{\bigcap_{i=1}^{n} A_i = \emptyset} \prod_{i=1}^{n} m_i(A_i) = \sum_{\bigcap_{i=1}^{n} A_i \neq \emptyset} \prod_{i=1}^{n} m_i(A_i) \tag{2}$$

We also defined a criterion for obtaining a crisp classification of each packet from the overall BPA, by means of a properly defined index. BPA in fact, only give indication regarding the overall degree of confidence in reporting the occurrence of each of the known events, while we are interested in knowing whether one of such events, has been detected or not. The function which allows us to transform the BPA in a detection result descends from observation of the relations between *Belief*, *Plausibility* and *Uncertainty*. Let $A, B \in \theta$; hence:

$$Bel(B) = \sum_{A \subset B} m(A) \; ; \; Pls(B) = \sum_{A \cap B \neq \emptyset} m(A) \tag{3}$$

$$Unc(B) = Pls(B) - Bel(B) \tag{4}$$

In the two-event case, we observe that

$$Bel(\{Normal\}) = m(\{Normal\}) \tag{5}$$

$$Pls(\{Normal\}) = m(\{Normal\}) + m(\{Normal, Attack\}) \tag{6}$$

$$Bel(\{Attack\}) = m(\{Attack\}) \tag{7}$$

$$Pls(\{Attack\}) = m(\{Attack\}) + m(\{Normal, Attack\}) \tag{8}$$

Hence,

$$Unc(\{Normal\}) = Unc(\{Attack\}) = m(\{Normal, Attack\}) \tag{9}$$

As said before, we aim at defining an index which allows us to associate a single label to each packet, even though the packet classification mechanism is inherently *fuzzy*. What we want is a *reliability index* R_I which tells us how much difference is there between the degree of belief the system has in stating each of the possible hypotheses.

Furthermore, such a reliability index should preferably have a direct dependency on the difference between the degrees of belief in each of the two simple hypotheses, and an inverse dependency on the degree of belief in the composite hypothesis, which explicitly measures the uncertainty associated to each decision. So, we defined R_I as:

$$R_I = \frac{Bel(\{Attack\})}{1 + Unc(\{Attack\})} - \frac{Bel(\{Normal\})}{1 + Unc(\{Normal\})} = \frac{m(\{Attack\}) - m(\{Normal\})}{1 + m(\{Normal, Attack\})}$$

(10)

The index R_I is defined in such a way that, if its value is $+1$, there is the highest reliability in detecting an ongoing malicious activity; if it is -1, it is quite sure that the observed traffic is normal; if it is 0, there's the maximum uncertainty, hence the packet will should be rejected.

In order to reject unreliably labeled packets, the value of R_I can be compared with a threshold τ which is related to the desired classification reliability. If it falls outside the range $[-\tau,\tau]$ described by such threshold, then the packet can be classified, with at least the specified degree of confidence; otherwise, the packet will fall inside an *uncertain* region. In that case, it will be rejected and eliminated from the labeled database we are interested to build. Note that the higher the threshold, the more reliable the classification of each packet, the higher the number of rejected packets.

Usually, the D-S combination rule is referred to as a technique which requires training at fusion level [9]. In fact, the BPA's are usually assigned according to the so-called *confusion matrix*, that describes the performance of a specific classifiers on a training set [17]. In our case, we don't have any training data available, hence we use a different method for assigning a BPA to each base classifier. In particular, we assign them BPA's related to the typical performance of the detection technique they implement. Then, starting from the category a base classifier belongs to (i.e., anomaly vs. misuse detection, unsupervised vs. supervised, etc.), we define some criteria for assigning a suitable BPA. In particular, we assign a higher value to $m(\{Attack\})$ if a signature-based misuse detector raises an alert. Such systems, in fact, are built to correctly detect the malicious behaviors described by the known signatures. On the other hand, the absence of alerts by a signature-based misuse detector is not necessarily related to the absence of any anomalies. A modified attack, in fact, can evade such detection technique. Thus, we assign low values to $m(\{Normal\})$ when the system notifies this kind of traffic.

Anomaly based signature detection systems, instead, have a dual behavior with respect to misuse detectors. On the other hand, detectors based on pattern recognition techniques generally attain worse performance in correctly detecting malicious behaviors, but also prove their ability to detect modified or novel attacks. For that reason, we assign lower belief in their classification with respect to signature based detectors, when an attack is detected. Moreover, an higher belief is assigned when a packet is attributed to the normal class with respect to the case in which it is attributed to the attack class.

In section 3 we will show how to assign reasonable value to the BPA of each chosen B-IDS, according to the above described criteria.

3.3 Experimental Results

In order to test the proposed approach, we used one day of the DARPA 99 traces (more than 1 million packets). To extract representative features from the raw traffic traces, as required by PR-based systems, we used the preprocessor plug-in for Snort^{TM} described in [5] and freely available on SourceForge [3]. It allowed us to extract 26 features from network traffic. Such features were derived from the *intrinsic* and *traffic* features defined by Lee and Stolfo in [11]. More details about the feature extraction process can be found in [5].

As B-IDS, we chose a signature-based IDS, namely Snort^{TM}, and two PR-based anomaly detectors, respectively a Rival Penalized Competitive Learning (RPCL) network and an one-class Support Vector Machine (SVM) [2]. The RPCL has only two neurons; after the unsupervised learning phase, we associate to the *Normal* class the neuron which won the competition the higher number of times. It is worth observing that, since Snort^{TM} works at packet level, we used it as a classifier for unprocessed raw tcpdump traffic. Moreover, since we used the version 2.2.4, we allowed its multiple detection feature. Snort^{TM}can then raise more than one alert for each packet. In this case, each alert is considered as an evidence supporting the event {*Attack*} for the current packet. The performance of Snort^{TM}and of the neural based classifiers on the chosen dataset are reported in table 1. Now, we are required to model the degree

	False Alarm Rate	Missed Detection Rate	Error Rate
Snort^{TM}	0.129%	21.789%	0.164%
RPCL	1.477%	21.997%	1.510%
SVM	0.924%	74.571%	1.044%

Table 1. Performance obtained by the chosen B-IDS

of belief associated to each base classifier reporting each of the observed events. As stated before, we do it by using the basic probability assignment. First of all, let's start by assigning a BPA to Snort^{TM}. As shown in table 2, we assume that Snort^{TM}is very reliable when reporting malicious activities. The probability that an attack actually occurs when Snort^{TM}reports it, is very high, due to its signature-based nature. According to that, we assigned the value 0.9 to $m(\{Attack\})$ when Snort^{TM} raises an alert.

	m({**Normal**})	m({**Attack**})	m({**Normal,Attack**})
Attack	0	0.9	0.1
Normal	0.6	0	0.4

Table 2. BPA's assigned to Snort^{TM}

---

[3]http://s-predator.sourceforge.net

Conversely, aware of Snort™'s low probability of detecting either a novel or modified attack, we don't really trust it too much when reporting normal activity.

Similarly to the case of Snort™, we considered the typical behavior of the neural-based classifiers we are using, in order to decide when and how much to trust it. Such classifiers, due to their unsupervised nature, are not supposed to perform extremely well on any class of traffic. Yet, on the other hand, they may also be able to detect novel attacks, thus compensating the lack of such ability for Snort™ and similar signature based B-IDS. In table 3 we observe the BPA's assigned to it.

By using such BPA's, and combining the results for the three considered B-IDS, we

	m({Normal})	m({Attack})	m({Normal,Attack})
Attack	0	0.5	0.5
Normal	0.6	0	0.4

Table 3. BPA's assigned to RPCL and SVM

are able to obtain a preliminary labeling of the raw traffic. To this regard, we verified that there are no differences in such a labeling if the above reported BPA's vary within a 5% range.

By varying the value of the reliability threshold and comparing it to the indicator defined in eq. 10, we finally obtain the error rates described in table 4. Here, *False Alarm Rate* and *Rejection Rate* are meant in the canonical way. When computing the *Missed Detection Rate*, we consider all the attack packets which were either misclassified as normal, or rejected. In other words, if an attack packet is rejected, we consider it as missed. By *Error Rate*, instead, we consider all the packets which are misclassified, regardless the number of rejections.

τ	False Alarm Rate	Missed Detection Rate	Error Rate	Reject Rate
0.00	0.278%	21.789%	0.313%	0%
0.24	0.027%	21.945%	0.063%	0.251%
0.78	0.015%	74.623%	0.051%	2.404%
0.88	0.015%	74.623%	0.015%	99.943%

Table 4. Performance obtained by combining the chosen B-IDS as a function of the threshold τ

In order to understand whether it is possible to use in practice a dataset labeled in this way, and for evaluating the effectiveness of the reliability index associated to each labeled packet, we used the dataset for training a supervised misuse detector. The chosen classifier is SLIPPER [3], a rule-based learning system that that creates a rule set by iteratively boosting a greedy rule-builder. In particular, we use three different datasets resulting from table 4: the first is the one obtained with the reliability threshold τ set to 0. In that case we consider all the packets, whatever the label assigned to them. As a second dataset, we chose the one made up of all the packets whose value for R_I

is greater than a reliability threshold equal to 0.24. Such choice allows a rejection rate below a reasonable level; the third dataset is the one obtainable when considering only packets whose R_I value exceeds 0.78. Other threshold values are not considered, since they would lead to discard too many packets from the database.

		False Alarm Rate	Missed Detection Rate	Error Rate
labels	$\tau = 0$	0.141%	21.997%	0.176%
obtained by	$\tau = 0.24$	0.034%	21.997%	0.070%
D-S approach	$\tau = 0.78$	9.570%	21.997%	9.590%
actual	10% of the dataset	0.045%	88.820%	0.190%
actual	20% of the dataset	0.025%	79.407%	0.154%
labels	30% of the dataset	0.004%	19.345%	0.036%
	100% of the dataset	0.013%	12.117%	0.032%

Table 5. SLIPPER performance as a function of the dataset used for training

In table 5 we show the results obtained by training SLIPPER on different instances of the considered dataset. Note that the results reported in the first three rows have been obtained by using labels provided by the proposed method, while in the last four rows different amounts of correctly labelled data have been considered.

The optimal threshold τ for the analyzed data corresponds to 0.24, as it allows us to attain the best performance. In this case, the difference with respect to the *ideal* training set (i.e., the whole database with actual labels) in terms of error rate turned out surely acceptable (only 0.03% with a recognition rate of 99.9%), thus confirming our claims. Moreover, it has to be pointed out that labels provided by our approach allow us to train a classifier that performs better than the one trained with the 20% of the whole database with actual labels, which exhibits an unacceptable missed detection rate. This is a significant result, since such a dataset is composed by over 230, 000 samples that have been labeled by hand, with a significant waste of time with respect to an automatic labeling. Finally, note that the performance obtained by SLIPPER trained with the dataset built by considering $\tau = 0.24$ are better than those obtained by the best B-IDS.

3.4 Conclusions

In this paper we deal with the problem of collecting labeled packets, in order to usefully train intrusion detection systems. We describe an architecture based on the Dempster-Shafer theory which, by analyzing raw packets, is able to assign labels to them. It is also able to point out how reliable each of the labels is, thus allowing to choose only the packets which satisfy a certain level of confidence. By training a supervised algorithm with data labeled in this way, we show that it is possible to obtain results which are similar to those obtained by using the actual class of all the packets.

As future developments, we deem it might be possible to extend the D-S based architecture, by adding further analysis stages including also semi-supervised classifiers and iterating the labeling process, thus attaining a better labeled dataset.

References

J. Beale, J.C. Foster, *Snort 2.0 Intrusion Detection*, Syngress Publishing, Inc., Rockland, MA, 2003.

C.-C. Chang, C.-J. Lin, LIBSVM: A Library for Support Vector Machines, 2001.

W.W. Cohen, Y. Singer. Simple, Fast, and Effective Rule Learner. In *Proceedings of the 16th National Conf. on Artificial Intelligence and 11th Conf. on Innovative Applications of Artificial Intelligence*, Orlando (FL), USA, pp. 335-342, July 18-22, 1999.

C. Elkan, Results of the KDD99 classifier learning, *ACM SIGKDD Explorations 1*, pp. 63-64, 2000.

M. Esposito, C. Mazzariello, F. Oliviero, S. P. Romano, C. Sansone, Real Time Detection of Novel Attack by Means of Data Mining Techniques. In: C.-S. Chen, J. Filipe, I. Seruca, J. Cordeiro (Eds.), *Enterprise Information Systems VII*, Springer-Verlag, pp. 197-204, 2006.

G. Giacinto, F. Roli, L. Didaci, Fusion of multiple classifiers for intrusion detection in computer networks, *Pattern Recognition Letters*, vol. 24, pp. 1795-1803, 2003.

J. Gordon, E.H. Shortliffe, The Dempster-Shafer Theory of Evidence, in B.G. Buchanan and E.H. Shortliffe (Eds.), *Rule-Based Expert Systems*, Addison-Wesley, pp. 272-292, 1984.

R. Kumar, E.H. Spafford, A Software Architecture to Support Misuse Intrusion Detection, in *Proceedings of the 18th National Information Security Conference*, pp. 194-204, 1995.

L.I. Kuncheva, J.C. Bezdek, R.P.W. Duin, Decision templates for multiple classifier fusion: an experimental comparison. In *Pattern Recognition*, vol. 34, pp. 299-314. 2001.

P. Laskov, P. Daussel, C. Schafer, K. Rieck, Learning intrusion detection: supervised or unsupervised?, in F. Roli and S. Vitulano (Eds.), *Lecture Notes in Computer Science, vol. 3617*, Springer-Verlag, Berlin, pp. 50-57, 2005.

W. Lee, S.J. Stolfo, A framework for constructing features and models for intrusion detection systems, *ACM Trans. on Information System Security*, vol. 3, no. 4, pp. 227-261, 2000.

Y. Liu, K. Chen, X. Liao, W. Zhang, A genetic clustering method for intrusion detection, *Pattern Recognition*, vol. 37, 2004.

J. McHugh, Testing Intrusion Detection Systems: A Critique of the 1998 and 1999 DARPA Intrusion Detection System Evaluations as Performed by Lincoln Laboratory, *ACM Transactions on Information System Security*, vol. 3, no. 4, pages 262-294, 2000.

M. Meier, S. Schmerl, H. Koenig, Improving the Efficiency of Misuse Detection. In K. Julisch, C. Kruegel (eds), *Proc. of the Second Intern. Conf. on Detection of Intrusions and Malware, and Vulnerability Assessment*, Vienna, Austria, July 7-8, pp. 188-205, 2005.

S. Singh, M. Markou, Novelty detection: a review - part 2: neural network based approaches. *Signal Processing*, vol. 83, n. 12, 2003.

B.K. Sy, Signature-based approach for intrusion detection. In: P. Perner, A. Imiya (eds) LNAI vol. 3587, *Proceedings of the 4th Intern. Conf. on Machine Learning and Data Mining in Pattern Recognition*, Leipzig, July 9-11, pp. 526-536, 2005.

L. Xu, A. Krzyzak, C.Y. Suen, Methods of Combining Multiple Classifiers and Their Applications to Handwriting Recognition. *IEEE Trans. on SMC*, Vol.22, pp. 418-435, 1992.

D. Yu, D. Frincke, Alert Confidence Fusion in Intrusion Detection Systems with Extended Dempster-Shafer Theory, *Proceedings of the 43rd Annual ACM Southeast Conference*, Kennesaw, Georgia, March 2005.

S. Zanero, Analyzing tcp traffic patterns using self organizing maps, in F. Roli and S. Vitulano (Eds.), *Lecture Notes in Computer Science, vol. 3617*, Springer-Verlag, Berlin, pp. 8390, 2005.

C. Zhang, J. Jiang, M. Kamel, Intrusion detection using hierarchical neural networks. *Pattern Recognition Letters* 26(6), pp. 779-791, 2005.

4 Use of Artificial Neural Networks and Effects of Amino Acid Encodings in the Membrane Protein Prediction Problem

Subrata K Bose[1], Antony Browne[2], Hassan Kazemian[3] and Kenneth White[4]

[1] MRC Clinical Sciences Centre, Faculty of Medicine, Imperial College London, UK
   subrata.bose@ic.ac.uk
[2] Department of Computing, School of Engineering and Physical Sciences, University of
   Surrey, Guildford, UK a.browne@eim.surrey.ac.uk
[3] Intelligent Systems Research Centre, Department of Computing, Communication
   Technology and Mathematics, London Metropolitan University, London, UK
   h.kazemian@londonmet.ac.uk
[4] Institute for Health Research and Policy, Departments of Health and Human Sciences,
   London Metropolitan University, London, UK kenneth.white@londonmet.ac.uk

Abstract - In biology it is a truism that in order to understand function it is necessary to understand structure. Membrane proteins (MPs) are no exception and although they constitute an estimated 30% of the total number of proteins encoded in mammalian genomes, they are considerably under-represented in structural databases, contributing less than 1% of the protein structures in the Protein Data Bank (www.rcsb.org/pdb). Many drug targets are membrane proteins that act as hormone or chemical messenger receptors and there is considerable interest in this class of proteins shown by the pharmaceutical industry. Structural analysis of membrane proteins is considerably disadvantaged by the difficulty in obtaining crystals. Bioinformatic analysis of protein amino acid sequences affords one route to the preliminary characterisation of protein structure and some of the oldest algorithms attempted prediction of the relatively short, about 25 amino acids, and discrete, transmembrane regions of proteins that span the lipid membrane of cells. Making use of training sets based on known structures of membrane proteins we describe here an application of Applied Neural Nets (ANN) to the identification of transmembrane regions in protein sequences. We focus on the problem of representing the 20 different amino acids in a machine-learning algorithm, comparing four binary representations. A 5-bit representation based on the five structural sub-groups of amino acids proved to be less reliable than one based on a simple 20-bit binary representation that had no grounding in the properties of the amino acid, but gave the best classification rate of 90.0% (89% sensitivity, 90% specificity) and Area under the Curve (AUC) is 0.9381. We conclude that, for the length of amino acid strings used in the Neural Nets, five, the type of encoding is not critical. However for longer strings, where potential functional features of a transmembrane sequence could be conserved, we speculate that the way in which amino acids are represented could influence the effectiveness of neural nets.

Keywords: Membrane Proteins, Neural Networks, Knowledge Discovery, Secondary Structure Prediction, Amino acid binary encoding, Receiver Operating Characteristics (ROC) and Area Under the Curve (AUC)
Availability: Algorithm and data used to generate the results are available upon request to the authors.

4.1 Introduction

Proteins are essential macromolecules of life that constitute about half of a living cell's dry weight (Parris and Onwulata 1995). They are polymers of one or more uncleaved chains of amino acids ranging typically from two hundreds to few thousands. Proteins play crucial roles almost in all-biological processes (Elliott and Elliott 1997).

A large number of researchers are investigating globular proteins because of the easy availability of the data, but the prediction of membrane protein structures is a key area that remains unsolved (Baldi and Pollastri 2002). The part of the protein which makes contact with the cell membrane is called the transmembrane domain (TM) or the membrane spanning region (MSR). Some of them are accountable for a number of key tasks in a living cell and comprise some extremely essential biochemical components for cell-cell signaling, transportations of nutrients, solvents and ions across the membrane, cell-cell adhesion and intercellular communication (Ito 2000). Due to the fact that many drugs or drug adjuvants may interfere with membrane dynamics and subcellular localisation of enzyme systems, the pharmacological and pharmaceutical importance of integral membrane protein structure is enormous.

Three dimensional structures of proteins derived by X-ray crystallography have been determined for about 15000 proteins, but only about 80 of these are membrane proteins, despite the fact that the human proteome is estimated to be comprised of about 30% proteins containing membrane spanning regions (MSRs). Due to the presence of the hydrophobic and hydrophilic region on the surface of membrane proteins, they are not soluble in aqueous buffer solutions and denature in organic solvent. Because of their hydrophobic characteristics, and the fact that detergent micelles form around the hydrophobic regions, it is hard to induce MPs to form well-ordered 3D crystals (Persson and Argos 1997).

A reliable bias free membrane protein topology prediction tool would provide very useful structural and functional classification of protein sequences in a genome. Though a wide array of tools are available for predicting the topology of transmembrane domains, current methods for prediction of membrane spanning regions are far away from achieving 95% reliability and developers have overrated the accuracy of their methods by 15%-50% (Ikeda et al. 2001; Bose et al. 2005; Bose et al. 2006).

Though neural networks have been considered as classification and regression systems whose inner working principles were very difficult to interpret it is now becoming apparent that ANN could be used as a very useful tool for biological data mining and classification, for their adaptive nature and ability to approximate collective nonlinear functions. Due to the architecture of the neural networks, learning from examples makes this technique interesting for a problem like classification of patterns in biological sequences because of the lack of experience but availability of the training data (Rost and Sander 1993).

In this study, we revisited the problem of amino acid encodings, discussed below, and propose a novel methodology to predict whether a particular segment belong to the transmembrane regions or not by using artificial neural network. We have investigated four amino acid encodings and evaluated their performances. The most up to date, redundancy reduced, membrane and non-membrane data sets are used to train the ANN and to test the network's performance.

4.2 System and Methods

4.2.1 Membrane and non-membrane dataset

The lack of desired performance of the membrane spanning regions prediction methods and the overrating of the accuracy of their methods could be mainly due to the lack of non-redundant membrane datasets which were used in the learning and tuning processes (Ikeda et al. 2003). The quality and reliability of the data are two important factors before the selection of a data set for any modelling technique, including neural networks. Prediction of the membrane spanning regions (MSR) in proteins using neural network (NN) techniques requires high quality, experimentally characterized transmembrane data for training, validating and testing the performance of the network. It has been experimentally observed that selection of the protein data set for test and training purposes can lead to large variation, so being able to obtain an unbiased result from the ANN largely depends on the quality of the membrane and nonmembrane data set. In a methodological study, it was found that larger data sets play an important role for protein secondary structure prediction using neural networks, with accuracy of prediction increasing from 63.6% to 67% comparing smaller with larger data sets, repectively (Chandonia and Karplus 1996).

To improve the accuracy, an effort to use larger well-characterized reliable datasets for both training and testing has been made. We used two protein datasets with known biochemical characterizations of membrane topology, assembled by Möller and in the TMPDB Release 6.2 (Möller et al. 2000; Shimizu and Nakai 1994; Kihara et al. 1998; Ikeda et al. 2002). From these two sets of data, we have identified proteins common to either set by unique ID and those are excluded from our experimental database. To train the ANN with negative sequences, the DB-NTMR dataset (Pasquier and Hamodrakas 1999a; Pasquier et al. 1999b) was chosen, which is freely available at http://biophysics.biol.uoa.gr/DB-NTMR.

4.2.2 Amino acid sequence encodings

A predicament of using ANNs to mine primary amino acid sequence is that most ANNs are unable to identify non-numerical character strings. So conversion of the amino acid sequences into real numbers in order to get numerical input vectors is an important critical step of constructing the model. Four binary encoding schemas are used in this study, an orthogonal distributed 20 binary bits, 16 binary bits, 9 binary bits and 5 binary bits. Out of these four encodings, only the 5 and 9 binary bit encodings are based on physico-chemical properties. In practice 20 binary bits is the most common distributed encoding method, in which each amino acid is represented by a unique 20-bit binary string consisting of nineteen 0s and one 1, since there are 20 amino acids (Qian and Sejnowski 1988; Yang and Chou 2004). For example, amino acid, 'Alanine' is represented by 10000000000000000000, 'Tyrosine' is represented by 00000000000000000001 and the position of 1 identifies the amino acid and 1 would move to the right alphabetically based on the one letter abbreviation of the amino acids.

The 16-bits schema is a product of a genetic search algorithm and 30% shorter than the traditional orthogonal representations (de la Maza 1994). 9 bits representation is a feature-based grouping of amino acids where hydrophobicity, positive charge, negative charge, aromatic side chain, aliphatic side chain, small size, bulk size properties are used (Brusic 1995). On top of that two correction bits are used to discriminate similar amino acids. 5 bits representation is designed based on a classification of 20 amino acids which unites hydropathy index, molecular weight , and pI values together (Yang and Wang 2003; Nelson and Cox 2000). Amino acids A, V, L, I and M fit in to a non-polar and aliphatic group, F, Y and W belong to the aromatic group, G, S, P, T, C, N, and Q belong to the polar and uncharged group, K,H and R are the positively charged group and D and E belong to the negatively charged group.

4.2.3   Architecture of Neural Networks

The first consideration in designing the application was the neural technique to be adopted. The type of problem where we want to link a set of inputs (sequences of amino acids) to an output (membrane or non-membrane) can be solved using a supervised neural technique. We have chosen feedforward multilayer Perceptrons (MLPs). Because by setting sufficient number of hidden units and accurate weights and biases from a compact region of input space it can approximate to arbitrary accuracy any continuous function (Hornik 1991).

The multi-layered feed-forward neural network used here consists of an input layer, a single hidden layer and an output layer and training was done by the scaled conjugate gradient algorithm (Fig.??).

4.2.4   Distribution of the data and training procedure

The amino acid dataset that contain sequences of MSR and non-membrane regions are converted by using the four encoding schemas described above. This algorithm was applied to all the encodings separately to identify the best encodings. The resulting encoded dataset has been randomized first and the training data for each NN model is randomly chosen from it by the algorithm. From the source data set about 75% of the source data was randomly taken for training the network, and the remaining 25% of the data were selected as the test data. To detect when the over-fitting starts and to prevent the over-fitting problem, the training set was further partitioned into two disjoint subsets: training and validation datasets. The training dataset was used in

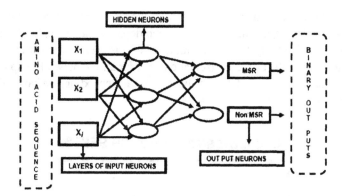

Fig. 1. Neural networks (NNs) architecture, amino acid sequences after converting according to the schemas are presented as input, the network's target output is either 0 or 1. 1 designates membrane spanning region (MSR) and 0 for nonmembrane.

the training process and the validation dataset was used to stop the training (before convergence) when the validation error rate started to increase instead of decreasing. The size of the validation data was about 25% of the training data. The size and ratio of distribution of the training, validation and test data was kept unchanged for all the four encoding schemas.

For each encoding schema, the NN model was trained by the combination of changing the learning rate within a range, along with changing the number of hidden units and a random starting weight initialization. During the training the validation dataset was used as an observer to check the progress of training after regular intervals. Once the validation accuracy rate decreased the training stopped and the best result obtained is saved. Initially we designed the experiment with a threshold value of 0.5 to get the most suited experimental parameters for the particular algorithm. Without changing the parameter of the best NN model, we have also investigated changing the threshold values ranging from 0.1 to 0.9.

4.2.5 Implementation

NNs models were implemented by using the neural network Toolbox and Netlab software under Matlab Version 13.0 for Windows platform. MSR and non-membrane data were extracted by a Perl scripts and the conversion of the amino acid sequences of both MSR and non-membrane data to binary strings was carried out by a piece of software developed by using Visual Basic 6.0.

4.3   Results and Discussion

All four algorithms produce a confusion matrix which can be used to critically analyze the performances of all the algorithms. Here in this study three parameters - classification rate (%), true positive ratio or hit rate (TPr), false alarm rate or false positive ratio

(FPr) are used for comparison of the algorithms. We also use the ROC curve to asses the robustness of the algorithms. An ROC graph depicts relative trade-offs between benefits and costs. To plot a ROC curve, hit rate (TPr) is used as the vertical axis (X) and false alarm rate (FPr) as the horizontal one(Y), for all the network output thresholds we investigated. For quantitative analysis from each encoding, we have calculated the area under the ROC curve using nine points.

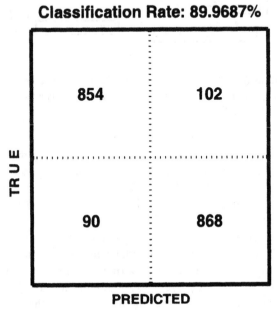

Fig. 2. Two-by-two confusion matrix (also called a contingency table) produced by best network for twenty binary representation

In our study ANNs trained with 20-binary-bit encoding produced the highest classification rate and AUC, hence superior robustness . We have observed a minor effect on the classification rate (~2% variance) and AUC when either altering the bit length of binary input data (from 5-bits to 20 bits) or increasing the hidden layer nodes after a certain level, or both.

Table 1. Best classification rate and area under the ROC curve on different binary encodings

Encoding Name	Classification Rate (%)	Area Under The Curve (AUC)
Five Binary	87.17	0.9302
Nine Binary	89.28	0.9373
Sixteen Binary	88.08	0.9323
Twenty Binary	89.96	0.9381

Of the four binary bit representations, the 5-bit binary approach attempts the use of, physico-chemical properties of amino acids, but applying this biological information into the input data didn't improve the prediction accuracy or AUC (in table 1 and fig 3).

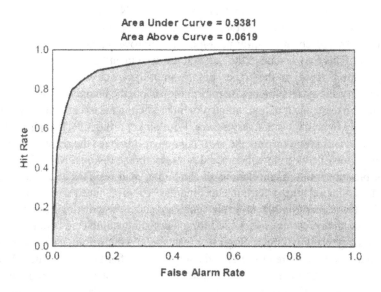

Fig. 3. Area Under ROC Curve report for 20-bit binary encoding

Our data suggest that the higher the dimension of binary input variables the greater the classifier's robustness. The results also suggest that by increasing the numbers of binary input variables a slightly higher classification rate and robustness may be achieved. This could be due to the fact that these binary encodings don't initiate any artificial ordering; uniform weight was given to each amino acid for the network learning purposes. If the amino acids were encoded with the values 0 (A), 1(R), 2(N) and so on, some algorithms might try to interpret the artificial ordering A<R<N among 20 amino acids. Binary encodings have the advantage of not importing any artificial correlations between the amino acids during the learning process. Some earlier research suggests that binary input data may improve an ANN's learning but according to the best of our knowledge, there is no recorded evidence on the effect of binary input data on the robustness of the ANNs, especially in the area of membrane protein prediction (Fausett 1994).

Due to the large number of network parameters of the 20-bit approach, theoretically the input space of the network's architecture should be enlarged and over-stretched which could eventually decrease the ratio of the sequence number over the space. Binary encodings with higher numbers of input variables could well make the ANN's architectures vulnerable to overfitting. Overfitting could eventually cause the ANNs to make a prediction decision that is totally irrelevant to the training data (Smith 1996). It could also generate anomalous predictions in multilayer perceptrons, even with noise-free data. It is also reported that with large input windows there are chances of attenuating parsed information available in the input data that is very significant for the prediction (Lund et al. 1997). Hypothetically all these problems could increase the complexity and diminish the classification performance of the ANNs.

This research clearly suggests that increasing the ANN's binary input vector's number may improve the classification rate and robustness of the system slightly, but incorporation of physico-chemical information didn't improve the network's performance dramatically. This may be due to the fact that the system and dataset are competent in identifying the mapping in the higher dimension of the space and due to the reduced dimensionality, the system might lose information about the boundary. Our results also suggest that in the context of membrane protein prediction the effect of the dimensionality of binary input data is not very severe. With binary orthogonal encoding, though the prediction was based on only the local context, it improved the network's capability to distinguish between membrane and non-membrane regions. But this encoding may not produce implicit correlations of the amino acid residues at all. It could be simply due to the fact that with this encoding the ANNs achieved finer capability for illustrating the scenario in higher levels which are superior in distinguishing different classes rather than creating artificial ordering among the amino acid residues. The results may suggest that taking biological information of the neighbouring residues in consideration is not a prerequisite to make a good classifier because in the 20-bit approach each prediction is based in isolation, taking no account of the predictions for adjacent residues and are hence uncorrelated. However the data may simply reflect that the biological properties implicit in the 5-bit encodings are too crude. Although transmembrane domains of proteins are overall hydrophobic in character, many contain individual polar or charged amino acids. These are often involved in interactions between transmembrane regions of the same or different proteins. Moreover, proteins involved in transport of ions across membranes must carry polar or charged amino acids in the transmembrane region to facilitate the transport. It seems likely that the transmembrane sequence reflects the function of the protein, which could vary from being a single hydrophobic "anchor" to keep the protein attached to a membrane, or being part of a complex ion channel made of several transmembrane regions from separate proteins.

4.4 Future Development

We propose to generate a dendrogram of the cluster analysis to detect the samples the network failed on. Ward's method of cluster analysis technique will be adopted to detect which features carry the most information when the tree splits between 'correctly classified' and 'incorrectly classified', to identify if there is any similarity between input sequences that the network fails to process correctly. An alternative technique would be to use a different kind of NN such as a self-organising map to do the clustering and identify any sub-cluster in the data that the feed-forward network is having problem with.

4.5 Conclusions

This research dealt with one of the most significant problems in structural molecular biology - the prediction of membrane spanning regions from primary amino acid sequences, by ANNs. The outcome of the research is threefold.

It is reported that almost all the current membrane protein prediction methods have been significantly overestimated in terms of their accuracy. This is mainly due to a failure to use well-characterised and reliable benchmarking data sets and also an appropriate unbiased performance evaluation metric. In this research we have tried to overcome these problems by presenting an experimentally confirmed, reliable membrane and non-membrane data set and by checking the robustness of the performance by setting very rigid and unbiased evaluation criteria.

Secondly, by constructing a standardised machine-learning framework we have developed a system that could be applied to the analysis of membrane spanning regions in the proteome with significant robustness. It transpired the correct classification rates were not essentially the most unbiased performance measure of MSR classifiers because the number of known globular proteins is far greater than that of the membrane protein. Therefore all-negative or all-positive classifiers may possibly indicate a high classification rate. To avoid these problem classifiers, performances were evaluated over the whole array of class distributions by using the ROC curve. The value of the area under the ROC curve clearly illustrated the universal performance of the classifier, given that it is not reliant on the threshold used for achieving a class level.

Thirdly, the results suggest that 20-bit binary encodings can achieve a higher classification accuracy and robustness compared with 5-bit and 9-bit encodings, indicating that use of simple physico-chemical parameters may not increase the robustness of the system more so than the binary encodings.

References

Baldi.P. and Pollastri, G. (2002). Machine Learning Structural and Functional Proteomics. IEEE Intelligent Systems (Intelligent Systems in Biology II).

Bose, S., Kazemian, H., White, K. & Browne., A. (2005). Use Of Neural Networks To Predict And Analyse Membrane Proteins in the Proteome. BMC Bioinformatics. ISSN 1471-2105 Vol. 6 (Suppl 3): P3.

Bose S., Kazemian H.B., White K. & Browne A. (2006), Presenting a Novel Neural Network Architecture for Membrane Protein Prediction. Proceedings 10th International Conference on Intelligent Engineering Systems, London, UK June 26-28(ISBN of printed proceedings:1-4244-9708-8 and ISBN of CD proceedings: 1-4244-9709-6)

Brusic V., Rudy G. and Harrison L.C. (1995). Prediction of MHC binding peptides using artificial neural networks. Complexity International volume 2, ISSN 1320-0682.

Chandonia, J M. and Karplus M (1996). The importance of larger data sets for protein secondary structure prediction with neural networks. Protein Science, 5, 768-774.

de la Maza M (1994). Generate, Test and Explain: Synthesizing Regulatory Exposing Attributes in Large Protein Databases. Proceedings of the Twenty-Seven Annual Hawaii International Conference on System Sciences.

Elliott, W. H. & Elliott, D. C. (1997). The structure of proteins. In: Biochemistry and Molecular Biology. pp. 23-37, NY: Oxford University Press.

Fausett, L. (1994). Fundamentals of Neural Networks, Englewood Cliffs,NJ: Prentice Hall.

Hornik, K.(1991). Approximation capabilities of multilayer feed-forward networks. Neural Networks 4, 251–257.

Ikeda, M., Arai, M., Okuno, T. and Shimizu, T. (2001). The prediction accuracy of trans-membrane topology is improved by a consensus method: An application to genome-wide analysis. 4th International Conference on Biological Physics (ICBP), pp. 60.

Ikeda, M., Arai, M., Lao, D. M. and Shimizu, T. (2002) Transmembrane topology prediction methods: A re-assessment and improvement by a consensus method using a dataset of experimentally-characterized transmembrane topologies. In Silico Biol., 2, 19-33.

Ikeda, M., Arai, M., Okuno, T. and Shimizu, T.(2003). TMPDB: a database of experimentally-characterized transmembrane topologies Nucleic Acids Res., January 1, 2003; 31(1): 406 - 409.

Ito A. (2000). Mitochondrial processing peptidase: multiple-site recognition of precursor proteins. TICB, 10:25-31.

Kihara, D., Shimizu, T. and Kanehisa, M. (1998) Prediction of membrane proteins based on classification of transmembrane segments. Protein Eng., 11, 961-970.

Lund, O., Frimand,J., Gorodkin,H., Bohr, J.,Hansen,J., and Brunak, S., Proteindistance (1997). Constraints predicted by neural networks and probability density functions. Prot.Eng., 10:1241-1248.

Möller S., Kriventseva, E. and Apweiler, R. (2000) A collection of well characterized integral membrane proteins. Bioinformatics 16, 1159-1160.

Nelson, D. and Cox,M.(2000) Lehninger Principles of Biochemistry Amino. Worth Publishers.

Qian, N. and Sejnowski, T. J. (1988). Predicting the secondary structure of globular proteins using neural network models. Journal of Molecular Biology. 202, 865-884.

Parris, N. & Onwulata, C. (1995). Food Proteins and Interactions. In: Molecular Biology and Biotechnology A comprehensive desk reference, (R. A. Meyers ed.) pp. 320-323, Cambridge UK: VCH Publishers.

Pasquier, C., and Hamodrakas, S. J. (1999a) An hierarchical artificial neural network system for the classification of transmembrane proteins, Protein Eng., 12(8), 631-4.

Pasquier C, Promponas VJ, Palaios GA, Hamodrakas JS, Hamodrakas SJ(1999b).A novel method for predicting transmembrane segments in proteins based on a statistical analysis of the SwissProt database: the PRED-TMR algorithm. Protein Eng. :12(5):381-5.

Persson, B and Argos, P (1997). Prediction of membrane protein topology utilizing multiple sequence alignments. Journal of Protein Chemistry 16(5): 453-7.

Rost, B. and Sander, C.(1993). Prediction of protein secondary structure at better than 70% accuracy. J Mol Biol, 232:584-99.

Shimizu, T. and Nakai, K. (1994) Construction of a membrane protein database and an evaluation of several prediction methods of transmembrane segments. In Miyano, S., Akutsu, T., Imai, H., Gotoh, O. and Takagi, T. (eds), Proc. Genome Informatics Workshop , Universal Academy Press, Tokyo, pp. 148-149.

Smith, M. (1996). Neural Networks for Statistical Modeling, Boston: International Thomson Computer Press, ISBN 1-850-32842-0.

Yang X. and Wang B. (2003). Weave Amino Acid Sequences for Protein Secondary Structure Prediction. Proceedings of the DMKD, San Diego, CA, USA (ACM 1-58113-763-x).

Yang, Z.R. and Chou, K.C. (2004). Predicting the O-linkage sites in glycoproteins using biobasis function neural networks. Bioinformatics, , vol. 20, pp. 903-908.

5 Computationally Efficient Graph Matching via Energy Vector Extraction

Ariel Amato[1], Murad Al Haj[1], Josep Lládos[1], Jordi Gonzàlez[2]

[1] Computer Vision Centre & Departament Informàtica, Universitat Autònoma de Barcelona ,
08193 Cerdanyola, Spain. Corresponding Author: *aamato@cvc.uab.es*
[2] Institut de Robòtica i Informàtica Industrial (UPC-CSIC), Edifici U, Parc Tecnològic de
Barcelona. C/ Llorens i Artigas 4-6, 08028 Barcelona, Spain

Abstract. This paper presents a method for graph matching based on domain knowledge by quantifying representative graph features. Our method searches and extracts the most relevant cues in different graphs. Once these cues are extracted and quantified, a new energy function is used to match the different graphs based on the obtained features values. This approach has been successfully applied for deformable template matching. As a result, the matching error and the computational cost are reduced by efficiently selecting and grouping representative features.

5.1 Introduction

Graphs hold a great representative power which makes them the most natural way to encode and symbolize any pattern [1]. All non-verbal human communications, ranging from hand gestures to written documents, include some concept of a graph. Many applications in computer vision include selecting and extracting information from graphs. Tombre proposed a method for analyzing engineering drawings [2], and Kruger, Potzsch, and Andmalsburg proposed a method for determining face position and pose based on labeled graphs [3].

Due to this power, graph matching is a logical way to compare and recognize different objects. The main challenge in any graph matching method is to extract representative segments of different graphs for comparison. Many approaches have been considered: some were based on one-to-one correspondence [1], while others were based on many-to-many correspondence [4]. However, these methods usually suffered from computational complexity and inefficiency while handling distortions. In this paper, we present a method for graph matching based on feature extraction to obtain a vector representation for each graph; this vector is later used for deformable template recognition. A new energy function is formulated to extract this vector based on the graph attributes. Then, a simple distance function is applied for the final matching. This method is robust to noise, segmentation errors, graphs with missing or extra edges, and graphs with missing or extra nodes.

This paper is organized as follows. Section 2 discusses briefly related works. Section 3 presents the feature extraction method while section 4 presents the matching method. In section 5, experimental results are discussed. Concluding remarks are made in section 6.

5.2 Related Work

Graph matching is usually addressed as a method for object recognition. Gold and Rangarajan [1] propose a one-to-one correspondence that is established through a graduated assignment. Kim and Kak [5] propose a bipartite graph matching using discrete relaxation for 3-D object reconstruction. Other algorithm uses a quadratic programming approach using a maximal clique framework [6]. Many-to-many correspondence has been also investigated [4], frequently in the context of edit-distance, [7]. A survey for graph matching in pattern recognition is presented in [8]. In [9], a robust point matching for nonrigid shapes is discussed; while in [10], a fast graph comparison technique was developed.

However, these methods are either computationally complex or do not support slight distortions in graphs. So, a small deformation in the graph to be matched introduces a lot of error in the matching process, unless the algorithm is computationally expensive.

In this paper, a robust method with a low computational cost is introduced. Its strength lies in its ability to assign quantitative values to representative graph features such that the matching process is only a simple distance function.

5.3 Energy Function

A graph $G = (N, E)$ can be interpreted as a set of basic forms, which are the nodes and the edges. Figure 1 shows an interpretation of a given object as a graph. The features used in matching different graphs are the information obtained from these nodes and edges.

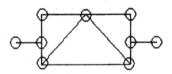

Fig. 1. Object representation as a set of nodes and edges

This method transforms a graph into a vector of energy values. An energy function is calculated at each node in the graph. This energy function aims at encoding the number of edges connected to each node, their relative length, their shape, and the average relative angle of each node. Then, each graph is represented as a vector of these calculated energy values.

Towards this end, we define a completely novel energy function as follows:

$$E(i) = \sum_{p=1}^{n} p * k1 + \frac{\sum_{p=1}^{n} L_{ip}}{\sum_{j=1}^{m}\sum_{p=1}^{n} L_{jp}} * k2 + \frac{\sum_{p=1}^{n} \theta_{ip}}{n} * \frac{k3}{2.\pi} + \frac{\sum_{p=1}^{n} A_{ip}}{\sum_{j=1}^{m}\sum_{p=1}^{n} A_{jp}} * k4 \qquad (1)$$

where n is the number of edges attached to node i, m is the number of nodes in the graph, L_{ip} is the length of the pth edge attached to node i, θ_{ip} is the angle the pth edge form with the horizontal, A_{ip} is the area enclosed by the edge in case it is not a straight line. This area represents the shape of the edge as shown in Fig. 2. The constants k1, k2, k3 and k4 are set experimentally.

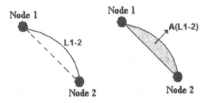

Fig. 2. Area enclosed by a circular edge between Node 1 and Node 2

5.4 Graph Matching

Let's assume a graph G_k is to be matched with a set of graphs $G_1, G_2, \ldots, G_n$. Once the energy vectors E_k and $E_1, E_2, \ldots, E_n$ are obtained, they are then sorted in descending order. The distance between E_k and each of the other energy vectors is calculated according to Eq. 2.

$$d_j = \sum_{i=1}^{n} | E_k(i) - E_j(i) | \qquad (2)$$

where d_j is the distance between G_k and G_j, n is the maximum number of nodes found in G_k and G_j .

5.4.1 Robustness

This method is robust to perturbations in the graph structure due to the fact that the energy function, Eq. 1, puts more weight on the representative features of the different graphs. The idea is to compare the most representative features of one graph to the most representative features of the second graph. Therefore, sorting the two energy vectors, and comparing them one-by-one (the first value in E_1 to the first value in E_2, the second value in E_1 to the second value of E_2, and so on) provide a very simple and effective way to compare the representative features. Any noise or distortion introduced will have low energy value and will appear at the end of the energy vectors; therefore, it will have a minimal effect on the matching process. Also, this matching process is independent on the size of the graphs, since the relative lengths of the edges are considered. Matching is also independent on the position of the graphs since relative angles are calculated.

5.4.2 Efficiency

The main advantage of this method is its computational efficiency since the matching is done in linear time. It is able to achieve robust detection in $O(n)$ where n is the maximum number of nodes found in the different graphs. This is considered a great achievement when compared with other methods that are considered low-cost yet they run in $O(lm)$, where l and m are the number of links in the two graphs [1].

5.5 Experimental Results

We worked with a database of four graphs from the International Symbol Recognition Contest (GREC'2003), shown in Fig. 3, and we tested our method with 512 samples which are distorted versions of such graphs, see Fig. 4.

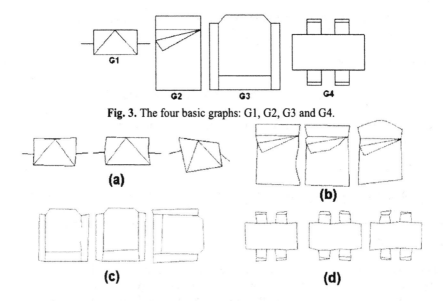

Fig. 3. The four basic graphs: G1, G2, G3 and G4.

Fig. 4. Samples corresponding to distorted versions of (a) G1, (b) G2, (c) G3, and (d) G4.

The purpose was to match each distorted graph with its original version. Setting experimentally k1 to 10, k2 to 5, k3 to 3, and k4 to 3, we were able to achieve a 100% recognition rate. Table 1 shows results of calculating the distance function between 16 distorted versions of G1 randomly selected and all four templates: G1, G2, G3 and G4. Each row represents the Euclidian distance between the distorted versions shown in Fig 4 and the four template graphs. It can be seen that the minimum distance (shown in bold) is obtained when comparing each distorted version of G1 with the template graph G1, thus indicating that the matching was correctly achieved. Tables 2, 3, and 4 show the same results for distorted versions of G2, G3, and G4, respectively.

TABLE 1: Distance Calculation for 16 samples (distorted versions) of G1

Sample (Distorted Versions of G1)	G1	G2	G3	G4
1	**9**	106	157	663
2	**12**	107	162	670
3	**12**	103	158	666
4	**8**	101	154	662
5	**10**	103	154	671
6	**11**	106	154	668
7	**11**	107	162	670
8	**9**	108	159	668
9	**10**	110	160	669
10	**12**	110	160	664
11	**8**	112	158	665
12	**8**	104	154	670
13	**12**	106	169	669
14	**11**	111	154	663
15	**10**	106	153	667
16	**9**	104	161	670

TABLE 2: Distance Calculation for 16 samples (distorted versions) of G2

Sample (Distorted Versions of G2)	G1	G2	G3	G4
1	94	**8**	172	660
2	96	**12**	176	664
3	94	**8**	172	660
4	96	**12**	176	664
5	96	**12**	176	663
6	94	**8**	172	660
7	96	**9**	172	660
8	94	**8**	176	663
9	97	**11**	174	665
10	97	**10**	174	663
11	95	**11**	175	660
12	94	**8**	176	662
13	95	**9**	175	664
14	96	**10**	173	660
15	94	**8**	175	664
16	94	**8**	174	663

TABLE 3: Distance Calculation for 16 samples (distorted versions) of G3

Sample (Distorted Versions of G3)	G1	G2	G3	G4
1	158	177	**8**	572
2	155	178	**4**	567
3	155	176	**5**	571
4	157	180	**3**	569

5	155	176	5	571
6	157	180	8	569
7	158	180	7	567
8	155	176	3	572
9	156	178	4	571
10	154	177	6	569
11	155	176	7	571
12	158	180	8	570
13	156	177	7	571
14	156	180	3	568
15	158	177	3	572
16	157	176	5	576

TABLE 4: Distance Calculation for 16 samples (distorted versions) of G4

Sample (Distorted Versions of G4)	G1	G2	G3	G4
1	667	676	571	33
2	667	686	577	31
3	669	678	569	23
4	670	679	570	24
5	670	679	570	28
6	668	675	568	24
7	670	678	571	17
8	669	678	570	22
9	668	679	569	25
10	671	675	568	29
11	669	676	573	23
12	670	684	567	19
13	667	682	568	28
14	670	680	572	30
15	669	679	570	26
16	671	677	569	25

5.6 Conclusions

In this paper, we present a computationally efficient graph matching technique based on feature extraction via energy vectors. This method has a very low order computational complexity O(n) and it is extremely robust to noise and distortion. The experimental results were impressive. In the future, this method will be tested with more graphs specifically those including non-linear edges.

Acknowledgements

This work has been supported by EC grants IST-027110 for the HERMES project and IST-045547 for the VIDI-Video project, and by the Spanish MEC under projects TIN2006-14606, DPI-2004-5414 and TIN2006-15694-C02-02. Jordi Gonzàlez also acknowledges the support of a Juan de la Cierva Postdoctoral fellowship from the Spanish MEC.

References

[1] Gold, S. and Rangarajan, A., "Graph Matching by Graduated Assignment", *IEEE Computer Society Conference on Computer Vision and Pattern Recognition(VCPR'96)*, pp. 239-244, June 1996. San Francisco, CA, USA.

[2] Tombre, K., "Analysis of Engineering Drawings: State of the Art and Challenges", *Graphics Recognition Algorithms and Systems, LNCS*, vol. 1389, pp. 257-264, 1998.

[3] Kruger, N., Potzsch, M., Andmalsburg, C.V.D., "Determination of Face Position and Pose with a Learned Representation Based on Labeled Graphs", *Image Vision Computing*, n. 15, pp. 665-673, 1997.

[4] Keselman, Y., Shokoufandeh, A., Demirci, M.F. and Dickinson, S., "Many-to-Many Graph Matching via Metric Embedding", *IEEE Computer Society Conference on Computer Vision and Pattern Recognition*, vol. 1, pp. 1-850 – 1-857, June 2003.

[5] Kim, W., and Kak, A.C., "3D object recognition using bipartite matching embedded in discrete relaxation", *IEEE Transactions on Pattern Analysis and Machine Intelligence*, 13(3):224-251, 1991.

[6] Pelillo, M., Siddiqi, K., and Zucker, S., "Matching hierarchical structures using association graphs", *IEEE Transactions on Pattern Analysis and Machine Intelligence*, 21(11):1105-1120, November 1999.

[7] Liu, T.L., and Geiger, D., "Approximate tree matching and shape similarity", *7th International Conference on Computer Vision*, pp. 456-462, 1999.

[8] Conte D., Foggia P., Sansone C., and Vento M. , "Thirty Years of Graph Matching in Pattern Recognition", *International Journal on Pattern Recognition and Artificial Intelligence*, vol. 18, no. 3, pp. 265-298, 2004.

[9] Zheng Y., and Doermann D., "Robust Point Matching for Nonrigid Shapes by Preserving Local Neighborhood Structures", *IEEE Transactions on Pattern Analysis and Machine Intelligence*, 13(3):224-251, 1991.

[10] Lopresti D. and Wilfong, G.T , "A Fast Technique for Comparing Graph Representations with Applications to Performance Evaluation", *International Journal on Document Analysis and Recognition*, vol. 6, no. 4, pp. 219-229, April, 2003.

6 A Validity Index Based on Cluster Symmetry

Sriparna Saha and Sanghamitra Bandyopadhyay

Machine Intelligence Unit,
Indian Statistical Institute,
Kolkata, India
Email:{sriparna_r,sanghami}@isical.ac.in

Abstract. An important consideration in clustering is the determination of an algorithm appropriate for partitioning a given data set. Thereafter identification of the correct number of clusters and the corresponding clustering needs to be performed. In this paper, a newly developed point symmetry distance is used to propose a new cluster validity index named *Sym*-index which provides a measure of "symmetricity" of the different partitionings of a data set. The index is able to address all the above mentioned issues, viz., identifying the appropriate clustering algorithm, determining the number of clusters and evolving the proper partitioning as long as the clusters possess the property of symmetry. A Kd-tree-based data structure is used to reduce the complexity of computing the point symmetry based distance. Results demonstrating the superiority of the *Sym*-index in appropriately determining the proper clustering technique as well as the number of clusters, as compared to two other recently proposed measures, namely the PS-index and *I*-index, are provided for three clustering methods viz., two recently developed genetic algorithm based clustering techniques and the average linkage clustering algorithm. Four artificial data sets and one real life data set are considered for this purpose.

Keywords: Unsupervised classification, cluster validity index, symmetry, point symmetry based distance, Kd tree.

6.1 Introduction

Clustering [4] is a core problem in data-mining with innumerable applications spanning many fields. The three fundamental questions that need to be addressed in any typical clustering scenario are: (i) what is a good clustering technique suitable for a given data set, (ii) how many clusters are actually present in the data, and (iii) how real or good is the clustering itself. It is well-known in the pattern recognition community that different algorithms are applicable for data with different characteristics. Given a wide choice of methods, determining an appropriate clustering algorithm for a particular data set presents a challenge. Once the proper clustering method has been identified, the next task is to determine the number of clusters and also the validity of the clusters formed [8]. The measure of the validity of clusters should be such that it will be able to impose an ordering of the clusters in terms of their goodness [9].

Several cluster validity indices have been proposed in the literature. These are Davies-Bouldin (DB) index [11], Dunn's index [11], Xie-Beni (XB) index [11], I-index [11] etc., to name just a few. Some of these indices have been found to be able to detect the correct partitioning for a given number of clusters, while some can determine the appropriate number of clusters as well. However, the effectiveness of these indices in determining the proper clustering algorithm has seldom been studied. Such an attempt has been made in the present paper. In this regard, a new cluster validity index is proposed which is found to be more effective than two other indices in determining the appropriate clustering method, the correct number of clusters and the proper clustering as well.

Most of the validity measures usually assume a certain geometrical structure in the shapes of all the clusters. But if different clusters possess different structural properties, these indices are often found to fail. It may be noted that one of the basic feature of shapes and objects is symmetry. It is considered as a pre-attentive feature which enhances recognition and reconstruction of shapes and objects [12]. As symmetry is so common in the natural world, it can be assumed that some kind of symmetry exists in the clusters which may be of different shapes. Based on this, Su and Chou have proposed a point symmetry (PS) distance, and a clustering algorithm that uses this PS-distance [12]. In [3], a modified PS-distance is suggested, based on which a new validity index called PS-index, is also proposed. It has been shown in [1] that both the definitions of the PS-distances in [12] and [3] have severe limitations, and a new PS-distance, d_{ps}, is proposed. Here we propose a symmetry based cluster validity index named Sym-index that uses the new distance d_{ps}. For A different clustering algorithms A_i, $i = 1, \ldots, A$, the number of clusters K varying from K_{min} to K_{max}, Sym-index is computed for each of the $A \times (K_{max} - K_{min})$ partitionings. The algorithm A^* and the number of cluster K^* for which Sym-index attains its maximum value indicate the most appropriate combination for the data set.

The performance of the proposed index is compared to that of PS-index [12] and I-index [11] for four artificially generated data sets with different characteristics and one real-life data set. For the purpose of comparison, the GAK-means algorithm [10], average linkage clustering algorithm [4], and the genetic PS-distance-based clustering algorithm (GAPS) [1] are used.

6.2 The Existing Point Symmetry Based Cluster Validity Index

The point symmetry distance (PS) proposed by Su and Chou in [12] is defined as follows: Given N patterns, x_j, $j = 1, \ldots N$, and a reference vector c (e.g., a cluster centroid), the "point symmetry distance" between a pattern x_j and the reference vector c is defined in [3] as

$$d_c(\overline{x}_j, \overline{c}) = d_s(\overline{x}_j, \overline{c}) \times d_e(\overline{x}_j, \overline{c}) \tag{1}$$

where

$$d_s(\overline{x}_j, \overline{c}) = \min_{i=1,\ldots N \text{ and } i \neq j} \left(\frac{\|(\overline{x}_j - \overline{c}) + (\overline{x}_i - \overline{c})\|}{\|(\overline{x}_j - \overline{c})\| + \|(\overline{x}_i - \overline{c})\|} \right) \tag{2}$$

and $d_e(\overline{x}_j, \overline{c})$ denotes the Euclidean distance between $\overline{x}_j$ and $\overline{c}$. Note that the minimum of the quantity within brackets on the right hand side of Equation 2 occurs when $x_i = x_j^*$, where $\overline{x}_j^*$ is the symmetrical/reflected point of $\overline{x}_j$ with respect to $\overline{c}$.

PS-index: The cluster validity index, PS-index, is defined as [3]

$$PS(K) = \frac{1}{K} \sum_{i=1}^{K} \frac{1}{n_i} \sum_{j \in S_i} \frac{d_s(\overline{x}_j, \overline{c}_i) \times d_e(\overline{x}_j, \overline{c}_i)}{min_{m,n=1,\ldots,K \text{ and } m \neq n} d_e(\overline{c}_m, \overline{c}_n)}$$

$$\Rightarrow \frac{1}{K} \sum_{i=1}^{K} \frac{1}{n_i} \sum_{j \in S_i} \frac{d_c(\overline{x}_j, \overline{c}_i)}{d_{min}} \tag{3}$$

where S_i is the set whose elements are the data points assigned to the ith cluster, n_i is the number of elements in S_i, or, $n_i = |S_i|$, d_{min} is the minimum Euclidean distance between any two cluster centers and $d_c(\overline{x}_j, \overline{c}_i)$ is computed by Equation 1. The smallest $PS(K)$ indicates a valid optimal partition with the optimal cluster number K.

It is evident from Equation 2 that this distance measure can be useful to detect clusters which have symmetrical shapes. But this distance measure will fail for datasets where clusters themselves are symmetrical with respect to some intermediate point. From equation 1, it can be noted that as $d_e(\overline{x}_j, \overline{c}) \approx d_e(\overline{x}_j^*, \overline{c})$, $d_c(\overline{x}_j, \overline{c}) \approx \frac{d_{symm}(\overline{x}_j, \overline{c})}{2}$, where $d_{symm}(\overline{x}_j, \overline{c}) = \|(\overline{x}_j - \overline{c}) + (\overline{x}_j^* - \overline{c})\|$. In effect, if a point $\overline{x}_j$ is almost equally symmetrical with respect to two centroids $\overline{c}_1$ and $\overline{c}_2$, it will be assigned to that cluster with respect to which it is more symmetric. Euclidean distance between the cluster center and the particular point has no effect. This is intuitively unappealing. Since a point may then be assigned to a very far off cluster centre, just because it happens to be marginally more symmetric with respect to it.

The drawbacks of d_s and d_c have been demonstrated theoretically and experimentally in [1]. Those could not be included here for lack of space. Since the point symmetry based distance d_c proposed in [3] has some inherent problem, and the PS-index is based on d_c, the PS-index also has the same drawbacks. In this article a new point symmetry based distance is used to propose a new symmetry based cluster validity index which overcomes these limitations.

6.3 *Sym*-index: Proposed Symmetry Based Cluster Validity Index

6.3.1 Symmetry Based Distance

In order to overcome the limitations of d_c, a new PS distance called $d_{ps}(x, c)$ corresponding to point x with respect to center c is defined as follows: Let a point be x. The symmetrical (reflected) point of x with respect to a particular center c is $2 * c - x$. Let us denote this by x^*. Let the first and second unique nearest neighbors of x^* be at Euclidean distances of d_1 and d_2 respectively from it. Then

$$d_{ps}^*(x, c) = \frac{(d_1 + d_2)}{2} * d_e(x, c) \tag{4}$$

where $d_e(\overline{x}, \overline{c})$ is the Euclidean distance between the point $\overline{x}$ and $\overline{c}$.

The basic differences between the PS based distances in [12] and [3], and the proposed point symmetry distance $d_{ps}(\overline{x}, \overline{c})$ are as follows:

1. Instead of computing the Euclidean distance between the original reflected point $\overline{x}^* = 2 \times \overline{c} - \overline{x}$ and its first nearest neighbor as in [12] and [3], here the average distance between $\overline{x}^*$ and its first and the second unique nearest neighbors have been taken. Consequently the term, $(d_1 + d_2)/2$ will never be equal to 0, and the effect of $d_e(\overline{x}, \overline{c})$, the Euclidean distance, will always be considered. Considering both d_1 and d_2 in the computation of d_{ps} makes the PS-distance more robust and noise resistant.

2. Considering both d_1 and d_2 in the computation of d_{ps} makes the PS-distance more robust and noise resistant. From an intuitive point of view, if both d_1 and d_2 of $\overline{x}$ with respect to $\overline{c}$ is less, then the likelihood that $\overline{x}$ is symmetrical with respect to $\overline{c}$ increases. This is not the case when only the first nearest neighbor is considered which could mislead the method in noisy situations.

The computation of point symmetry based distance is highly complex. In order to compute the nearest neighbor distance of the reflected point of a particular data point with respect to a cluster center efficiently, we have used Kd-tree based nearest neighbor search. ANN (Approximate Nearest Neighbor), which is a library written in C++ (obtained from http://www.cs.umd.edu/~mount/ANN), is used for this purpose. Here ANN is used to find d_1 and d_2 in Equation 4 efficiently. The Kd-tree structure can be constructed in $O(n\log n)$ time and takes $O(n)$ space.

6.3.2 The Proposed Cluster Validity Measure

Definition

Consider a partition of the data set $X = \{\overline{x}_j : j = 1, 2, \ldots n\}$ into K clusters and the center of each cluster $\overline{c}_i$ can be computed by using $\overline{c}_i = \frac{\sum_{j=1}^{n_i} x_{ij}}{n_i}$, where n_i ($i = 1, 2, \ldots, K$) is the number of points in cluster i, and x_{ij} is the jth point of the ith cluster. The new cluster validity function *Sym*-index is defined as:

$$Sym\text{-index}(K) = \left(\frac{1}{K} \times \frac{1}{\mathcal{E}_K} \times D_K \right). \tag{5}$$

Here,

$$\mathcal{E}_K = \sum_{k=1}^{K} E_k,$$

such that

$$E_k = \sum_{j=1}^{n_k} d_{ps}^*(\overline{x}_{kj}, \overline{c}_k),$$

and

$$D_K = max^K_{i,j=1} \|\bar{c}_i - \bar{c}_j\|.$$

D_K is the maximum Euclidean distance between two cluster centres among all centres. $d^*_{ps}(\overline{x_{kj}}, \overline{c_k})$ is computed using Equation 4 with the following constraint: the first two nearest neighbors of the reflected point of $\overline{x_{kj}}$ with respect to $\bar{c}_k$ are searched only among the points which are assigned to the kth cluster, i.e., the first and second nearest neighbors of the reflected point should belong to the kth cluster. The objective is to maximize this index in order to obtain the actual number of clusters. It may be mentioned that Sym-index is inspired by the $\mathcal{I}$-index developed in [11].

Explaination

As formulated in Equation 5, Sym-index is a composition of three factors, $1/K$, $1/\mathcal{E}_K$ and D_K. The first factor increases as K decreases; as Sym-index needs to be maximized for optimal clustering, it will prefer to decrease the value of K. The second factor is a measure of the total within cluster symmetry. For clusters which have good symmetrical structures, $\mathcal{E}_K$ value is less. Note that as K increases, the clusters tend to become more symmetric. Moreover, as $d_e(x, c)$ in Equation 4 also decreases, $\mathcal{E}_K$ decreases, resulting in an increase in the value of the Sym-index. Since Sym-index needs to be maximized, it will prefer to increase the value of K. Finally the third factor, D_K, measuring the maximum separation between a pair of clusters, increases with the value of K. Note that value of D_K is bounded by the maximum separation between a pair of points in the data set. As these three factors are complementary in nature, so they are expected to compete and balance each other critically for determining the proper partitioning.

The use of D_K, as the measure of separation, requires further elaboration. Instead of using the maximum separation between two clusters, several other alternatives could have been used. For example, if D_K was the sum of pairwise inter cluster distances in a K-cluster structure, then it would increase largely with the increase in the value of K. This might lead to the formation of maximum possible number of clusters equal to the number of elements in the data set. If D_K was the average inter cluster distance then it would decrease at each step with K, instead of being increased. So, this will only leave us with the minimum possible number of clusters. The minimum distance between two clusters may be another choice for D_K. However, this measure would also decrease significantly with increase in the number of clusters. So this would lead to a structure where the loosely connected sub-structures remain as they were, where in fact a separation was expected. Thus maximum separability may not be attained. In contrast, if we consider the maximum inter cluster separation then we see that this tends to increase significantly until we reach the maximum separation among compact clusters and then it becomes almost constant. The upper bound of this value, which is equal to the maximum separation between two points, is only attainable when we have two extreme data elements as two single element clusters. But the terminating condition is reached well before this situation. This is the reason why we try to improve the maximum distance between two maximally separated clusters.

Table 1. Optimum values of the *Sym*-index, PS-index and $\mathcal{I}$-index for *Data1*, *Data2*, *Data3*, *Data4* and Iris using the three algorithms. (Entries in the brackets indicate the number of clusters corresponding to which the index gets its optimum value.) The best value of the indices, across the algorithms, are mentioned in bold face.

Data set	GAPS			GAK-means			Average linkage		
	Sym	PS	$\mathcal{I}$	Sym	PS	$\mathcal{I}$	Sym	PS	$\mathcal{I}$
Data1	**0.049(2)**	**0.0024(2)**	663.85(8)	0.014(8)	0.029(8)	1101.25(5)	0.011(7)	0.04(7)	993.05(6)
Data2	**0.057(3)**	0.018(6)	7.2(8)	0.051(9)	0.05(8)	**7.24(6)**	0.019(4)	0.04(4)	3.27(5)
Data3	0.012(5)	0.037(6)	1315.88(6)	**0.014(5)**	0.031(7)	1276.29(5)	0.013(5)	0.039(5)	1240.83(4)
Data4	**0.0076(5)**	0.022(5)	**12095.52(5)**	0.004(7)	0.015(7)	10259.18(8)	0.0076(5)	0.022(5)	12095.52(5)
Iris	**0.049(3)**	0.084(7)	691.29(3)	0.046(4)	0.107(4)	633.82(3)	0.046(3)	0.088(2)	653.95(3)

6.4 Experimental Results

Several artificially generated and real-life data sets were used to experimentally demonstrate that the *Sym*-index is not only able to find the proper cluster number for different types of data sets, but is also able to indicate the suitable clustering method. Due to lack of space results have been shown here only for one real-life and four artificially generated data sets. Three clustering algorithms viz., a newly developed point symmetry based genetic clustering technique (GAPS) [1], GAK-means algorithm [10] and the Average-linkage clustering algorithm [7] are used as the underlying partitioning techniques. The number of clusters, K is varied from 2 to 10 for each algorithm, and the variation of the *Sym*-index is noted. Its maximum value indicates the appropriate algorithm and the appropriate number of clusters. Finally comparisons are made with two other recently developed cluster validity indices, i.e., a point symmetry based PS-index [3] and $\mathcal{I}$-index [11] in terms of the number of clusters and the clusterings obtained. The parameters of the genetic algorithms (GAPS and GAK-means) are as follows: population size is equal to 100, crossover and mutation probabilities for GAK-means are kept to be equal to 0.8 and 0.01, respectively. For GAPS, the mutation and crossover probabilities are selected adaptively. Both the algorithms are executed for a maximum of 30 generations. Table 1 shows the optimum values of three validity indices, *Sym*-index, PS-index and $\mathcal{I}$-index and the number of clusters obtained after application of the three algorithms, GAPS, GAK-means and Average Linkage on different data sets.

1. *Data1*: This data set, used in [1], contains 400 points distributed on two crossed ellipsoidal shells. The clustering result obtained after application of GAPS on this data set is shown in Figure 1(a). As expected, GAPS is able to detect the proper clustering since the data is symmetrical. The values of *Sym*-index and PS-index are the optimum for $K = 2$ (see Table 1). $\mathcal{I}$-index could not identify the optimal clustering with any of the algorithms. Irrespective of the index used, GAK-means fails here since the clusters are non-convex. Again, Average linkage also fails here as the clusters have a little overlap.

2. *Data2*: This data set, used in [1], consisting of 350 points, is a combination of ring-shaped, spherically compact and linear clusters. The clustering result obtained after application of GAPS on this data set is shown in Figure 1(b). As the clusters present here are symmetrical, GAPS performs well for this data set. Again GAK-

means and Average linkage are found to fail here. *Sym*-index is able to detect the proper clustering after application of GAPS with $K = 3$ (see Table 1). $\mathcal{I}$-index and PS-index both could not find the proper clustering with any of the algorithms.

3. *Data3*: This data set consists of 250 points distributed over 5 spherically shaped highly overlapping clusters, each consisting of 50 points, used in [10]. The clustering results obtained after application of GAK-means and GAPS on this data set are shown in Figures 2(a) and 2(b), respectively. Although, *Sym*-index is able to detect 5 clusters for all the three algorithms (see Table 1), it attains the maximum value after application of GAK-means (Figure 2(a)). Its value for $K = 5$ with GAPS is poorer. Indeed, the clustering obtained here (Figure 2(b)) is not completely perfect. This again reveals the fact that *Sym*-index is able to indicate a suitable clustering algorithm for a given data set. As can be seen from Table 1, PS-index is able to detect the proper cluster number along with GAPS. But optimal value of PS-index corresponds to $K = 7$ with GAK-means. $\mathcal{I}$-index also attains its optimum value with GAPS for $K = 6$.

4. *Data4*: This data set contains 850 data points distributed over five clusters. The clustering result obtained after application of Average linkage on this data set is shown in Figure 3. As the clusters present here are symmetric and nonoverlapping, GAPS and Average linkage perform well. GAK-means fails here as all the clusters are non-convex. *Sym*-index, $\mathcal{I}$-index and PS-index are able to find the proper clustering with GAPS and Average linkage with $K = 5$ (see Table 1). But PS-index attains its optimum value with GAK-means for $K = 7$.

5. Iris: This data set, obtained from [6], consists of 150 data points distributed over 3 clusters. Each cluster consists of 50 points. This data set represents different categories of irises characterized by four feature values [5]. It has three classes Setosa, Versicolor and Virginica. It is known that two classes (Versicolor and Virginica) have a large amount of overlap while the class Setosa is linearly separable from the other two. Here as the data set is of dimension 4 so no visualization is possible. For this data set we have calculated the *Minkowski Score* (MS) [2] of the clustering result obtained after application of all the three algorithms with $K = 3$ since it is not possible to demonstrate the clustering results for this 4-d data set pictorially. MS is a measure of the quality of a solution given the true clustering. Let T be the "true" solution and S the solution we wish to measure. Denote by n_{11} the number of pairs of elements that are in the same cluster in both S and T. Denote by n_{01} the number of pairs that are in the same cluster only in S, and by n_{10} the number of pairs that are in the same cluster in T. *Minkowski Score* (MS) is then defined as:

$$MS(T,S) = \sqrt{\frac{n_{01} + n_{10}}{n_{11} + n_{10}}}. \tag{6}$$

For MS, the optimum score is 0, with lower scores being "better". Smaller value of MS means better clustering. The MS scores are 0.58, 0.61 and 0.62 for GAPS, GAK-means and Average linkage, respectively. From the obtained MS values it is clear that GAPS is able to find the best clustering among the three algorithms and for this particular partitioning, *Sym*-index and $\mathcal{I}$-index obtained their best values. PS-index is unable to find the proper clustering with any algorithms.

Interestingly, it was observed that for all the data sets, *Sym*-index was able to detect the proper number of clusters as well as the suitable clustering algorithm. For example, for *Data2* where GAPS should perform the best for $K = 3$, the value of *Sym*-index is the maximum for GAPS (0.57) as compared to those for GAK-means (0.51) and Average linkage (0.019) thereby indicating the suitable clustering technique. Again, for *Data3*, where GAK-means should perform the best for $K = 5$, the value of *Sym*-index is the maximum (see Table 1) for this case. The other indices are sometimes misled in this regard. For example, for *Data3*, $\mathcal{I}$ value is more for GAPS with 6 clusters, (=1315.88) as compared to GAK-means with 5 clusters (=1276.29). Again, for *Data4*, GAPS with $K = 5$ should be the appropriate choice (one that is correctly indicated by *Sym*-index), PS-index attains its minimum value for GAK-means with $K = 7$. These results, therefore, point at the significant superiority of the proposed index.

6.4.1 Effectiveness of Using Kd-tree for Nearest Neighbor Search

Note that the above implementations of GAPS and *Sym*-index used a Kd-tree structure to reduce computational time of identifying the nearest neighbors. In order to actually demonstrate this, GAPS was also executed without using Kd-tree data structure for the four artificial data sets. The computational times for those data sets (GAPS is implemented in C and was executed in a machine having linux platform, PIV processor, 1.6GHz speed) are mentioned in Table 2. As is evident, incorporation of Kd-tree significantly reduces the computational burden of the process. In order to examine whether the proposed scheme scales up with the dimensionality, a 20-dimensional artificial data set, consisting of 3000 points, is generated. The data has three clusters-two hyperellipsoidal shaped and one hyperspherical (containing 1000 points in each). GAPS with Kd-tree took 6 minutes to execute the first generation where as GAPS without Kd-tree didn't complete its first generation even in 250 minutes. This example shows that using Kd-tree based GAPS is effective in reducing the computational complexity even for 20-dimensional data.

Table 2. Execution Time (GAPS is implemented in C and executed in Linux platform, PIV processor, 1.66 GHz speed) in seconds by GAPS with and without Kd-tree based search

Data set	GAPS with Kd-tree	GAPS with out Kd-tree
Data1	30	1714
Data2	30	1652
Data3	62	2268
Data4	266	9112

6.5 Conclusion

A new symmetry based cluster validity index is proposed in this article that is able to indicate both the appropriate number of clusters as well as the clustering algorithm. Its effectiveness is demonstrated on four artificially generated data sets and one real life data set. As a part of future work, the effectiveness of the proposed index needs to be studied extensively with more data sets and algorithms. It also needs to be compared with other validity indices. A theoretical study also needs to be conducted to analyze its performance.

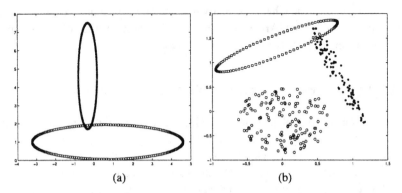

Fig. 1. Clustering obtained by GAPS on (a) *Data1* for $K = 2$ (b) *Data2* for $K = 3$

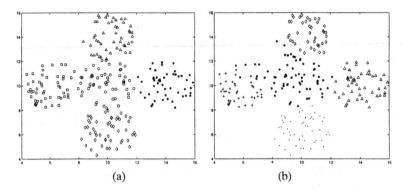

Fig. 2. Clustered *Data3* for $K = 5$ obtained by (a) GAK-means (b) GAPS

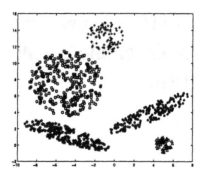

Fig. 3. Clustering obtained by Average linkage on *Data4* for $K = 5$

References

Bandyopadhyay, S. and Saha, S. (2007) GAPS: A Clustering Method Using A New Point Symmetry Based Distance Measure. Pattern Recognition. (accepted). Available online: http://dx.doi.org/10.1016/j.patcog.2007.03.026.

Ben-Hur, A. and Guyon, I. (2003) Detecting Stable Clusters using Principal Component Analysis in Methods in Molecular Biology. M.J. Brownstein and A. Kohodursky (Ed.). Humana press, pp. 159–182.

Chou, C. H., Su, M. C. and Lai, E. (2002) Symmetry as A new Measure for Cluster Validity. 2nd WSEAS Int. Conf. on Scientific Computation and Soft Computing. Crete, Greece, pp. 209–213.

Everitt, B. S., Landau, S. and Leese, M. (2001) Cluster Analysis. London: Arnold.

Fisher, R. A. (1936) The Use of Multiple Measurements in Taxonomic Problems. Annals of Eugenics. 3, 179–188.

http://www.ics.uci.edu/~mlearn/MLRepository.html

Jain, A. K., Dubes, R. C. (1988) Algorithms for Clustering Data. Prentice-Hall, Englewood Cliffs, NJ.

Jain, A. K., Duin, P.W. and Jianchang, M. (2000) Statistical Pattern Recognition : A Review. IEEE Transactions Patt. Anal. Machine Intell. 22(1), 4–37.

Jain, A. K., Murthy, M.N. and Flynn, P.J. (1999) Data Clustering: A Review. ACM Computing Reviews.

Maulik, U. and Bandyopadhyay, S. (2000) Genetic Algorithm Based Clustering Technique. Pattern Recognition. 33, 1455–1465.

Maulik, U. and Bandyopadhyay, S. (2002) Performance Evaluation of Some Clustering Algorithms and Validity Indices. IEEE Transactions on Pattern Analysis and Machine Intelligence. 24(12), 1650–1654.

Su, MuChun and Chou , Chien-Hsing (2001) A Modified Version of the K-means Algorithm with a Distance Based on Cluster Symmetry. IEEE Transactions on Pattern Analysis and Machine Intelligence. 23(6), 674–680.

7 Introduction of New Expert and Old Expert Retirement in Ensemble Learning under Drifting Concept

Indrė Žliobaitė

Faculty of Mathematics and Informatics,
Department of Informatics, Vilnius University, Vilnius
Indre.Zliobaite@mif.vu.lt

Abstract. In the paper the role of new expert and expert retirement conditions are analysed. In this paper we take Kolter/Maloof [6] algorithm as a basis. The main our suggestions are: 1) variable new expert weight with expert retirement in order to overcome relative weight reduction problem of the "right" experts; 2) diversity based old expert retirement. Such option lets to achieve the same (sometimes better) classification accuracy as infinite expert system but using lower computational resources and in cases this outperforms "the oldest" and "the weakest" expert retirement methods.

Keywords: Concept drift, classification, ensemble learning

7.1 Introduction

During the past decade significant deal of attention in the field of pattern recognition is drawn to the *concept drift* problem, formulated by [1]. Other researchers [2] refer to this problem as *changing environment*. Environmental changes include fluctuations in underlying probability distributions of the classes, random noise, random trends (or gradual changes), random substitutions or systematic trends (reoccurring contexts).

The problem arises when the environment is changing during the model lifetime; therefore the models needs be adaptable during the time of operation. Starting from very basic example, this problem can be illustrated by classification task, where male from female need to be separated. An algorithm is trained to perform well on present sample; however, new fashion comes into play, male start to wear long hair, while some of female start to wear short haircut. This new fashion can be seen as environmental change (or external change), due to which algorithm may need to be retrained. "Spam" categorization is a classical example of concept drift problem, as "spam" definition as well as "spam" content changes over time.

The problem of changing environment is apparent for time varying data domains. Environmental changes are considered to have happened before some time moment t with respect to time moment t_0 where we had initial environmental domain.

Therefore, when facing the problem of changing environment in classification of prediction tasks, we mostly deal with time series. To deal with this problem on-line learning is used, i.e. the algorithm is retrained during the time of operation.

For a review of the main findings in the field of pattern recognition under concept drift the reader is referred to comprehensive review by A.Tsymbal [3]. He classified the algorithms for handling concept drift into three main categories: 1) instance selection, where the goal is to select the instances relevant to the current concept (e.g. sliding window approach), 2) instance weighting where instances are weighted (e.g. according to their age or competence regarding current concept), 3) ensemble learning based, which maintains a *set* of concept descriptions and final decision is made according to the weighted voting or selection of the fittest description.

In this paper we focus on the ensemble learning based model for classifying data with presence of concept drift. We focus on ensemble learning models as they allow to keep diversity and preserve "old" information, fit to the current environmental situation. Although measures of diversity in classifier ensembles and their relationship with the ensemble accuracy have been widely analysed in the field [4], here we focus on the classification algorithms for dealing with concept drift.

7.1.1 New expert addition and old expert retirement – problem formulation

Pattern recognition decisions under changing environment often need to be made either in on-line mode or in batches after retraining the algorithm. If an ensemble of classifiers is used for final decision (one expert = one classifier), one needs to decide not only if the number of experts in the ensemble is fixed or it may vary, but also is completely new experts can be introduced during the algorithm operation. The new experts are introduced after environment change is observed, as they can be more fit to the present state of environment.

On the other hand, if we assume infinite algorithm operation, the number of experts may increase sky high, making algorithm operation computationally difficult and inefficient. Therefore, the conditions need to be set, under which existing experts are withdrawn from the ensemble (we call this action "retirement").

The problem of new expert addition is introduced in our paper [5]. In this paper we present continuation of previous research, concentrating on expert retirement problem, while discussing along with new expert addition problem. There are three main issues related to new expert weight. The *first* is the percentage weight of newly introduced expert in the total ensemble. If we assign more than 50% of total ensemble votes to new expert the ensemble decision would fully depend on new expert vote. Empirically the new expert need to be weighted 0-50% in the total ensemble, as close to 0% would make little sense of adding new expert. The *second* issue is if the new expert starts full participation in the decision making from introduction moment or later. Empirically it could be given full responsibility since introduction; however, the expert needs to be pre-trained.

The *third* issue of the new expert addition is directly related to old expert retirement. The question is if an expert weight needs to be fixed or variable during algorithm operation period and if the weight of new expert needs to be dependent on the number of present experts. Empirically the new expert contributes missing information to the ensemble as a whole and depends on the ensemble performance.

If we operate a dynamic system, the number of experts is getting larger and larger; inevitably we have to start withdrawing (or retiring) the experts so that the number of decision makers is limited.

Using multiple classifier system we need the experts to be diverse, otherwise, if all experts are similar, we could use single expert decision making, instead of voting. New experts are dynamically added depending on information embedded in recent portion of the data. If the environment has changed, that means expert addition (and expert training before addition) is based on the newest portion of data. This last portion of data is different from previous portions due to environmental changes occurred, therefore the new expert pre-trained on this last portion of data would be in a way different from the existing experts. Still the "oldest" expert might be similar to the "newest" expert due to reoccurring contexts.

There is a need to measure expert diversity, otherwise, we might be adding and using experts to the system, which are similar to each other and do not give much value added to the system. Empirically we state, that the criterions for expert retirement need to be based on diversity measures, rather than expert age (the oldest), or strength (the weakest).

7.1.2 Contribution

In this paper expert retirement conditions in line with new expert addition to the system were analysed. The main contributions are: suggested expert "retirement" condition based on expert diversity rather than age or strength (for on-line classification algorithms operating in changing environment) in line with variable new expert weight, which lets to overcome relative weight reduction problem of the "correct" experts in the algorithm operating process.

In this paper we focus on a problem of expert retirement in the ensemble learning. Taking Kolter/Maloof [6] algorithm as a basis.

7.2   Ensemble Based Algorithms for dealing with Concept Drift

Recently pattern recognition algorithms for dealing with concept drift problem gain more and more attention in the field. We construct specific framework to compare the algorithms within the dimensions we are interested in. The dimensions are as follows: a – the decision rule, b – the rules for adding new expert in the ensemble, c – the rules for discarding old experts, d – retraining of existing experts. In the presented algorithms all experts are retrained on the last batch of data, therefore we do not repeat d dimension for each algorithm. We purposely omit the base learner (e.g. neural networks, decision trees) from the list of dimensions, as the focus of present paper is on the ensemble interaction here any base learner could be used.

K.O. Stanley in Y2003 [7] proposed an algorithm called Concept Drift Committee (CDC). The algorithm starts from single expert, but when the number of experts reaches user-fixed population, the new expert is added only if an old one is discarded. An expert can be removed if it reached preset maturity. The dimensions for CDC:

    a.   Majority voting, the weights of experts are equal.

    b.   Add new expert if there is a free place available in the ensemble, i.e. if the ensemble has not reached population limit yet or if an old expert has just been discarded.

    c.   An expert is discarded if all criterions are positive: i) it has the lowest accuracy in the ensemble measured on the latest testing batch; ii) has performance record below user-fixed threshold; iii) is mature.

In Y2001 Street and Kim [8] proposed ensemble-based algorithm, which they called SEA (Streaming Ensemble Algorithm). They use a decision tree as a base learner and employs heuristic replacement strategy to increase classifier accuracy. One important idea proposed by the authors is to favour classifiers, which are correct at times when the ensemble is nearly undecided. The benchmarks are as follows:

    a   The quality score is increased (in case an expert is right) or decreased in proportion to how close the ensemble voting was to 0,5. Credit or blame is given to a single expert, if the ensemble was homogeneous.

    b and c   Add new expert if there is a free place available in the ensemble (independently on the ensemble performance), or if there is an expert, the quality of which measured according to prior specified criterions, is lower than quality of the new expert, the old expert is replaced by new.

Kolter and Maloof inY2005 presented [6] additive expert ensemble algorithm, which is an extension of Weighted Majority Algorithm, formalized by Littlestone and Warmuth inY1994 [9], Kolter and Maloof extended this to streaming data case, allowing the number of experts change dynamically. The main idea of the algorithm is to add a new expert only after the ensemble makes a mistake. For benchmarking purposes here we analyse the discreet case of Kolter and Maloof algorithm. The context of our framework:

    a   Majority voting. The weights of wrong experts in the ensemble are decreased by multiplier $\beta \in [0,1]$.

    b   The new expert is added if the ensemble makes mistake as a whole. The weight of new expert is wt+1 new=Wt* γ, here Wt is the total weight of the ensemble at time t and $\gamma \in [0, 1]$ is new expert multiplier.

    c   Initial version did not have expert discarding, later they introduced two discarding options to avoid over-fitting the system with experts: discarding the oldest expert or discarding the worst performing expert.

There has not been systematic focus on expert retirement and new expert addition problem for algorithms operating under concept drift so far; however, these issues have been addressed in some algorithms along with other issues analysed.

7.3   The Balance of Expert Weights During Algorithm Operation

We take Kolter and Maloof [6] algorithm for discreet case as a basis for present analysis. These authors have variable expert weights and rather simple although theoretically based interpretation of their chosen approach. They derive this approach suited for the domains affected by concept drift directly from Majority Vote Algorithm for stationary cases [9].

The authors have chosen the weight decay and new expert multipliers (as it was defined before) to be bounded β, $\gamma \in [0,1]$. In fact, the ratio between total weight of *right*[1] experts, *mistaken* experts and the *new* expert are determined by those two multipliers. γ is the main direct influencer for *new* expert weight in the ensemble while β is primary influencer for *existing* expert retirement in one of the options suggested by Kolter/Maloof.

According to Kolter and Maloof framework, $W_t = \sum_{i=0}^{N_t} w_{t,i}$ is the total weight of the ensemble at time t, here $w_{t,i}$ is the weight of the ith expert at time t. In our modification the weight of the system at time $t + 1$ would be $W_{t+1} = W_{t,right} + \beta * W_{t,wrong} + \gamma * W_t - W_{t,retired}$, in case the ensemble made a mistake at time t and $W_{t+1} = W_{t,right} + \beta * W_{t,wrong}$, if the ensemble was right, where $W_{t,right}$ is the sum of the right expert weights at time t and $W_{t,wrong}$ is the sum of the wrong expert weights, $W_{t,retired}$ is the weight of an expert, which was retired at time t (if there were no retirement at time t, $W_{t,retired} = 0$).

Kolter and Maloof analysed only the case when $\beta + 2\gamma < 1$. As it is shown in [6], $W_{t+1} \leq \frac{1}{2} (1 + \beta + 2\gamma)W_t$. Let us define A := $\frac{1}{2} (1 + \beta + 2\gamma)$. The authors must have chosen A so that W_{t+1} is kept bounded, i.e. $W_{t+1} \leq W_t$. It can be shown that A $\geq \frac{1}{2}$. We decompose A into three cases choosing different β and γ for the model:

I. $\frac{1}{2} < A < 1$. This is narrowed Kolter and Maloof approach, they derived [6]:

$$M \leq \frac{m\log(1/\beta) + \log(1/\gamma)}{\log(2/(1+\beta+2\gamma))}, \tag{1}$$

where M is the number of mistakes an ensemble makes between two time steps t_0 and t, while m is the number of mistakes made by the new expert, which was added at time t_0. From (1), the number of mistakes made by the system is bounded. It can be proven [5] that

---

[1] By "right" experts we mean the experts which were correct in their classification at time t, and by "mistaken" experts we mean the experts which made a mistake in their classification at time t

$$m < \frac{m \log(1/\beta) + \log(1/\gamma)}{\log(2/(1+\beta+2\gamma))}. \qquad (2)$$

To conclude, the boundary for γ and β parameters chosen so that $\frac{1}{2} < A < 1$ cannot guarantee that ensemble system outperforms single expert in terms of mistakes made in a continuous piece of data stream independently of whether expert retirement is used or not.

II. A = 1. If a mistake is made by the ensemble at time t, $W_{t+1} = W_t - W_{t,\text{retired}}$. If the ensemble is right at time t, then $W_t (1+\beta)/2 \le W_{t+1} \le W_t$. It does not guarantee M outperformance against m.

III. $1 < A \le 2$, the upper boundary is guaranteed by $\beta \le 1$ and $\gamma \le 1$.

Therefore $W_{t+1} \ge W_t - W_{t,\text{retired}}$, if a mistake was made at time t, but $W_{t+1} \le W_t$ in case there was no mistake at time t. This generally gives $M \ge (m \ln \beta + \ln \gamma) / \ln A$. But $(m \ln \beta + \ln \gamma) / \ln A \le 0$, it is obvious that $M \ge 0$ this inequality has no value added.

The limits used by the authors of [6] differently from WMA [9], do not guarantee ensemble will outperform single expert neither without nor with expert retirement, because of γW_t addition to the total weight if an ensemble has made a mistake. In order inconsistencies can not eliminate the expert, which in general is fit and experienced, β needs to be chosen > 0.

7.4   Suggested Modification I – Variable γ

In [6] the weight of new expert added to the system was fixed (γW_t). In [5] we suggested using *variable* γ, in this paper we add expert retirement factor to this consideration. The suggested modification is unique, because it is variable (so far the decay constants were fixed). The uniqueness is not variability itself, but the fact that it solves the problem of relative weight decay, which is present in other ensemble algorithms for dealing with concept drift, especially when the number of experts is not bounded (e.g. no retirement). In such case there is a great difference if there are 10 or say 1000 experts in the ensemble for decision making at the moment. In case of fixed decay. The main principle behind our modification is to take the size and the number of experts into account and eliminate relative weight decay of *right* experts.

In expert-based system the proportion between the weights of *mistaken* experts, *right* experts and the *new* expert is a decisive factor. Depending on size of the *mistaken* expert population (might vary from $\frac{1}{2} W_t$ to $1 W_t$), the larger was the *wrong* expert population relatively larger weight is got by the new expert, as the "right" expert weights remain unchanged. We suggest the following options of variable γ:

A $\gamma = (W_{t\text{wrong}} - W_{t\text{right}} - W_{t,\text{retired}}) / (W_t - W_{t,\text{retired}})$, here $W_{t\text{wrong}}$ is the total weight of *mistaken* experts, $W_{t\text{right}}$ the weight of *right* experts and $W_{t,\text{retired}}$ is the weight of retired expert at time t. Here the new expert comes with the weight, which would have been lacking in order *right* experts win at time t. Here we can overcome the problem of reducing relative weights for *right* experts.

B $\gamma = W_{tw}(1- \beta) / (W_t - W_{t,retired})$. This preserves $W_{t+1} = W_t - W_{t,retired}$ in case of ensemble mistake, i.e. the weight decayed by β are replaced by the weight of new expert. This also preserves the *same* relative weights for the *right* experts.

C $\gamma = \max\{0,(W_{tw} \cdot \beta - W_{tr}) / (W_t - W_{t,retired})\}$. This preserves relative weights of *right* experts and even increases them similarly to the IIa case. The main difference between IIa and IIc is that in IIc that after weight decay the weights of *right* experts might exceed the weights of *mistaken* experts.

7.5 Suggested Modification II – Retirement Based on Diversity

If classification algorithm operates on-line and new expert is added each time when the ensemble makes a mistake, the number of experts might grow to infinity, therefore old experts need to be withdrawn. The main our suggestion is to withdraw (retire) one of the two most similar experts, measured using particular diversity measures. Such option lets to achieve the same classification accuracy as infinite expert system with much lower computational resources and in cases of relatively weaker mistaken expert decay term β, "the oldest" and "the weakest" methods suggested in [6] are outperformed. In either case the retired expert might have been either right or wrong in the last decision making task.

We choose the three methods for measuring ensemble diversity, which were summed up in Tsymbal et al in [11] firstly due to their property to measure classifier diversity pair-wise (for comparability) and secondly because they all take correct/incorrect classification of instances as an input.

The first measure is *fail/non-fail disagreement* [later *divP*], it is equal to the ratio of instances classified correctly by strictly one from two classifiers over total number of instances. Let us define N^{ab} – the number of instances in the testing set classified correctly (a=1) or incorrectly (a=0) by the first classifier and correctly (b=1) or incorrectly (b=0) by the second. Then $divP = (N^{01}+N^{10}) / (N^{11}+N^{10}+N^{01}+N^{00})$.

The second measure is called Q *statistic* [later *divQ*], where similarity of two classifiers output is measured [11]. Using the same notation, $divQ = (N^{11}*N^{00} - N^{01}*N^{10}) / (N^{11}*N^{00} + N^{01}*N^{10})$. For *divQ* to give result [0,1] we apply the following function: $divQ = (1 - divQ) / 2$ before using the result.

The third measure is *correlation coefficient* [later *divC*] between outputs, which is calculated: $divC = (N^{11}*N^{00} - N^{01}*N^{10}) / \text{sqrt}((N^{11}+N^{10})(N^{01}+N^{00})(N^{11}+N^{01})(N^{10}+N^{00}))$. We normalize this measure to [0,1] values the same way as *divQ*.

The oldest and the weakest methods for retirement used in [6] correspondingly indicate the oldest expert or an expert with the smallest weight for retirement. We challenge these approaches by adding diversity-based retirement, as the value of ensemble is in its diversity, the weakest and especially the oldest experts might be still useful due to reoccurring contexts.

7.6   Experimental Design and the Algorithm Used

Kolter and Maloof called their algorithm [6] for discreet cases without expert removal AddExp.D. We make one principle modification for this algorithm, which was not discussed in this paper. We do not retrain old experts after new one is added to keep the experts diverse. Let us call the algorithm used AddExp.D2:

Table 1. Steps of AddExp.D2 algorithm:

AddExp.D2($\{x,y\}^T$, β, γ), here y is a class label $\{0,1\}$
Initial number of experts $N_1 = 1$; Initial expert weight $w_{1,1} = 1$
For $t = 1,2,..,T$:
   Get expert predictions $\xi_{t,1},..., \xi_{t,Nt} \in \{0,1\}$
   Output prediction $y^\wedge_t = \text{argmax}_{c \in \{0,1\}} \sum^{Nt}_{i=1} w_{t,i}^{[c = \xi t,i]}$
   update expert weights $w_{t+1,i} = w_{t,i} * \beta^{[yt \neq \xi t,i]}$
   if $y^\wedge_t \neq y_t$ then
        if N_t = maximum number of experts, retire old expert
      add new expert: $N_{t+1} = N_t + 1$; $w_{t+1,i} = \gamma W_t$
   Train the latest expert on new sample x_t, y_t

We run the experiment on expert retirement in line with new expert addition in the following categories:
1.   Retirement of *the oldest*.
2.   Retirement of *the weakest* (smallest expert weight at time *t*)
3.   −5. Retirement of older of the two most similar (we compare pair-wise all "alive" experts the newest one), we use the three measures of diversity detailed in the section 6: *divP*, *divQ* and *divC*.
6.   −7. Benchmark experiments: $\beta=1$, $\gamma=0$ what correspond to single expert system and $\beta=0$, $\gamma=1$ what corresponds to single expert system as well, but the expert is permanently replaced by the new one as soon as it makes the first mistake.

We use 50 days history to train new expert on in the experiments. It is similar to window-based approach to concept drift handling, but this needs to be implemented in order the expert to be fully capable of making a decision when needed.

In the experimental set up we use $\beta=0,7$ and we use the Ist framework from section 3. We chose these parameters for retirement experiment presentation, as under these conditions the best result in new expert addition experiment without retirement was achieved [5].

We perform each experiment with different number of experts for comparison. We make 3, 7, 15, 31 and 63 expert experiments, this works for the next experiment as present number of experts times 2 plus 1, to make the number of experts uneven.

7.7   Experimental Results and Discussion

The data for real experiment are taken from [10]. These consist of 2956 observation dates 1673 and 1283 in each of the classes correspondingly (the data was shortened as compared to the original in order to avoid estimating missing values) and 7 dimensions: week day {1,..7}, period (continuous), 2 x price (cont.), 2 x demand (cont.), transfer (cont.) and the class labels discrete {up, down} – electricity consumption. The task is to classify the days into days of increase and days of decrease in electricity consumption.

Experimental results are presented in the table below as the percentage of instances where the algorithm made mistakes in total testing set. The experimental results are not statistically significant (standard deviation is about 0,4-0,5%), however, qualitative results are of major importance here.

Table 2 Experimental results. The top results are market in grey.

Maximal number of experts	3	7	15	31	63	retirement	one expert Always	new expert
divP	5,31%	5,55%	5,31%	5,55%	5,31%	5,28%	18,34%	5,58%
divQ	5,45%	5,24%	5,31%	5,28%	5,24%	5,28%	18,34%	5,58%
divC	5,51%	5,28%	5,28%	5,28%	5,28%	5,28%	18,34%	5,58%
the oldest	5,28%	5,28%	5,28%	5,28%	5,28%	5,28%	18,34%	5,58%
the weakest	5,51%	5,28%	5,28%	5,28%	5,28%	5,28%	18,34%	5,58%

First of all, the experiments show that the ensemble learning system (formalized in [6]) outperforms single expert classifier ($\beta=1$, $\gamma=0$) and "always new expert" algorithm ($\beta=0$, $\gamma=1$), but this is not the result of present paper.

Secondly, in most of the cases all the ensembles employing expert retirement perform not worse than the system without expert retirement. Using *divQ* diversity measure leads to the best system accuracy ever, outperforming the system without retirement.

Moreover, it can be noted from the results provided that *divQ* and *divC* diversity measures used for expert retirement often outperform *divP* (fail/non-fail disagreement) system. The same was seen in the additional experiments performed. *divQ* and *divC* employ more sophisticated relationship between correct and mistaken classification instances than *divP*, putting more emphasis on the borderline cases.

Furthermore, we provide the results using the best performing parameters for new expert addition. We know this is the best result from additional experiments performed with new expert addition. From additional experiments we note that the worse accuracy is achieved by the ensemble as compared to the best possible accuracy, the better is the effect on accuracy by diversity based expert retirement.

In addition, it can be noted from additional experiments performed that the largest effect of diversity based expert retirement is achieved when we have relatively low weight decay (i.e. high weight decay term β), in such case the weights of old experts do not decrease so quickly when the mistakes are made during algorithm operation. If we have relatively quick weight decay, in such case both the oldest and the weakest experts have little influence to the total ensemble decision and therefore we get no improvement in accuracy when retirement is introduced (however, we get improvement in computational resources needed, otherwise the number of experts would theoretically grow to infinity). Diversity based expert retirement allows saving computational power and achieving ensemble diversity by retiring the experts "duplicating" information.

If the expert system makes a mistake, but only once-off random drift in data happens (atypical instance). In this case new expert is added, and the weight of mistaken experts are decayed. In the next algorithm step the data is "back" to the previous normal state, however, we have one more expert added which in principle is very similar to the one before previous expert. These two experts "duplicate" each other and one of them might be retired.

Finally, the diversity measurement under changing environment differ from diversity measurement for ordinary ensembles of classifiers, as in changing environment case experts are introduced at different times therefore have different lengths of performance history. In present research we used "the oldest" approach if the common performance history was to short to make diversity calculations. We will perform deeper study of the pair-wise diversity measures for classifiers having different performance length in the future.

To sum, expert retirement based on diversity measures do not outperform the result of "no retirement" in general case, but in certain cases diversity based approaches outperform the result of "the oldest" and "the weakest" expert retirement methods. Moreover, this research implementing diversity based expert retirement and suggesting variable weight for new expert addition with retirement gives important insights into the problems discussed and serves as a prototype for further research.

7.8   Conclusion

In this paper we analysed the problems of expert retirement conditions and new expert weight with old expert retirement in the light of changing environment or concept drift. We did not peg to a specific pattern recognition algorithm, for testing purposes we used Fisher LDF to classify electricity consumption data into two classes.

Various combinations of old expert weight decay and new expert addition coefficient based on Kolter/Maloof [6] previous work were analysed. Firstly we suggested variable weight for new expert introduction with expert retirement, which lets to overcome the problem of relative reduction of correct expert weights.

The second suggestion was to retire experts using diversity measures; this lets to achieve the same (sometimes better) classification accuracy as infinite expert system but using lower computational resources and in cases this outperforms "the oldest" and "the weakest" expert retirement methods.

This research is more of qualitative than quantitative nature and serves as a prototype for future modelling. We will continue working on the argumentation for old expert refusal and the criterions of old experts keeping and ranking in the system.

References

1. Widmer, G., Kubat, M. (1996). Learning in the Presence of Concept Drift and Hidden Contexts. Machine Learning 23(1): 69-101
2. Kuncheva L.I., Classifier ensembles for changing environments, Proceedings 5th International Workshop on Multiple Classifier Systems, MCS2004, Cagliari, Italy, in F. Roli, J. Kittler and T. Windeatt (Eds.), Lecture Notes in Computer Science, Vol 3077, 2004, 1-15.
3. Tsymbal A. The problem of concept drift: definitions and related work, Technical Report TCD-CS-2004-15, Department of Computer Science, Trinity College Dublin, Ireland, 2004.
4. Kuncheva L.I., C.J. Whitaker. Measures of diversity in classifier ensembles, Machine Learning , 51 , 2003, 181-207.
5. Žliobaitė, I. (2007). Ensemble Learning for Concept Drift Handling – the Role of New Expert. To appear in the proceedings of MLDM 2007.
6. Kolter, J.Z., Maloof, M. A. (2005). Using Additive Expert Ensembles to Cope with Concept Drift. In Proceedings of the Twenty-Second International Conference on Machine Learning.
7. Stanley, K (2003). Learning Concept Drift with a Committee of Decision Trees. The University of Texas at Austin, Department of Computer Sciences. AI Technical Report 03-302. September 2003.
8. Street, W.N., Kim, Y. (2001). A streaming ensemble algorithm (SEA) for large-scale classification. Seventh ACM SIGKDD International Conference on Knowledge Discovery & Data Mining (KDD-01), p. 377-382, San Francisco, CA, August 2001.
9. Littlestone, N., Warmuth, M. K. (1994). The Weighted Majority Algorithm. Inf. Comput. 108(2): 212-261
10. Gama, J. (2004). Datasets for Concept Drift. Retrieved from World Wide Web 2006 12 30 from http://www.liacc.up.pt/~jgama/ales/ales_5.html
11. Tsymbal, A., Pechenizkiy, M. and Cunningham, P. (2004). Diversity in search strategies for ensemble feature selection. Information Fusion, 6 (1), 2005, 3-4

8 Comparison of Three Feature Extraction Techniques to Distinguish Between Different Infrasound Signals

José Chilo[1], Thomas Lindblad[2], Roland Olsson[3] and Stig-Erland Hansen[4]

[1]Department of Physics, Royal Institute of Technology, S-106 91 Stockholm, Sweden and Department of Electronics, University of Gävle, S-801 76 Gävle, Sweden
jco@hig.se
[2]Department of Physics, Royal Institute of Technology, S-106 91 Stockholm, Sweden
lindblad@particle.kth.se
[3]Faculty of Computer Science, Ostfold University College, N-1757 Halden, Norway
roland.olsson@hiof.no
[4]Faculty of Computer Science, Ostfold University College, N-1757 Halden, Norway
stig-erland.hansen@hiof.no

Abstract: The main aim of this paper is to compare three feature extraction techniques, Discrete Wavelet Transform, Time Scale Spectrum using Continuous Wavelet Transforms, and Cepstral Coefficients and their derivatives, for the purposes of classifying time series type signal data. The features are classified by two types of neural networks. The paper draws a number of important conclusions on the suitability of these features for analysis, and provides a good comparative evaluation on four different data sets.

8.1 Introduction

Infrasound is a low frequency acoustic phenomenon typically in the frequency range 0.01 to 20 Hz. Due to an increasing number of infrasound stations being deployed around the world, more and more infrasound data is likely to become available in the next few years. Automation of the detection and classification process is important to manage a continuous flow of data from infrasound sensors. In this paper, we explore the use of three feature extraction algorithms in combination with neural networks to achieve a system for automatic identification and classification of infrasound events. The goal is a system that is easy to implement in hardware with, for example, FPGAs.

Infrasound produced by natural and man made sources has been observed in the recordings made by the Swedish Infrasound Network (SIN) for several decades (Liszka 2003). In fact, infrasound events are not only studied by SIN but also by other networks, e.g. the IMS infrasound network (Campus 2004). The SIN has recently been converted into the Swedish-Finnish Infrasound Network and consists of 4 stations located in Kiruna, Jämtön and Lycksele in Northern Sweden and Sodankylä in Finland. Each station has an array of three modified Lidström-microphones with a 7 Hz low-pass filter, so that the effective frequency range is 0.5 – 6 Hz. A sampling rate of 18 Hz is used at all stations. A typical recording of a bolide is shown in Fig. 1.

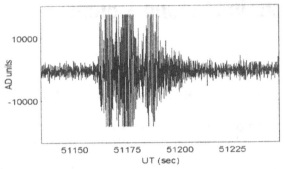

Fig. 1. The signal from the meteorite event as recorded by the SIN station in Kiruna on January 17, 2004

A selection of infrasonic measurements from SIN is used here to do some fundamental data pre-processing, namely: (1) Discrete Wavelets Transforms (DWTs), (2) Time Scale Spectra (TSSs) using Continuous Wavelet Transforms (CWTs), and (3) Cepstral Coefficients and their Derivatives (CCDs). Then, we use linear logistic discriminants, support vector machine (SVM) classifiers and two rather conventional neural network algorithms to classify this data. The neural networks used are back-propagation neural networks (BPNN) and radial basis function networks (RBFNN).

8.2 Data pre-processing

8.2.1 Discrete Wavelets Transforms (DWTs)

DWTs are well known (Fonseca, Guido, Silvestre, and Pereira 2005; Schumacher and Jun 1994) and are included in many computational tools, e.g. MatLab. It has been noted previously (Schmitter 2006) that the energies of the wavelet scales together with the time series skewness and kurtosis (i.e. the 3rd and 4th moments of the value distribution) form a suitable feature vector for signal classification. In this paper, the energies of the Daubechies (DAUB4) wavelet scales 2 to 9 are used for a feature vector that in total has 10 components as inputs to the classifiers. The other two components are skewness and kurtosis. Skewness is sensitive to unipolarity of the signal. Kurtosis is a measure of the tail of the distribution.

Figure 2 shows an infrasound signal from meteorite (2048 components, 114 sec at 18 Hz sampling rate) with its DWT sum, detail coefficients and energy. Figure 3 shows four sets of feature vectors for each of the four types of infrasound signals that are to be classified.

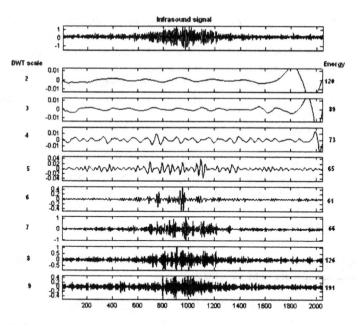

Fig. 2. The infrasound signal from a meteor (top), the resulting discrete wavelet coefficients from large to small scale, and the energies (right).

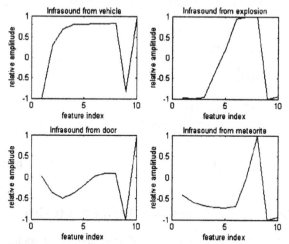

Fig. 3. Infrasound feature vectors using DWT for data pre-processing

8.2.2 Time Scale Spectrum (TSS) using Continuous Wavelet Transforms (CWT)

The data pre-processing steps to extract feature vectors using continuous wavelet transforms methods (Liszka and Holmström 1999) are as follows.

1. The Morlet wavelet transform is applied to the time series using 128 dilations.

2. A "kind of band-pass filtering" of wavelet coefficient magnitudes is then performed. The entire range of coefficient magnitudes from zero to maximum is divided into 20 equal intervals. For each interval the corresponding inverse wavelet transform is performed, which means that a new version of the original time series is created for every interval. This time series is what the signal would look like if only a narrow range of spectral densities were present in the signal.

3. A real-valued matrix, consisting of times series from step (2) as rows is created.

4. Each row of the matrix created in step (3) is wavelet transformed. The resulting matrices are time-averaged (average along rows) leading to arrays with 128 elements. A 20 x 128 matrix is constructed with time-averages as rows. This matrix is what we call the Time Scale Spectrum (TSS) of the time series.

Figure 4 shows four sets of feature vectors for each of the four types of infrasound signals that are to be classified.

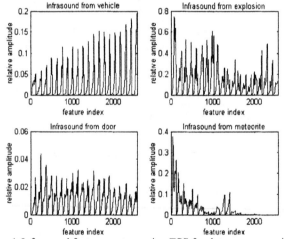

Fig. 4. Infrasound feature vectors using TSS for data pre-processing

8.2.3 Cepstral Coefficients and their Derivatives (CCD)

A set of Mel-frequency scale cepstral coefficients and their associated derivatives for each infrasound signal are used to form a set of feature vectors (Ham and Park 2002; Ham, Rekab, Park, Acharyya, and Lee 2005; Mammone, Zhang, and Ramachandran 1996). The data pre-processing steps are as follows:

1. The mean value from the time series is removed.
2. The hamming window is applied to the time series.
3. Power Spectra Density (PSD) is computed.

4. We apply Mel-frequency scaling to every PSD using

$$S = 1125 * \log_e(0.000003 * PSD).$$

5. The inverse discrete cosine transform is performed on every S. The first 25 elements of the transform are the cepstral coefficients.

6. We take the derivative sequence of the result from the inverse discrete cosine transform. The first 15 elements of the derivative are the derivative terms that we use.

7. The 15 derivatives terms are concatenated with the 25 cepstral coefficients to form the feature vector of each time series. Then, the logarithm of the absolute value of the feature vector is computed. The mean value is removed from the feature vector and last, the feature vector is rescaled between [-1, 1].

Four vectors for the types of infrasound signals to be classified are presented in Fig. 5.

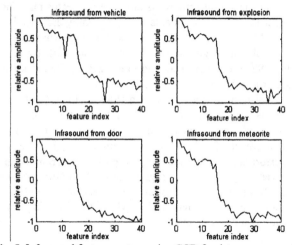

Fig. 5. Infrasound feature vectors using CCD for data pre-processing

8.3 Time series data sets

In the present study, we have applied the classification algorithms to four data sets. The first data set consists of infrasonic signals produced by four meteors and detected at SIN namely Jokkmokk, Bygdsilium, Karelia and Finnmark meteorites. After a study of the recordings we chose infrasonic signals from each microphone. The original data were segmented into smaller windows of 2048 samples spanning 114 seconds each at 18 Hz.

The second data set was obtained from man-made explosions. The third data set was collected from opening and closing doors (ten different doors). The last data set was obtained from three different vehicles. Data was collected using Lidström-microphones, digitized at 200 Hz and low-pass filtered with a cutoff frequency of 7 Hz.

8.4 Algorithms

Two neural networks were used in this approach, back-propagation and radial basis function networks. Back-propagation neural networks (BPNNs) typify supervised learning, where the task is to learn to map input vectors to desired output vectors. The back-propagation learning algorithm modifies feed-forward connections between the input and the hidden units, and the hidden and outputs units, so that when an input vector is presented to the input layer, the output layer's response should be the desired output vector (Perlovsky 2001). Anther popular type of feed-forward network is the radial basis function (RBF) network. It has two layers, not counting the input layer, and differs from a BPNN in the way that the hidden units perform computations. Each hidden unit essentially represents a particular point in input space, and its output, or activation, for a given instance depends on the distance between its point and the instance, which is just another point (Witten and Frank 2005).

In order to compare the neural net approach with other learning algorithms, we have included linear logistic discriminants and support vector machines in the investigation. The linear logistic discriminants that we employ are based on building and using a multinomial logistic regression model with a ridge estimator to guard against over fitting by penalizing large coefficients, based on work by le Cessie and van Houwelingen in 1992 (Landwehr, Hall and Frank 2003). This classifier builds linear logistic regression models with built-in attribute selection.

Platt's sequential minimization algorithm (SMO) (Platt 1999) is a fast iterative algorithm that is easy to implement for training Support Vector Machines (SVMs). In the last few years, there has been a surge of interest in SVMs (Keerthi, Shevade, Bhattacharyya and. Murthy 2001). SVMs have empirically been shown to give good generalization performance on a wide range of problems. Training an SVM requires the solution of a very large quadratic programming (QP) optimization problem. SMO breaks this large QP problem into a series of smallest possible QP problems. These small QP problems are solved analytically, which avoids using a time-consuming numerical QP optimization as an inner loop.

8.5 Experiments and results

The experiments were conducted with WEKA (Witten and Frank 2005). Each classifier was trained using DWT, TSS and CCD feature vectors of 30 samples of meteorites, 27 samples of opening and closing doors, 27 samples of vehicles and 24 samples of man-made explosions. The classification results are shown in tables 1-3. We used ten-fold cross validation in our experiments, which means that each dataset was divided into ten equal sized folds and ten independent runs of each algorithm were conducted for each dataset. For the ith run, the ith fold was designated as the test set and the patterns in the remaining nine folds were used for training. At the end of training the classifier's generalization was measured on the test set.

Table 1. Classification results using DWT

	Door	Vehicle	Meteor	Explo-sion	Total (%) Correctly Classified	Time (sec) taken to build model
BPNN	17/27	23/27	24/30	12/24	70.0	2.27
RBFNN	23/27	24/27	26/30	13/24	80.0	0.13
SimpleLogistic	23/27	26/27	26/30	14/24	83.0	0.50
SMO	18/27	25/27	21/30	4/24	63.0	0.99

Table 2. Classification results using TSS

	Door	Vehicle	Meteor	Explo-sion	Total (%) Correctly Classified	Time (sec) taken to build model
BPNN	27/27	27/27	30/30	21/24	97.2	1037.7
RBFNN	27/27	27/27	26/30	15/24	88.0	2.52
SimpleLogistic	27/27	27/27	27/30	21/24	94.5	65.65
SMO	27/27	27/27	30/30	18/24	94.4	2.08

Table 3. Classification results using CCD

	Door	Vehicle	Meteor	Explo-sion	Total (%) Correctly Classified	Time (sec) taken to build model
BPNN	27/27	27/27	30/30	24/24	100.0	18.75
RBFNN	23/27	25/27	26/30	19/24	86.1	0.28
SimpleLogistic	27/27	27/27	30/30	24/24	100.0	0.94
SMO	27/27	27/27	30/30	22/24	98.2	1.41

The BPNN showed best overall performance in the classification of infrasound signals. The total classification accuracy using BPNN is about 97% in the TSS case, which means that it is better than the others classifiers. In the CCD case, the total classification accuracy is 100% both for BPNN and SimpleLogistic.

8.6 Conclusions

Features based on discrete wavelets together with skewness and kurtosis (DWT), continuous wavelet transforms (TSS), and Mel-frequency scale cepstral coefficients and their associated derivatives (CCD) methods proved efficient for analysis and characterization of infrasound signals and as input into a classification algorithm that is trained to discriminate and characterize infrasonic events.

The main conclusion from this study is that the TSS method appears to be a very good procedure to pre-process infrasound signals for a subsequent BPNN classifier. The TSS method shows robustness with respect to record length, sampling frequency, signal amplitude and time sequence length that is not shown by the DWT and CCD methods. In addition, it provides suitable inputs to a BPNN.

References

Campus, P. (2004) The IMS Infrasound Network and its Potential for Detection of Events: Examples of a Variety of Signals Recorded Around the World, *Newsletter No 06, Inframatics*.

Fonseca, E.S., Guido, R.C., Silvestre, A.C. and Pereira, J.C. (2005) Discrete wavelet transform and support vector machine applied to pathological voice signals identification, *Seventh IEEE International Symposium on Multimedia*, pp. 12-14.

Ham, F. and Park, S. A (2002) Robust Neural Network Classifier for Infrasound Events Using Multiple Array data, *IEEE International Joint Conference NN*, Vol. 3, pp. 2615-2619.

Ham, F., Rekab, K., Park, S., Acharyya, R. and Lee, Y. (2005) Classification of infrasound Events Using Radial Basis Function Neural Network, *IEEE International Joint Conference NN*, Vol. 4, pp. 2649-2654s.

Keerthi, S.S., Shevade, S.K., Bhattacharyya, C. and Murthy, K.R.K. (2001) Improvements to Platt's SMO Algorithm for SVM Classifier Design, *Neural Computation*, Vol 13, pp. 637-649.

Landwehr, N., Hall, M. and Frank, E. (2003) Logistic Model Trees, *16th European Conference on Machine Learning*.

Liszka, L. (2003) Cognitive Information Processing in Space Physics and Astrophysics, *Pachart Publishing House*, Tucson, Az, USA, ISBN 0-88126-090-8.

Liszka, L. and Holmström, M. (1999) Extraction of a deterministic component from ROSAT X-ray data using a wavelet transform and the principal component analysis, *Astron. Astrophys. Suppl. Ser.*, Vol. 140, pp. 125-134.

Mammone, R.J., Zhang, X. and Ramachandran, R.P. (1996) Robust Speaker Recognition: A Feature-Based Approach, *IEEE Signal Processing Mag.*, Vol. 13:5, pp. 58-71.

Platt, J.C. (1999) Using Analytic QP and Sparseness to Speed Training of Support Vector Machines, *NIPS conference*, pp. 557-563.

Perlovsky, L.I. (2001) Neural Networks and Intellect: Using Model-Based Concepts, *Oxford University Press, Inc.*, ISBN 0-19-511162-1.

Schumacher, P. and Jun, Z. (1994) Texture classification using neural networks and discrete wavelet transform, *ICIP-94 IEEE International Conference*, Vol. 3, pp. 903-907.

Witten, I.H. and Frank, E. (2005) Data mining: Practical Machine Learning Tools and Techniques, 2nd Edition, *Morgan Kaufmann Publishers*, San Mateo, CA.

9 Developing Trading Strategies based on Risk-analysis of Stocks

Martin Sykora and Sameer Singh

Research School of Informatics,
Loughborough University, Loughborough, UK
M.D.Sykora@lboro.ac.uk, S.Singh@lboro.ac.uk

Abstract: Risk Management has always been of fundamental importance to financial markets. The aim of all good trading strategies is based around minimising possible risk and at the same time achieving most profit. A balance between these two factors must be struck for different risk – profit profiles. In this paper we describe an innovative way for visually quantifying risk, and we show how our method can be used as a tool for developing trading strategies to help manage risk. We run our algorithm on selected historical FTSE-100 stocks and pick some companies for a more detailed study of trading strategies. The method shows considerable promise for future research work.

9.1 Introduction

For many years now the most widely used method for measuring risk in financial assets has been standard deviation of univariate time-series data [1, 2]. This method and its derivatives are used by traders, brokers and professional fund managers all around the world because of its simplicity and well-known statistical properties. Standard deviation measures the spread of distribution about its mean, and as such does not take into account any of the investors' ability to predict asset price moves. Standard deviation is a very rough measure in the financial context and can be misleading, and there is still disagreement on what constitutes risk and how best to quantify it [2].

We propose a method to quantify risk in a more meaningful way for those investing in stock markets. The core characteristic of our approach is based on the postulation that risk is a function of our ability to forecast an asset, time-horizon over which risk is measured and stock data complexity, $Risk = f(\alpha, \beta, \gamma)$, where α is Predictor, β is Time-Horizon and γ is Complexity. To illustrate this let us assume that an investment agent is able to anticipate future moves with good accuracy. Hence the agent would most likely feel confident making an investment. On the other hand if an agent has little idea of whether a market will move up or down it is probably best to stay out of the market. The basic idea that risk is directly related to our prediction ability is intrinsic to many trading decisions. However we are not aware of any meaningful or novel attempts at quantifying risk in this manner.

The rest of this paper is structured as follows; in the next section we discuss our risk quantification method, in section 9.3 we show how we can use the method to select trading strategies, section 9.4 presents results to illustrate the potential benefit of the method and in section 9.5 we present key conclusions of our work.

9.2 Risk Quantification

We propose a risk quantification strategy based on Prediction Engineering and Risk Limitation (PEARL) model. The key elements of our approach involve modeling and visualization of risk based on our ability to predict several time steps ahead because we can develop trading strategies that are based on finding the right time in the future to sell or buy. Our strategy builds a RQG (Risk Quantification Graph) which a trader can visualize or an automated trading software can use directly to invest in the stock markets. A sample RQG is shown in Figure 1. The x-axis of the graph measures the amount of risk involved in trading t time steps ahead, and the y-axis measures the profits or benefits involved with that, provided we use n predictors (e.g. non-linear regressor such as neural network) for a maximum of n time step ahead forecasts. It is important to note that in this approach for a j step ahead prediction, where $j \leq n$, predicted values obtained from all predictors predicting 1 to $j-1$ steps ahead are used as input for the forecast. The maximum time horizon n also determines the duration within which RQG has any value, i.e. the trader should trade within this period to make use of the graph. Our risk quantification method is based on several processing steps which are described in the following sections.

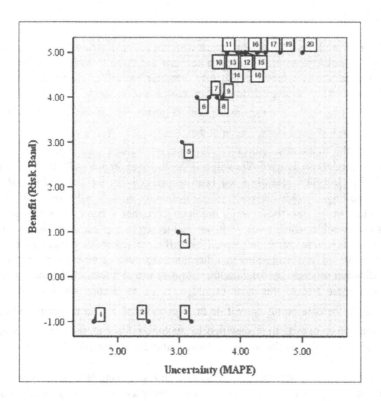

Fig. 1. (Wolseley 8/11/2006 – 5/12/2006) Risk Quantification Graph. 1 – 20 day Ahead predictions and associated uncertainty are plotted above.

9.2.1 Developing Forecast Models

We first divide the data into three parts: training, validation and test set. The first step is to develop a total of n predictors for a given stock. The aim is to use the training data to teach our j th predictor how to perform j time steps ahead forecast, where $(1 \le j \le n)$, use the validation set optimize the parameters of the predictor (e.g. in Brown's Double Exponential Smoothing predictor we need to optimize for α), as well as determine uncertainty associated with each of the predictors (this is explained in detail in section 9.2.5), and finally use the test set with our trading strategy as explained in section 9.3 to judge how well we can both predict as well as effectively trade to make profits and minimize risk.

The overall process of developing predictors involves the following steps:

9.2.2 Choose a predictor

A number of predictors are available that work on univariate time-series data. In this paper such prediction is our immediate concern and the interested reader for multivariate forecasting is referred to [3]. Any predictor has an input and an output. The input data is often the lagged time series values. For example, consider your time series to be $(x_1, x_2, ...x_i ....x_N)$ with N data points. To predict data point x_i, we can use the last m time steps, i.e. input data is $(x_{i-1-m} .... x_{i-1})$ and the output is x_i. Since both the input data and output are numeric values, any linear or non-linear regression model can be used. We will call the above approach as Real Value Prediction (RVP). However, recently it has been recognized that for developing and using effective trading strategies it is not necessary to have an accurate forecast of the true stock value. In the very basic form, predicting whether a stock price will go up or not, or the extent to which prices will vary (let us say using fuzzy linguistic variables *very high, high, low, very low*) would be sufficient for making trading decisions. Lindsay et al. [4] have suggested that therefore regression problem can be treated as a classification problem by banding the output values in a total of B bands, and then using the input data of the form $(x_{i-1-m} .... x_{i-1})$ to predict which of the bands $(B_1, ..., B_L)$ the data point x_i will lie in. The value of L can be optimized on the validation set or can be user specified to maximize the benefits with the selected trading strategy. We call this approach Band Value Prediction (BVP).

In this paper we have selected one example with RVP, using Brown's Double Exponential Model, and another example with BVP using a k-nearest neighbour classifier. Browns Double Exponential Smoothing model [5, 6] model is essentially averaging last m points based on a parameter, α and it also caters for the trend in a series. The method is not able to predict turning points in the series because it only models simple linear relationships, but the method works reasonably well in predicting stable trends [5]. For a more complete description of the model please consult the two sources, referenced above. Due to the stock markets' non-linear nature [7], predictors that model non-linear relationships would likely perform better. The second predictor we have used is a kNN or k nearest neighbor classification algorithm [8]. kNN however needs considerably more data than Brown Double Exponential model.

Since our trading strategy, as well as Risk Quantification Graph is designed to use the predicted value in banded regions (i.e. rather than specifying x_i we specify its corresponding band), we use a banding approach (which is different to BVP) on the output of RVP. Our output banding approaches are explained next.

9.2.3 Data preparation for Real Value Prediction

A given time series $(x_1, x_2, \ldots x_i \ldots x_N)$ can be predicted either on its actual values or after making it stationary. Difference and log operators are often used to stationarise time series. We recommend that all time series data should be made stationary, especially with respect to the mean before predictions are performed. When we chose to use Brown's Double Exponential Model we found that better results were obtained without making the data stationary, and hence we have decided to use the data as given. The output x_i is now banded as follows. We take the data $(x_{i-1-20} \ldots x_{i-1})$, and find its minimum (a) and maximum (b). A total of 11 bands of size $\left(\dfrac{b-a}{11} \right)$ are centred around x_{i-1}. The prediction success of the model is based on whether the actual and predicted output value bands are the same or not, or can be based on mean absolute percentage error of predicted returns.

9.2.4 Data preparation for Band Value Prediction

We have used a k-nearest neighbour classifier for band-value prediction. In this specific case we find that differencing the time-series twice and predicting this is better than predicting original value. A first differenced time series is of the form $(x_2 - x_1, x_3 - x_2, \ldots x_i - x_{i-1} \ldots x_N - x_{N-1})$. Let us denote the final differenced time series to be predicted as $(y_1, y_2, \ldots y_j \ldots y_{N-2})$. The difference between the minimum and maximum of the training data is given by minimum (a') and maximum (b'). We experiment with $L = 2,4,6$ bands and these are centred on the x_{i-1} with a width of $\left(\dfrac{b'-a'}{L} \right)$. The predictive ability is now measured based on whether the actual and predicted output value bands are the same or not.

9.2.5 Measuring Uncertainty of Forecast Models

The RQG is generated with the basic assumption that forecast ability determines risk. If you have a perfect predictor for the future, there is no risk. Otherwise the level of risk is dependent on the quality of predictor, data complexity, and how far we wish to predict. In fact all of these three factors are correlated. The x-axis of RQG quantifies the risk involved by predicting above 1, 2, ... n steps ahead. Hence uncertainty associated with predicting m steps ahead can be measured as the accuracy on validation set that is achievable with a predictor model trained to predict m steps ahead. To illustrate this, let's say for a j step ahead forecast, on a total of m validation data points, the error will be measured m times as $\left(e_1^{(j)}, e_2^{(j)}, \ldots, e_m^{(j)} \right)$. The average error estimate will be $\hat{e}(j) = \sum_{p=1}^{m} e_p^j$. This is our measure of uncertainty on j step

ahead forecast.

9.3 Trading Strategies

After generating the RQG described in previous section we can now attempt to visually interpret it and discuss its role in trading strategies. Figure 1 shows an example
graph where the most optimal investment situation is the far top left corner corresponding to the most benefit and least uncertainty. This is an ideal high profit – low
risk situation. It is generally believed that financial-agents are risk-averse investors
[2],which means that investors prefer more wealth to less but to accept more risk
they also require higher expectations of returns. Hence it is of interest to find situations with an appropriate risk – return balance.

In order to rank trading time-horizons on most optimal risk – return we can compute
Euclidean distances (Eq. 2) from a given point (x_i, y_i) on the scatter-plot to the most
optimal point (left – top corner, coordinate $(0, 5)$). Before we compute the distances
we use standard min-max normalisation to transform uncertainty and benefit into
$0...1$ ranges. With the Euclidean distances known we can now rank our trading time-
horizons based on the minimum distance. Table 1 and Figure 2 illustrates this (do not
worry at this point in time how the figure was derived).

$$d = \sqrt{(x_i - 0)^2 + (y_i - 5)^2} \qquad (2)$$

Some investors are more risk averse than others this can be because of age,
family/cash flow situation and other motivations. To cater for this we can also
compute weighted Euclidean distances instead (Eq. 3), where a weight in range of
$0...1$ is given to uncertainty (w_1) and a weight in range of $0...1$ is given to the benefit
(w_2). This causes the rankings of time horizons to change to new most optimal
rankings. For example when a weight of 0.3 is assigned to benefit and weight of 0.7
to uncertainty, this indicates that it is important for us not to take on much risk, and a
weight of 0.3 on profit means that our goal are not high returns but returns do carry
some importance

$$d = \sqrt{w_1(x_i - 0)^2 + w_2(y_i - 5)^2} \qquad (3)$$

Table 2 shows rankings of different weights for Fig. 2, where two sets of weights
were used. In the first set of weights, (uncertainty) $w_1 = 0.7$ and (benefit) $w_2 = 0.3$, in
the second set of weights $w_1 = 0.3$ and $w_2 = 0.7$. The row ranking, represents the

order of best to worse trading horizons as based on Euclidean distances, where ranking *1* stands for the smallest Euclidean distance. In the first set of weights, the ranking of trading horizons is biased towards minimising uncertainty, and hence position of the points on y-axis plays less of a role. The second set of weights favors profit over uncertainty, hence for example point 3 is ranked before 1, or point 19 before 12.

RQG can be used in various interesting ways to implement real trading strategies. When time-horizons are above the no-profit/loss line, see Fig. 2, then, this indicates that predictions for those investment-horizons are in positive returns. Hence a possible trading strategy would be to buy a stock for all time-horizons above the no-profit/loss line. So essentially we would buy at time t and sell at time $t+h$, where h is a time-horizon above no-profit/loss line, this means we would buy and sell as many times as there are time-horizons above the line $y=0$.

This strategy can very much be reversed, where we sell stocks for all time-horizons below no-profit/loss line and buy them back at their relevant time-horizons. This process is known as *short* selling and is a commonly used trading method [9]. Further we could fine-tune the strategy by only trading time-horizons with low uncertainty, where given some readiness to risk we only consider trades with uncertainty lower then an appropriate threshold. In Fig. 2 we see a vertical line at $x=4$, based on which we filter out all other trades but everything that is to the left of the line.

Time Horizons

Ranking	1	2	3	4	5	6	7	8	9	10	11	...
	2	3	1	4	5	12	19	18	7	15	8	...
continued...	12	13	14	15	16	17	18	19	20			
	20	6	16	17	10	11	9	13	14			

Table 1. Time-horizon ranking based on Euclidean distances

Weights	Time Horizons															
Ranking	1	2	3	4	5	6	7	8	9	10	11	12	13	14	15	...
U=0.7 B=0.3	2	1	3	4	5	12	7	8	6	10	11	9	19	18	15	...
U=0.3 B=0.7	2	3	1	4	5	19	18	20	12	15	16	17	7	8	6	...

Table 2. Time-horizon ranking (top 15) based on Euclidean distances

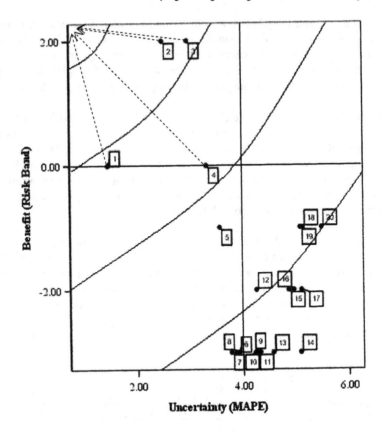

Fig. 2. (AstraZeneca 6/12/2006 – 5/1/2007) RQG, Desirability of trading 1 – 4 steps ahead can be based on Euclidean distance between their position and ideal (0, 2) position shown above

One obvious strategy that can be personalized to an agent's investments needs and requirements follows directly from assigning different weights on uncertainty and risk. Suppose an investment agent has motivation for high profits, then such weights would be set that $w_2 = r$ and $w_1 = 1\text{-}r$ and $w_2 > w_1$, where w_2 is the weight for benefit. Then the top m time-horizons from the resulting ranking based on least weighted Euclidean distances would be selected as the suitable time-horizons to trade, where m is some arbitrary integer. It is worth mentioning that when we run this strategy on a few stocks, the actual percentage returns had tendency to be less volatile when more weight was put on uncertainty. Further we need to only trade time-horizons above $y=0$ line, or for short selling, below the line.

9.4 Experimental Details

In the following sections we first detail the purpose of the experiment(s), data used and any additional design details. Section 9.5 will show results on the basis of the following.

9.4.1 Experimental Objectives

The main objective of our experiment is to show that there is some pragmatic benefit in using RQG method. We use a naïve trading strategy to demonstrate the utility of our proposal.

9.4.2 Data

The data used in our experiments were the daily split adjusted, close prices from Wolseley, a FTSE-100 company. Data was separated into training set, validation set and test set, as indicated on Figure 3.

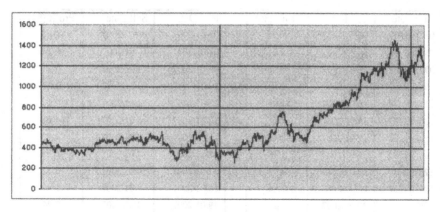

Fig 3. 10 years of Wolseley time-series data (training/validation/test sets, respectively)

9.4.3 Experimental Set-up and Methodology

We implemented a simple naïve trading strategy based on RQGs for both prediction models (Browns and kNN) described in section 9.2. Figure 4 illustrates the trading strategy; for a particular day j_i an RQG is generated showing predicted output and uncertainty over the next two days. We buy the stock at j_i and either sell on j_{i+1} or j_{i+2}, based on the shortest Euclidean distance as described in section 9.3. We do this for 19 consecutive trading days, at each day we must buy and sell on either of the next two days. In section 9.5 we present returns in percentages for this.

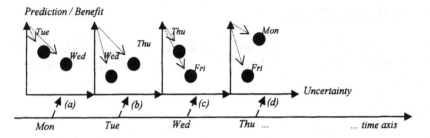

Fig 4. Naïve 2 day strategy, predicting on Monday, Tuesday, Wednesday, Thursday...

9.5 Results

Percentage returns for our naïve trading strategy are presented for Wolseley, for the period 8th Jan 07 – 2nd Feb 07.

Buy Date	Sell Date	Profit (%)	Buy Date	Sell Date	Profit (%)
05/01/2007	08/01/2007	-0.78	05/01/2007	08/01/2007	-0.78
08/01/2007	10/01/2007	0.24	08/01/2007	10/01/2007	0.24
09/01/2007	10/01/2007	-1.55	09/01/2007	11/01/2007	0.54
10/01/2007	12/01/2007	2.59	10/01/2007	12/01/2007	2.59
11/01/2007	15/01/2007	1.85	11/01/2007	12/01/2007	0.46
12/01/2007	16/01/2007	-0.08	12/01/2007	16/01/2007	-0.08
15/01/2007	17/01/2007	-1.81	15/01/2007	17/01/2007	-1.81
16/01/2007	18/01/2007	1.38	16/01/2007	17/01/2007	-0.38
17/01/2007	19/01/2007	3.77	17/01/2007	19/01/2007	3.77
18/01/2007	22/01/2007	1.96	18/01/2007	19/01/2007	1.96
19/01/2007	22/01/2007	0	19/01/2007	23/01/2007	0.74
22/01/2007	23/01/2007	0.74	22/01/2007	23/01/2007	0.74
23/01/2007	25/01/2007	-2.06	23/01/2007	25/01/2007	-2.06
24/01/2007	26/01/2007	-2.37	24/01/2007	26/01/2007	-2.37
25/01/2007	26/01/2007	-0.97	25/01/2007	26/01/2007	-0.97
26/01/2007	30/01/2007	0.37	26/01/2007	30/01/2007	0.37
29/01/2007	30/01/2007	0.15	29/01/2007	31/01/2007	-0.23
30/01/2007	31/01/2007	-0.38	30/01/2007	31/01/2007	-0.38
31/01/2007	02/02/2007	2.12	31/01/2007	02/02/2007	2.12
Total:		5.18	Total:		4.49

Table 3. Profits (in %), for kNN on the left Browns on the right

As expected kNN, performs slightly better than Browns model. A simple buy-and-hold strategy for the same period would provide 5.15%, our kNN does slightly better. The RQG method has potential, as there seems to be some benefit in using RQG with even a very simple naïve trading strategy.

9.5 Conclusion

This paper proposes an innovative way of looking at risk. Several trading strategies were proposed based on the risk-quantification plots. The forecast system used is central to the accuracy of RQG and the success of any related trading strategies. The better the forecast system the more accurate will our proposed risk quantification be. We believe the method discussed is showing potential for further study within future work on visual risk quantification methods of stock markets and related financial assets.

References

1. Grinold R.C. and Kahn R.N. (2000) Active Portfolio Management, McGraw-Hill, ISBN 0-070-24882-6
2. Pilbeam K. (1998) Finance & Financial Markets, ISBN 0-333-62945-0
3. Hair, Anderson, Tatham and Black (1998) Multivariate Data Analysis, Prenrtice Hall, ISBN 0-138-94858-5
4. Lindsay D. and Cox S., Effective Probability Forecasting for Time series Data using standard Machine Learning Techniques, ICAPR 05 proceedings, pages 35-44
5. Delurgio S. (1998) Forecasting: Principles and Applications, McGraw-Hill, ISBN 0-256-13433-2
6. Makridakis S., Wheelwright S.C. and Hyndman R.J. (1998) Forecasting: Methods and Applications, John Wiley & Sons, ISBN 0-471-53233-9
7. Trippi R. (1995) Chaos and Nonlinear Dynamics in the Financial Markets, Irwin, ISBN 1-557-38857-1
8. Han J. and Kamber M. (2006) Data Mining: Concepts and Techniques, Morgan Kaufmann, ISBN 1-55860-901-6
9. Burns R. (2005) The Naked Trader: How anyone can make money Trading Shares, Harriman House Publishing, ISBN 1-897-59745-2

Part II
Biometrics

10 Facial Image Processing with Convolutional Neural Networks

Christophe Garcia and Stefan Duffner

France Telecom R&D, 4 rue du Clos Courtel, 35512 Cesson-Sévigné, France,
{christophe.garcia,stefan.duffer}@orange-ftgroup.com

Abstract. We present a generic machine-learning technique based on Convolutional Neural Networks and describe how it can be successfully applied to different facial processing applications like face detection, facial feature detection, face alignment, gender classification and face recognition. We experimentally show that the proposed approach outperforms state-of-the-art techniques based on Adaboost, SVMs or AAMs, as it conjointly learns feature extraction and classification parameters, making it very robust to noise, lighting variations and partial occlusions while being naturally and efficiently implemented on embedded platforms.

10.1 Introduction

Facial image processing is an area of research dedicated to the extraction and analysis of information about human faces, information which is shown to play a central role in social interactions including recognition, emotion and intention. Over the last decade, it has become a very active research field due to the large number of possible applications, such as model-based video coding, image retrieval, surveillance and biometrics, visual speech understanding, virtual characters for e-learning, online marketing or entertainment and intelligent human-computer interaction. With the introduction of new powerful machine learning techniques, statistical classification methods and complex deformable models, recent advances have been made on face detection and tracking, person identification, facial expression and emotion recognition, gender classification, face coding and virtual face synthesis. However, lots of progress has still to be made to provide more robust systems, in order to cope with the variability of facial image appearances due to lighting conditions, poses and expressions, image noise and partial occlusions, in an unconstrained, real-world context.

Many approaches to tackle these problems have been proposed in the literature. They can roughly be divided into two groups: local and global approaches. Early local approaches used simple visual features like color (Saber and Tekalp, 1996), edges (Jesorsky, Kirchberg, and Frischholz, 2001) or geometric features (Brunelli and Poggio, 1993). There are also many methods that employ Gabor wavelets to extract features, e.g. Wiskott, Fellous, Krüger, and von der Malsburg (1997) and Perronnin, Dugelay, and Rose (2005). Further, local template matching-based approaches have been proposed by Moghaddam and Pentland (1997); Lin and Wu (1999); Jesorsky, Kirchberg, and Frischholz (2001). Mostly, these local features are then combined using global models, like probabilistic models (Reinders, Koch, and Gerbrands, 1996), deformable graphs (Wiskott, Fellous, Krüger, and von der Malsburg, 1997) or Hidden Markov Models (HMM) (Perronnin et al., 2005).

On the other hand, most global approaches process the face image as a whole and mostly perform statistical projections into lower-dimensional linear subspaces. For instance, Turk and Pentland (1991) use Principal Component Analysis (PCA) and Belhumeur, Hespanha, and Kriegmann (1997) Linear Discriminant Analysis (LDA). Other global methods are based on non linear classifiers. For the specific case of face detection, Rowley, Baluja, and Kanade (1998) propose a MLP neural network-based approach and Viola and Jones (2001) a technique based on Adaboost using Haar wavelets.

More recent approaches make use of the so-called Active Appearance Models (AAM), e.g. Edwards, Taylor, and Cootes (1998), that build independent statistical models of shape and texture and finally combine them into a global one.

We propose an approach that is fundamentally different from existing techniques. It is based on Convolutional Neural Networks (CNN), a specific type of neural network introduced by LeCun, Bottou, Bengio, and Haffner (1998). This approach tightly couples local feature detection, global model construction and classification in a single architecture where all parameters are learned conjointly. Thus, it alleviates the problems of feature extraction and selection, by automatically learning optimal filters and classifiers that are very robust to noise. In the following, we will show that CNNs are very effective for facial image processing by presenting different architectures, designed for face detection, facial feature detection, face alignment, gender classification and face recognition. The remainder of this paper is organized as follows. In Sect. 2, we describe CNNs in general and in Sect. 3 several variants for different applications are presented as well as experimental results. Section 4 describes how these architectures can be implemented efficiently on embedded platforms. Finally, conclusions are drawn in Sect. 5.

10.2 Convolutional Neural Networks

The main Convolutional Neural Network architecture which will be adapted depending on the targeted applications is shown in Fig. 1. It consists of six layers, excepting the input plane (retina) that receives an image area of fixed size to be processed. Layers C_1 through S_2 contain a series of planes where successive convolutions and subsampling operations are performed. These planes are called feature maps as they are in charge of extracting and combining a set of appropriate features. Layer N_1 contains a number of partially connected neurons and layer N_2 contains the output units of the network (one unit in the example). These last two layers carry out the classification task using the features extracted in the previous layers.

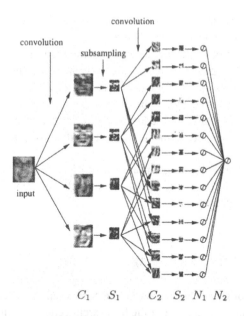

$$C_1 \quad S_1 \quad\quad C_2 \quad S_2 \quad N_1 \quad N_2$$

Fig. 1. The basic Convolutional Neural Network architecture

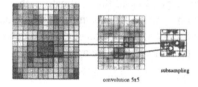

Fig. 2. Example of a 5 × 5 convolution map followed by a 2 × 2 subsampling map

Each unit in a layer receives input from a set of units located in a small neighborhood in the previous layer as shown in Fig. 2. The idea of connecting units to local receptive fields on the input was largely inspired by the discovery of locally-sensitive, orientation-selective neurons in the cat visual system (Hubel and Wiesel, 1962), and local connections have been used many times in neural models of visual learning (Fukushima, 1975; LeCun, 1989; Mozer, 1991). With local receptive fields, neurons can extract elementary visual features such as oriented edges, end-points, or corners. These features are then combined by the subsequent layers in order to detect higher-order features.

Distortions or shifts of the input can cause the position of salient features to vary. In addition, elementary feature detectors that are useful for one part of the image are likely to be useful for the entire image. This knowledge is applied by forcing a set of units, whose receptive fields are located at different locations in the image, to have identical weight vectors (LeCun, 1989). Units in a layer are organized in planes within which all the units share the same set of weights. Therefore, each feature map has a fixed feature detector that corresponds to a convolution with a trainable kernel, applied over the planes in the previous layer. Several feature maps (with different weight vectors) are used in each layer so that multiple features can be detected at each location. These feature maps form convolutional layers C_i.

Once a feature has been detected, its exact location is less important. Only its approximate position relative to other features is relevant, as absolute positions are likely to vary in the different instances of the patterns to classify. Hence, each convolutional layer C_i is typically followed by a subsampling layer, S_i, that performs local averaging and subsampling operations, reducing the resolution of the feature maps and, therefore, reducing the sensitivity of the output to shifts, distortions and variations in scale and rotation.

Using appropriate training sets, representative of the application to build, all parameters (convolution filters, subsampling factors, classification layers) are learned automatically via backpropagation.

10.3 Applications for facial image processing

In the following, we describe the various architectures used for different facial processing applications. They all make use of the basic architecture described in the previous section, consisting of several alternating convolution and subsampling layers followed by neuron layers. However, depending of the application, the dimensions and number of the feature maps or neurons vary as well as the type of the output layer.

Further, we briefly outline the training procedure for each of the described neural networks and, the way the trained systems are applied.

10.3.1 Face detection

In Garcia and Delakis (2004), we presented a face detection method called Convolutional Face Finder (CFF) which is able to localize multiple faces with a minimum size of 20×20 pixels, rotated up to $\pm 20°$ in the image plane and turned up to $\pm 60°$.

The basic architecture is the one described in Sect. 2, i.e. two alternating convolutional and subsampling layers C_1, S_1 and C_2, S_2 followed by two neuron layers N_1 and N_2 (see Fig. 1). The size of the retina is 36×32 pixels.

Layer C_1 is composed of four feature maps of size 28×32 pixels. Each unit in each feature map is connected to a 5×5 neighborhood into the input retina of size 32×36. Each feature map unit computes a weighted sum of its input by 25 (5×5) trainable coefficients, i.e. the convolution kernel, and adds a trainable bias.

Layer S_1 is composed of four feature maps of size 14×16 pixels, each connected to one feature map in C_1. The receptive field of each unit is a 2×2 area in the previous layer's corresponding feature map. Each unit computes the average of its four inputs, multiplies it by a trainable coefficient, adds a trainable bias, and the result passes through a hyperbolic tangent function, the activation function of the unit.

Layer C_2 contains 14 feature maps performing 3×3 convolutions. Here, outputs of different feature maps are fused in order to help in combining different features, thus in extracting more complex information. Each of the four subsampled feature maps of S_1 provides inputs to two different feature maps of C_2. This results in the first eight feature maps of C_2. Each of the other six feature maps of C_2 takes input from one of the possible pairs of different feature maps of S_1. Therefore, layer C_2 has 14 feature maps of size 12×14.

Layers N_1 and N_2 contain classical neural units. These layers act as a classifier, the previous ones acting as feature extractors. In layer N_1, each of the 14 neurons is fully connected to all units of only one corresponding feature map of S_2. The single neuron of layer N_2 is fully connected to all neurons of layer N_1. The units in layers N_1 and N_2 perform the classical dot product between their input vector and their weight vector, to which a bias is added. A hyperbolic tangent function is used to produce an output between -1.0 and $+1.0$. The output of neuron N_2 is used to classify the input image as a non-face, if its value is negative, or as a face, if its value is positive.

In order to train the neural network, we use a set of about 3,700 manually cropped, highly variable face images extracted from various sources of the Internet of from scanned images of newspapers. The set of initial negative (i.e. non-face) examples is built by randomly cropping regions out of images that do not contain any face. Then, this set is gradually augmented by a so-called bootstrapping procedure which, every 60 training iterations, applies the neural network on scenery images not containing any face and collects the false alarms which give a response above a certain threshold. This threshold is decreased at each step. Thus, the frontier between positive and negative examples is gradually refined. The training algorithm is the standard online Backpropagation with momentum which was slightly adapted to cope with weight sharing (Garcia and Delakis, 2004).

After training, the neural network can be applied on complex images containing faces of different sizes. To this end, the input image is repeatedly subsampled by a factor of 1.2, resulting in a pyramid of images. Each image of the pyramid is then filtered by the convolutional neural network, i.e. the entire images are convolved and subsampled at once to avoid redundant computation. Face candidates (pixels with positive values in the result image) in each scale are then mapped back to the input image scale. They are then grouped according to their proximity in image and scale spaces. Each group of face candidates is fused in a representative face whose center and size are computed as the centroids of the centers and sizes of the grouped faces, weighted by their individual network responses.

Finally, a face candidate is classified as face if its corresponding volume (i.e. the sum of positive answer values in a small pyramid around its center) is greater than a given threshold.

Table 1 lists the detection rates for various numbers of false detections for our system as well as for other published systems on the CMU test set (Rowley et al., 1998). It can be observed that our method compares favorably with the others, especially for low numbers of false alarms. This shows that face and non-face spaces are robustly separated. Figure 3 shows some detection results on the CMU test set.

10.3.2 Facial feature detection

CNNs can also be used to detect characteristic facial feature points. We developed a system to detect four facial features in face images: the eyes, the nose tip and the

Face detector	False alarms				
	0	10	31	65	167
Rowley et al. (1998)	–	83.2%	86.0%	–	90.1%
Schneiderman and Kanade (2000)	–	–	–	94.4%	
Li et al. (2002)	–	83.6%	90.2%	–	–
Viola and Jones (2001)	–	76.1%	88.4%	92.0%	93.9%
Convolutional Face Finder	88.8%	90.5%	91.5%	92.3%	93.1%

Table 1. Comparison of selected methods for various numbers of false alarms on the CMU test set (Garcia and Delakis, 2004)

Fig. 3. Some face detection results obtained on the CMU test set

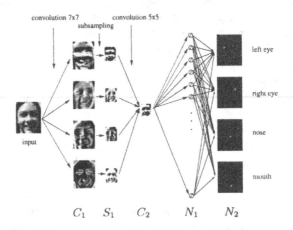

Fig. 4. The architecture of the facial feature detection system

mouth center (Duffer and Garcia, 2005). The architecture of this convolutional neural network is depicted in Fig. 4. The particularity of this neural network is that it has four output maps consisting of an array of neurons with the same dimensions as the retina. The system is trained to highlight for a given input face image the position of each of the four facial features in the respective output maps, i.e. for a given facial feature,

Fig. 5. Some facial feature detection results

the output neuron that corresponds to the feature position is trained to respond with $+1$ and all the others in the respective map with -1. Except for the output layer, the architecture is very similar to the one of the CFF. However, the size of the retina is 46×56, C_1 and S_1 contain four feature maps, C_1 performing a 7×7 convolution. C_2 contains only one feature map which is fully connected to the feature maps of S_1 and having convolution kernels of size 5×5. There is no layer S_2, and N_1 contains 40 fully connected neurons.

The training set consists of about 3,000 face images of various public face databases with manually annotated feature positions. Once the neural network has been trained, it can be applied to face images of any size by just rescaling the input image to the size of the retina and linearly projecting the resulting positions, i.e. the maxima in the output maps, into the original image. Experiments showed that the system is able to precisely and robustly detect facial features in face images with considerable variations in pose, illumination, facial expressions as well as noise and partial occlusions. We obtained a detection rate of 98.2% on the AR database with a maximum error of 15% of the bounding box width. Cristinacce and Cootes (2004) compared two feature detection approaches using the BioID database: one based on Adaboost, where they obtained a detection rate of 96%, and the other based on AAMs, where they report 92% of successful detection. Figure 5 shows some detection results on very complex images.

10.3.3 Face alignment

Most face recognition methods require the facial area to be well-centered within the segmented image in order to perform effectively. Slight mis-alignments in terms of position, rotation and scale cause a considerable performance drop. Many recognition methods try to tackle this problem by detecting characteristic facial feature points and then globally aligning the face image with respect to the feature positions. In fact, the method described in the previous section can be employed for this purpose. However, we propose a different approach that circumvents the difficult task of explicitly localizing facial features. For a given face image, we assume that the face has been roughly localized by the face detection method CFF. The face image is then cropped according to the respective bounding box and presented to the convolutional neural network,

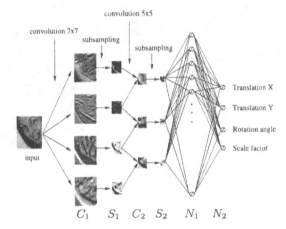

Fig. 6. The architecture of the face alignment system

Fig. 7. Some face alignment results. *Black rectangle:* desired bounding box. *White rectangle, left image:* original bounding box (by CFF). *White rectangle, right image:* aligned bounding box.

illustrated in Fig. 6. This neural network, once trained, estimates simultaneously translation, rotation and scale parameters of the transformation the input face image has undergone. To align the face image, the inverse transformation with the estimated parameters is applied to the initial bounding box. The architecture of the neural network is very similar to the face detector described in Sect. 3.1. The difference is that layer C_2 and S_2 only contain three feature maps connected as illustrated in Fig. 6 and that layer N_2 contains four neurons. Moreover, the feature maps in layer C_1 perform a 7×7 convolution and the ones in layer C_2 a 5×5 convolution.

The neural network is trained with about 30,000 annotated face images, artificially mis-aligned, and is able to correct translations of up to 13% of the bounding box width, $\pm 30°$ of rotation and $\pm 10\%$ of scale variations.

Experimental results show that 94% of the face images of the BioID database and 80% of the images of a difficult test set extracted from the internet are aligned with an error of less than 10% of the face bounding box width. We also compared the results with the alignment based on the feature detection method presented in the preceding section, and we measured an increase in precision of about 18%. Figure 7 shows the alignment results on some examples.

Fig. 8. Examples of training images for gender classification. *Left:* men, *right:* women

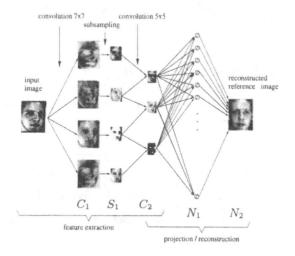

Fig. 9. The architecture of the face recognition system

10.3.4 Gender classification

We have used the CFF architecture to perform gender recognition. Only the size of the retina was changed to 46×56. The training set was constructed using cropped and histogram-equalized frontal face images of the FERET database (Philips, Wechsler, Huang, and Rauss, 1998) where 2541 images where used for training and 400 images for testing. Figure 8 shows some examples of training images.

The classification rate obtained with this architecture is 97.4% which is comparable to the results obtained by Baluja and Rowley (2007) who report a classification rate of 97.1% using a SVM-based and 96.4% using a AdaBoost-based approach.

10.3.5 Face recognition

Finally, CNNs can also be used for face recognition. We propose an approach that learns to reconstruct, from any face image of a person, a reference face image that is chosen beforehand for each person. More precisely, among all images of a each person, the example that is the closest to the mean image in terms of the Euclidean distance is selected as the reference image. Figure 9 shows the architecture of this neural network. It is similar to the face alignment system described in the preceding section with slight differences: layer N_1 contains 60 neurons and layer N_2 is a neuron array of the size of the retina, i.e. 46×56, with linear activation functions. Further, there is no layer S_2. It is important to note that layer N_1 contains much fewer neurons than its preceding and its following layers and thus represents a so-called "bottle-neck" layer. This type of architecture actually learns a non-linear projection of the face images into a sub-space of lower dimension and then reconstructs the respective reference images from this compressed representation.

After training, a given face image can be identified by calculating the distances between the projected vector in the intermediate layer (N_1) of the network and the projected vectors of the person's reference images and finally by performing a simple nearest neighbor classification.

We tested the system on two public face databases: the Olivetti Research Ltd. (ORL) face database (Samaria and Harter, 1994) and the Yale database (Belhumeur et al., 1997) and compared it to the well-known Eigenfaces approach (Turk and Pentland, 1991). Table 2 shows the overall recognition rates obtained using a leave-one out validation and an average over 30 test runs.

	ORL	Yale
Eigenfaces	89.7%	77.9%
proposed approach	**93.3%**	**88.0%**

Table 2. Recognition rates of the CNN-based approach compared to the Eigenfaces method

10.4 Implementation on embedded platforms

The CFF system has been successfully implemented on various embedded platforms like ARM (Xscale, IMX21), DSP (Starcore) and SPVM 3000 orange (Mamalet, Roux, and Garcia, 2006). To this end, extensive memory and computational optimizations have been conducted. For example, all parameters and calculations have been transformed from floating point to fixed point arithmetic without any loss of precision and effectiveness. Further optimizations exploiting the parallel computation of embedded processors have been performed as well as some algorithmic optimization merging the convolution and subsampling operations.

Finally, an overall speed-up factor of 55 has been achieved on the Xscale platform using these optimization techniques. Table 3 shows the processing speed on different platforms.

	Xscale PXA27x @ 624MHz	Starcore SC140 @ 275MHz	Pentium IV @ 3.2GHz
Floating point version	0.3 fps	-	10 fps
Optimized version	16.5 fps	35 fps	180 fps

Table 3. Execution speed of the CFF on different platforms (in frames per second)

The facial feature detection system described in Sect. 3.2 has also been implemented on embedded platforms using similar optimization techniques. Here, a speed-up factor of 700 has been obtained and the feature detection system runs at 68.7 faces per second on a Pentium IV with 3.2GHz and at 12.8 faces per second on a Xscale PXA27x with 624 MHz.

10.5 Conclusion

We presented a generic machine-learning technique based on Convolutional Neural Networks and described how it can be successfully applied to face detection, facial feature detection, face alignment, gender classification and face recognition.

   Experimental results showed that the proposed neural architectures are very appropriate for facial image processing, outperforming other systems based on Adaboost, SVMs or AAMs.

   CNNs are indeed very powerful, especially because they tightly couple local feature detection, global model construction and classification in a single architecture where all parameters are learned conjointly.

   Finally, we also showed that CNNs can be naturally and efficiently implemented on embedded platforms, allowing fast processing, without any loss of precision.

References

S. Baluja and H. Rowley. Boosting sex identification performance. *International Journal of Computer Vision*, 71(1):111–119, 2007.

P. Belhumeur, J. Hespanha, and D. Kriegmann. Eigenfaces vs fisherfaces: Recognition using class specific linear projection. *IEEE Transactions on Pattern Analysis and Machine Intelligence*, 17(7):711–720, 1997.

R. Brunelli and T. Poggio. Face recognition: Features versus templates. *IEEE Transactions on Pattern Analysis and Machine Intelligence*, 15(10):1042–1052, 1993.

D. Cristinacce and T. Cootes. A comparison of shape constrained facial feature detectors. In *Proc. of the 6th Int. Conf. on Automatic Face and Gesture Recognition*, pages 375–380, Seoul, Korea, 2004.

S. Duffer and C. Garcia. A connexionist approach for robust and precise facial feature detection in complex scenes. In *Fourth International Symposium on Image and Signal Processing and Analysis (ISPA)*, Zagreb, Croatia, September 2005.

G. Edwards, C. Taylor, and T. Cootes. Interpreting face images using active appearance models. In *Autom. Face and Gesture Rec.*, pages 300–305, 1998.

K. Fukushima. Cognitron: A self-organizing multilayered neural network. *Biological Cybernetics*, 20:121–136, 1975.

C. Garcia and M. Delakis. Convolutional face finder: A neural architecture for fast and robust face detection. *IEEE Transactions on Pattern Analysis and Machine Intelligence*, 26(11):1408–1423, 2004.

D. Hubel and T. Wiesel. Receptive fields, binocular interaction and functional architecture in the cat's visual cortex. *Journal of Physiology*, 160:106–154, 1962.

O. Jesorsky, K. Kirchberg, and R. Frischholz. Robust face detection using the hausdorff distance. In *Third International Conference on Audio- and Video-Based Biometric Person Authentication (AVBPA)*, pages 90–95, Halmstad, Sweden, 2001.

Y. LeCun. Generalization and network design strategies. In R. Pfeifer, Z. Schreter, F. Fogelman, and L. Steels, editors, *Connectionism in Perspective*, Zurich, 1989.

Y. LeCun, L. Bottou, Y. Bengio, and P. Haffner. Gradient-based learning applied to document recognition. *Proceedings of the IEEE*, 86(11):2278–2324, 1998.

S. Li, L. Zhu, Z. Zhang, A. Blake, H. Zhang, and H. Shum. Statistical learning of multi-view face detection. In *Conference on Computer Vision*, pages 67–81, 2002.

C.-H. Lin and J.-L. Wu. Automatic facial feature extraction by genetic algorithms. *IEEE Transactions on Image Processing*, 8(6):834–845, 1999.

F. Mamalet, S. Roux, and C. Garcia. Embedded convolutional face finder. In *International Conference on Multimedia and Expo*, pages 285–288, 2006.

B. Moghaddam and A. Pentland. Probabilistic visual learning for object representation. *IEEE Trans. on Pattern Analysis and Machine Intelligence*, 19(7):696–710, 1997.

M. C. Mozer. *The perception of multiple objects: a connectionist approach*. MIT Press, Cambridge, MA, USA, 1991.

F. Perronnin, J. Dugelay, and K. Rose. A probabilistic model of face mapping with local transformations and its application to person recognition. *IEEE Transactions on Pattern Analysis and Machine Intelligence*, 27(7):1157–1171, 2005.

P. Philips, H. Wechsler, J. Huang, and P. Rauss. The feret database and evaluation procedure for face recognition algorithms. *Image and Vision Computing*, 16(5): 295–306, 1998.

M. Reinders, R. Koch, and J. Gerbrands. Locating facial features in image sequences using neural networks. In *Proceedings of the Second International Conference on Automatic Face and Gesture Recognition*, pages 230–235, 1996.

H. Rowley, S. Baluja, and T. Kanade. Neural network-based face detection. *IEEE Transactions on Pattern Analysis and Machine Intelligence*, 20(1):23–38, 1998.

E. Saber and A. Tekalp. Face detection and facial feature extraction using color, shape and symmetry-based cost functions. In *Proceedings of the International Conference on Pattern Recognition*, 1996.

F. Samaria and A. Harter. Parametrisation of a stochastic model for human face identification. In *IEEE Worksh. on Applications of Comp. Vision*, pages 138–142, 1994.

H. Schneiderman and T. Kanade. A statistical model for 3D object detection applied to faces and cars. In *IEEE Conference on Computer Vision and Pattern Recognition*, volume 1, pages 746–751, 2000.

M. Turk and A. Pentland. Face recognition using eigenfaces. In *Computer Vision and Pattern Recognition*, pages 586–591, 1991.

P. Viola and M. J. Jones. Rapid object detection using a boosted cascade of simple features, 2001. Proc. Intl. Conference on Computer Vision and Pattern Recognition.

L. Wiskott, J.-M. Fellous, N. Krüger, and C. von der Malsburg. Face recognition by elastic bunch graph matching. *IEEE Transactions on Pattern Analysis and Machine Intelligence*, 19(7):775–779, 1997.

11 Time-dependent Interactive Graphical Models for Human Activity Analysis

Marco Cristani and Vittorio Murino

Università degli Studi di Verona, Dipartimento di Informatica, Verona, Italy,
cristanm|murino@sci.univr.it

Abstract. Automatically monitoring and classifying human activities is one of the most challenging problems currently faced in machine learning. In this paper, we propose a statistical model aimed at modeling interactions among human subjects, in particular, conversational audio data is here analyzed. The proposed model, called Coupled Hidden Duration Semi Markov Model, takes inspiration from the large literature on Hidden Markov Models and its variants. The novelty introduced by the model is the capability of dealing with interacting state processes, where 1) states that characterize a single process exhibit different time durations, and 2) different processes involved in an interaction are not synchronized, i.e., their states do not begin/end at the same time instants. Comparative synthetical and real data experiments are presented, showing that the proposed model is able to tackle difficult interactive situations, not otherwise manageable by the state-of-the-art algorithms.

11.1 Introduction

Automatic activity recognition can be considered a recent growing area in automatic surveillance and monitoring research fields. In this context, the primary task is to classify multimodal patterns as simple human actions and, subsequently, starting from modeling individual actions, the last challenge is to actually cope with group activities, evidencing and quantifying the causal interactions among the individuals.

Dynamic Bayes Nets (DBN) (Jordan 1999) offer an elegant mathematical framework to combine the observations of the activities to be modeled (bottom-up) with complex behavioral priors (top-down), in order to provide expectations about the processes and dealing properly with the uncertainty.

A widely known DBN is the Hidden Markov Model (HMM) (Rabiner 1989), that models single Markov processes whose states are not directly visible. In the last years, several HMM extensions have been proposed, which can be roughly subdivided in two main families. First, there are models managing processes whose states are assumed to remain unchanged for some random time duration before their transitions, such as the

Hidden Semi Markov Model (HSMM) (Murphy 2002; Hongeng and Nevatia 2003). The second family of HMM extensions copes with the interaction among Markov processes (Brand, Oliver, and Pentland 1997; Jordan 1999; Basu, Choudhury and Pentland 2001) in which various interaction aspects are considered. For instance, it is possible to extract the influence that *a whole process* exerts on another (Basu et al. 2001), or simply the inter-processes *state* conditional probabilities (Brand et al. 1997).

In this paper, we try to couple the two families of HMM extensions explained above, considering interactions among semi Markov processes. The modeling of such kinds of interactions is hard; actually, the interaction among "simple" Markov processes is evaluated at each time step, because at each time step every process makes a state transition, i.e., the processes are "transition" synchronized. In the case of interaction among semi Markov processes, the "transition" synchronization may be missed: roughly speaking, it may happen that a process continuously maintains a state while another interacting process performs several state transitions. Therefore, the computation of inter-chain conditional probabilities needs particular care in determining which are the states that condition or are conditioned by other states.

In order to deal with such a situation, we propose a novel framework, called Coupled Hidden Duration Semi Markov Model (CHD-SMM).

The aim of the paper is to use a CHD-SMM to capture and learn the nature of a *global process* (GP) formed by interacting semi Markov *individual processes* (IPs), highlighting aspects of the interaction present within.

In order to cope with complexity issues, the basic hypotheses over which a CHD-SMM can work are twofold. First, the whole global process modeled is formed by various *visible* semi Markov IPs. In other words, at each time step we can gather a shot of the different *visible* state labels assumed by every IP. The second hypothesis is that the IPs are interacting, in the sense that a transition of an IP towards one state is conditioned on the past story of all the other IPs.

In the experimental section, after reporting a synthetical example, we face the problem of recognizing high-level multiple audio activities, or conversational styles, where different human speech segments are modeled as IPs, whose visible states model periods of silence/speech of different duration. To the best of our knowledge, this is the first attempt to model such kinds of high-order interdependent dynamics, thus representing an improvement in the state of the art of the automatic monitoring literature.

The rest of the paper is organized as follows. In Section 2, the needed theoretical background is presented and Section 3 details the proposed model. Section 4 presents experimental results and concludes the paper.

11.2 Fundamentals

11.2.1 Hidden Markov Models

The entities characterizing an Hidden Markov Model λ are: the set S of the N hidden states; the transition matrix $\mathbf{A} = \{a_{ij}\}$, where $a_{ij} = P(S_t = j|S_{t-1} = i), 1 \leq i, j \leq N$ with $a_{ij} \geq 0$, $\sum_{j=1}^{N} a_{ij} = 1$ and the variable S_t indicating the state at time t; the emission matrix $\mathbf{B} = \{P(O|j)\}$ indicating the probability that the state

j emits the symbol O, and the initial state probability distribution $\pi = \{\pi_i\}$, where $\pi_i = P(S_1 = i), 1 \leq i \leq N$ with $\pi_i \geq 0$ and $\sum_{i=1}^{N} \pi_i = 1$. For convenience, we denote an HMM as a triplet $\lambda = (\mathbf{A}, \mathbf{B}, \boldsymbol{\pi})$.

The learning of the HMM's parameters can be performed in two ways: as a direct derivation of the EM algorithm (the Baum-Welch procedure (Rabiner 1989)), or as a standard constrained optimization process (Zhong 2002).

11.2.2 HMM coupling architectures

The most intuitive structure of HMM coupling is represented by unstructured Cartesian product HMMs (Jordan, Ghahramani, Jaakkola, and Saul 1999), i.e. a group of HMMs in which the state of one model at time t depends on the states of all models (including itself) at time $t-1$, i.e.

$$P(^{c}S_t|^{1}S_{t-1}, ..., ^{C}S_{t-1}). \tag{1}$$

The state transition probability for C processes is described by a $(C+1)$ dimensional matrix leading to N^C free parameters (assuming a common number of hidden states N). In the Coupled HMMs (Brand et al. 1997), the joint conditional dependency of Eq.1 is substituted by the product of all marginal conditional probabilities. Another solution is the Influence Model (IM) (Basu et al. 2001): here the full transition probability is modeled with a linear combination of singular inter-chains transition probabilities, where the weights θ represent the influence among chains (*not among the states of the chains*). In formulae:

$$P(^{c}S_t|^{1}S_{t-1}, ..., ^{C}S_{t-1}) = \sum_{d=1}^{C} \theta_{(cd)} P(^{c}S_t|^{d}S_{t-1}) \tag{2}$$

with $1 \leq c, d \leq C$, $\theta_{(cd)} \geq 0$, $\sum_{d=1}^{C} \theta_{(cd)} = 1$. In this case, the advantage is a good compromise between number of parameters needed ($CN^2 + C^2$, where the term CN^2 corresponds to the free parameters of the intra-chain transition tables, and C^2 for the influence coefficients) and expressivity of the model. In practice, the IM is able to model each interaction between pairs of chains, but is not able to model the joint effect of multiple chains together.

11.3 Coupled Hidden Duration Semi Markov Model

As pointed out in (Murphy 2002), Semi Markov processes can be approached as Markov processes whose *generalized* states (simply pointed out as *states* in this paper) are pairs of the form $S_{\langle t_k \rangle} = <S_{t_k}, D_{t_k}>$, where the variable S_{t_k} expresses the automaton *state label* occurring at time t_k, which is observed consecutively for D_{t_k} time instants, and $\langle t_k \rangle$ indicates the time interval $[t_k, t_k + D_{t_k}[$. In this paper, we model a GP composed by C interacting semi-Markov IPs. To do this, we suppose that the IPs are directly *visible*, i.e., an observation over an IP, at whatever instant t_k, permits deterministically to individuate its current state label S_{t_k}. To ease the reading, we describe the case of $C = 2$ IPs, adding the apex $'$ to the quantities related to the second IP. The joint probability of a GP states sequence is:

$$P\left(S_{\langle t_1 \rangle}, S_{\langle t_2 \rangle}, \ldots, S_{\langle t_M \rangle}, S'_{\langle t'_1 \rangle}, S'_{\langle t'_2 \rangle}, \ldots, S'_{\langle t'_{M'} \rangle}\right) \tag{3}$$

where, in general, the number of occurring states per chain can be different, i.e., $M \neq M'$, and $t_k \neq t'_k$, which means that no synchronization is present among state transitions. Anyway, we start the analysis supposing the states as perfectly synchronized (see Fig. 1(a)). In this case, we can rewrite Eq.3 dropping the apex $'$ from the time indexes, being them equal by definition. Subsequently, we first consider the factorization of the joint probability of a semi Markov process proposed in (Murphy 2002), which considers transition probability factors of the form $P(S_{\langle t_k \rangle} | S_{\langle t_{k-1} \rangle})$. Inspired by this, we rearrange Eq.3 as a product of coupled probability transition terms, assuming the form :

$$P(S_{\langle t_k \rangle} | S_{\langle t_{k-1} \rangle} S'_{\langle t_{k-1} \rangle}), \tag{4}$$

Such term considers the probability of being in state $S_{\langle t_k \rangle}$, given the previous own semi Markov state, and the semi Markov states assumed by the other synchronized IPs. In this case, evaluating Eq.4 is equivalent to the unstructured Cartesian HMM case, reaching a $O(N^C)$ space-complexity bound (see Fig. 1(b)). If the states are not synchronized (Fig. 1(c)) we can reach the exponential bound of $O((N^C)^L)$ (Fig. 1(c)), where L is the maximum state duration allowed. This happens when, during the interval $\langle t_{k-1} \rangle$ of length $D_{t_{k-1}}$, we have transitions in the other IP among different states at each time instant.

The situation can be better faced if we suppose that a transition among different states of one particular IP contributes to an evolution of the whole GP, introducing the concept of *implied transition*. Technically, we force a state transition of all the IPs whenever a single IP performs a transition between states having different label. This causes a state fragmentation, i.e., a state of an IP $S_{t_{k-1}}$ becomes two states $S_{\langle t_h \rangle}, S_{\langle t_{h-1} \rangle}$ if a transition between different states occurs at instant $t_h \in \langle t_{k-1} \rangle$ (Fig. 1(d)). Generalizing, in this framework the joint transition probability (4) can be fragmented in the following form:

$$P(S_{\langle t_k \rangle} | S_{\langle t_h \rangle}, S'_{\langle t_h \rangle}) \cdot$$
$$P(S_{\langle t_h \rangle} | S_{\langle t_{h-1} \rangle}, S'_{\langle t_{h-1} \rangle}) P(S'_{\langle t_h \rangle} | S_{\langle t_{h-1} \rangle}, S'_{\langle t_{h-1} \rangle})$$
$$\vdots$$
$$P(S_{\langle t_{h-n+1} \rangle} | S_{\langle t_{h-n} \rangle}, S'_{\langle t_{h-n} \rangle}) P(S'_{\langle t_{h-n+1} \rangle} | S_{\langle t_{h-n} \rangle}, S'_{\langle t_{h-n} \rangle}) \tag{5}$$

where $\sum_{i=1}^{n} \langle t_{h-i} \rangle = \langle t_{k-1} \rangle$; it is worth to notice that the time indexes are equal for both the processes, being them common (See Fig. 1(d), and Fig. 2(a), 2(b)).

The effects of this factorization are: 1) an enrichment of the state space, due to the fact that we break each $S_{\langle t_k \rangle} = < S_{t_k}, D_{t_k} >$, forming generalized states with the same state label but different smaller durations. Therefore, if an original IP had N states we reach a state cardinality of $\tilde{M} > N$; 2) the complexity of the transition matrix goes down to

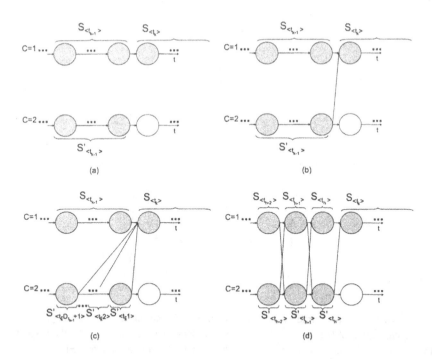

Fig. 1. Coupled semi Markov processes: (a) the states considered in Eq.3 are here perfectly synchronized; (b) the perfect synchronization permits to factorize into transition probabilities terms as written in Eq.4; (c) worst synchronization: the lower chain performs state transitions along all the time interval $\langle t_{k-1} \rangle$; (d) factorization obtained using the instants of implied transition: at each IP transition, every other IP performs also a state transition.

$O(\tilde{M}^C)$ instead of $O((N^C)^L)$. Nevertheless, the space complexity $O(\tilde{M}^C)$ results to be *unnecessarily* high, because several states segments with the same label but slightly different durations are present (see Fig. 2(a)).

Consequently, we decide to perform Gaussian clustering of all the existing durations (Fig. 2(c); in this way, starting from a set of fragmented states $\{< i, d >\}$ (indicating a possible pair of state label, state duration values), we obtain a novel set of generalized (hidden) states that we call $\{< i, \tilde{d} >\}$, where $\tilde{d} \sim \mathcal{N}(\mu_w, \sigma_w)$ $w = 1 \ldots, W$, where W indicates the number of temporal clusters individuated. Therefore, the states of an IP are no more directly observable, being now the duration of a generalized state a quantity affected by uncertainty. Therefore, once we observe a sequence of state labels S_{t_k}, which is d elements long, we suppose it has been generated by a *hidden duration state* $< S_{t_k}, \tilde{D}_{t_k} >= \tilde{S}_{\langle t_k \rangle}$.

We call the model that permits to deal with such a modified IP as Hidden Duration Semi Markov Model (HD-SMM). This is a hybrid HMM, where the observed state label S_{t_k} indicates a state label which associated duration is modelled by a particular hidden state, that in this case we model with a Gaussian function (various forms of du-

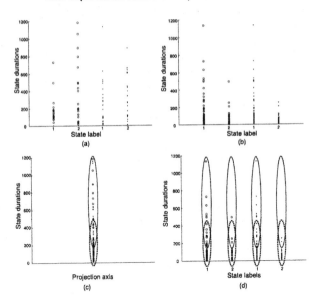

Fig. 2. Clustering of the durations, example with two (2-state labels) processes: (a) the first two columns represent the state labels of the first process (called 1 and 2) with the respective durations, before the time fragmentation. The third and fourth columns are related to the second process; (b) duration fragmentation: the number of smaller durations has grown; (c) projection on the temporal axis and clustering of the durations; (d) re-projection of the duration clusters on the state label axes, to ease the understanding.

rations are present in literature, starting from discrete mass functions, to Gaussian distributions, until the most recent Coaxian functions (Duong, Bui, Phung, and Venkatesh 2005). Here we use Gaussians as first explorative test, obtaining encouraging results as presented in Sec.4). The HD-SMM is indicated with $\lambda^{\text{HD-SMM}} = \{\mathbf{A}_d, \mathbf{B}_d, \pi\}$, where $\mathbf{A}_d$ indicates a $NW \times NW$ transition matrix, where N is the number of visible state labels, and W the number of temporal clusters individuated; the matrix $\mathbf{B}_d$ contains the Gaussian parameters that individuate different state durations. The analogy with the ordinary HMM machinery permit us to inherit all the classical inference and learning formulae.

Finally, connections among different HD-SMM lead to the Coupled Hidden Duration Semi Markov Model (CHD-SMM). In specific, HD-SMM are coupled together as occurs for normal HMMs, employing the coupling mechanism proposed in (Zhong 2002), that expresses the joint transition probability as convex combination of "IP to IP" influences coefficients. Rewriting the first term of Eq.5 we obtain:

$$P(S_{\langle t_k \rangle} | S_{\langle t_{k-1} \rangle}, S'_{\langle t_{k-1} \rangle})$$
$$= \theta_{11} P(S_{\langle t_k \rangle} | S_{\langle t_{k-1} \rangle}) + \theta_{12} P(S_{\langle t_k \rangle} | S'_{\langle t_{k-1} \rangle}) \tag{6}$$

and the same applies for the other elements of Eq.5. In conclusion, we remark that the learning of the CHD-SMM is performed in the same way as suggested in (Zhong 2002) for the Distance Coupled Hidden Markov Models: the training procedure is a constrained optimization process able to calculate separately transition parameters, influence factors and prior probabilities using Mean Field approximation, not reported here because deeply addressed in literature.

11.4 Experiments and discussion

11.4.1 A synthetic example

To evaluate the effectiveness of our model, we first show results on synthetic data. Data was generated by sampling 3 interacting 3-state semi Markov models, namely $c = 1, 2, 3$, whose states are named $^{(c)}S_{\langle t_k \rangle}$, with state label $S_{t_k} = 1, 2, 3$. The interaction has been exploited as follows: the process $c = 1$ is the "Leader" that evolves independently from the other processes with a flat transition table. All the state durations of the several models are modelled by different Gaussian pdfs, the mean values ranging from 10 to 70, with common standard deviation $\sigma = 2$.

The states of the leader are the *important* states, i.e. states that the other two processes, $c = 2, 3$, want to copy. When a transition of the leader occurs, a random time interval is extracted from an arbitrary Gaussian distribution with $\mathcal{N}(\mu_r = 2, \sigma_r = 0.4)$, that simulates a "reaction time" needed by processes 2 and 3 to notice the occurred change. After that, the 2 processes assume the same state of the leader. The length of the state sequences is 5000. The training stage of the CHD-SMM converged after 20-30 iterations.

Every state $S_{\langle t_k \rangle}$ of the semi Markov IPs, after the fragmentation caused by the presence of implied transitions and the subsequent clustering operation, turns into W new states, each one formed by the same state label S_{t_k}, and duration $D_{t_{k,w}}$, $w = 1, \ldots, W$ modeled by a different Gaussian distribution. In this experiment we chose $W = 2$ in order to represent long and short state durations, obtaining $D_{k,1} = \mathcal{N}(4.7868, 1)$ and $D_{k,2} = \mathcal{N}(70.0996, 10)$. The choice of dividing each state sequence using exactly 2 states is motivated by the intuitive need to model "short" and "long" state durations. Choosing a larger number of states (up to 4), does not change the quality of the results.

The transition matrix and the influence matrix obtained after the training are meaningful, in the sense that they mirror precisely the process modeled. In the following (Fig. 3), we show some interesting intra and inter-chain transition matrices, where ^{ij}A indicates the transition state conditional probabilities that chain C_i exerts on C_j. The matrices have to be observed considering couples of successive rows: the first couple indicates the probabilities to depart from the first state, considered in its short (first row) and long (second row) duration, and so on for the other rows.

As one can notice (see coefficients in bold), matrix ^{11}A depicts correctly the modelled behavior of the leader. A short duration state, triggering the transition of the other two chains, is followed with high certainty by the same state, but with longer duration. After that, the choice of the next state is equally allocated to states two and three. Similar considerations can be done for the other two states.

The second matrix, ^{12}A, expresses the high inter-chain dependency that the leader chain exerts on process no. 2, for both the durations of the states. Finally, matrix ^{21}A

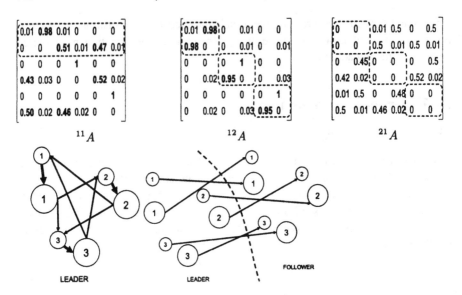

Fig. 3. Synthetical example: some learned transition matrices. In the matrix ^{11}A, the dashed boxes indicate the transition probabilities *from* the state label S_1 of the chain $c = 1$, both in the short-duration exemplar (first row) and in the longer one (second row). Below in the same column, the graphical depiction of ^{11}A is proposed, where the little (big) circles indicates the states with label i=1,2,3 and short (long) durations. Thick arrows represent high probabilities; some unimportant arrows are not reported for clarity. In ^{12}A the boxes highlight the strong conditional probabilities of each state of the leader on the follower. Below in the same column, the graphical depiction of ^{12}A is proposed; some unimportant arrows are not reported for clarity. The last matrix (^{21}A) shows that the leader does not follow the states assumed by the followers at all. The same results apply on Follower 3.

shows that the states of the follower are not able to probabilistically determine the states of the leader chain.

The obtained influence matrix is

$$\Theta_{\text{CHD-SMM}} = \begin{bmatrix} 1 & 0 & 0 \\ 0.99 & 0.008 & 0.002 \\ 0.99 & 0.001 & 0.009 \end{bmatrix} \tag{7}$$

that shows clearly the influence among the chains, where the coefficients θ_{ij} indicate the influence of the chain j over the chain i, with θ_{11} the auto-influence of the leader process on itself, and so on.

In order to compare our approach with the state of the art, we learn an Influence Model (IM) using directly the state sequence as if each state sequence would have been generated from Markov processes. This means that we have for each chain exactly three states, corresponding to the three different state labels and resulting in 3×3 transition matrices (In this case, we have exactly the same example as the one proposed in Basu et al. 2001). After the training, the resulting parameters are qualitatively different. As one can expect, the auto-transition probabilities dominates over the intra chain matrix, producing also high dependencies of the leader chain with respect to the other two processes. This can globally be visible in the influence matrix, that in this example assumes the values

$$\Theta_{IM} = \begin{bmatrix} 0.83 & 0.04 & 0.13 \\ 0.22 & 0.78 & 0 \\ 0.23 & 0 & 0.77 \end{bmatrix} \tag{8}$$

in which the auto influence dominates and a comparable influence is present among different IPs, without an emerging leader.

11.4.2 Conversational style classification

In this experiment, we show the ability of the CHD-SMM to model and classify different styles of conversations. We have 2 subjects, A and B, involved in several conversation sessions that hold for around 5 minutes each. Our class-library is formed by different conversation moods, labeled as follows:

1) *Flat discussion*: A and B are discussing calmly together.

2) *Successful interrogation*: A asks questions, and B answers promptly.

3) *Unsuccessful interrogation*: A asks questions but B does not respond promptly, producing longer periods of silence before (eventually) answering.

4) *Fight*: A and B are arguing.

The training data set is formed by 20 conversations sessions, for each conversation mood. Each session lasts 5 minutes circa, and is performed by actors. We ask them to improvise the fourth situation written above. To validate the semantic content of the audio sequences, we ask 10 testers to manually classify all the sequences, using the labels listed above. Subsequently, we perform a voice-unvoice test on the sample sequences, in order to obtain data-sets of voice/silence values. Therefore, the mood classes are modeled by CHD-SMM trained with the labeled data-sets. After the fragmentation of the data set, we perform Gaussian clustering using 2 clusters, in order to model "long" and "short" segments of state labels, for each state label. The learning time has been 10 sec. for each sequence, with 20-30 iterations before to converge.

In order to get better insight into the proposed method, we compare the CHD-SMM with the Influence Model, using as training sequences the same used for the CHD-SMM. Moreover, we explicitly model the turn taking dynamics of the conversation, by transforming the original training sequences. In practice, we reduce the data set, by maintaining for all the IPs only the states labels occurring in the instant of implied transition. With such data, we train an Influence Model similar to that proposed in (Basu et al. 2001), that we call Turn Taking Influence Model (TTIM).

The classification is performed using a Maximum Likelihood classifier, and the classification accuracy has been estimated using the Leave One Out (LOO) scheme (Duda, Hart and Stork 2001). The results of the classification are visible in Tab. 1. One can notice that the classification results based on the Influence Model show that, even with not-so-high accuracy, the conversation style "Successful Interrogation" (situation 2) and "Unsuccessful Interrogation" (situation 3) are better classified, compared to the other two situations. This is due to the different auto-transition probabilities (relative to the long silence periods for situation 3 and long speech periods for situation 2),

Test	IM	TTIM	CHD-SMM
1)	76%	85%	91%
2)	85%	65%	98%
3)	84%	70%	93%
4)	75%	90%	92%

Table 1. LOO classification accuracies for the four different problems.

which likely help to get a good discrimination. Anyway, the strong auto-transition probabilities overwhelm the transition probabilities among different states of the other two conversation situations 1 and 4, producing low classification accuracies. This is actually a problem because auto-transitions smooth away the turn-taking dynamics that strongly characterizes a conversation style. This effect is also visible by observing the resulting influence matrix of each sequence, mainly exhibiting auto-influences.

In the TTIM based classification, situations 2 and 3 show low accuracy, principally because the turn taking data does not represent any modeling of duration.

Globally, both the TTIM and the IM schemes exhibit worse performances with respect to our approach, that instead is able to model both a rough idea of duration of the states and exploiting well the inter-chain influences.

One drawback of the proposed method is that the exact duration of the states of each single IP is lost, due to the implied fragmentation of the state segments. In any case, the good classification performances encourage us to perform further testing of the model.

References

S. Basu, T. Choudhury and A. Pentland, "Towards measuring human interactions in conversational settings," in *IEEE Int'l Workshop on Cues in Communication (CUES 2001)*, Hawaii, CA, 2001.

M. Brand, N. Oliver, and S. Pentland, "Coupled hidden markov models for complex action recognition," in *Proc. of IEEE Conf. on Computer Vision and Pattern Recognition*, 1997.

R. Duda, P. Hart, and D. Stork, *Pattern Classification.* John Wiley and Sons, 2001.

T. Duong, H. Bui, D. Phung, and S. Venkatesh, "Activity recognition and abnormality detection with the switching hidden semi-markov model," in *CVPR (1)*, 2005, pp. 838–845.

M. I. Jordan, *Learning in graphical models.* MIT Press, 1999.

M. I. Jordan, Z. Ghahramani, T. Jaakkola, and L. Saul, "An introduction to variational methods for graphical models," *Machine Learning*, vol. 37, no. 2, 1999, pp. 183–233.

K. Murphy, "Hidden semi-markov models (hsmm's)," November 2002, available at www.ai.mit.edu/~murphyk.

S. Hongeng and R. Nevatia, "Large-scale event detection using semi-hidden markov models," in *Proceedings of the IEEE International Conference on Computer Vision*, Nice, France, October 2003, pp. 1–8.

L. Rabiner, "A tutorial on Hidden Markov Models and selected applications in speech recognition," *Proc. of IEEE*, vol. 77, no. 2, 1989, pp. 257–286.

S. Zhong and J. Ghosh, "Hmms and coupled hmms for multi-channel eeg classification," in *Proc. IEEE Int. Joint Conf. on Neural Networks*, 2002, pp. 1154–1159.

12 A New Lexicon-based Method for Automated Detection of Terrorist Web Documents

Menahem Friedman[1], Doron Havazelet[2], Dima Alberg[1,3], Abraham Kandel[4], Mark Last[1]

[1]Department of Information Systems Engineering
Ben-Gurion University of the Negev
Beer-Sheva 84105, Israel
{fmenahem, alberg, mlast}@bgu.ac.il
[2]Base Unit of DDR&D
Israel Ministry of Defense
doronhav@netvision.net.il
[3]Department of Industrial Engineering and Management
Sami Shamoon College of Engineering
Beer-Sheva, Israel.
[4]Department of Computer Science and
Engineering,
University of South Florida
Tampa, FL 33620, USA
kandel@csee.usf.edu

Abstract: Anomaly detection is an important tool for detecting abnormal, potentially criminal behavior in real-world data such as web documents, credit card transactions or other personal data. In this study, we assume having two labeled collections of normal and anomalous documents downloaded from normal and terrorist web sites respectively. Each document is represented by a set of *keyphrases* (words or short expressions) and their associated weights. By using a clustering method two separate sets of centroids are induced. In this paper, we propose a lexicon-based approach for labeling a new incoming document. It compares the document's list of keyphrases with two *strict lexicons* – the disjoint sets of keyphrases used only in the normal or the terrorist documents respectively and a *common* lexicon of the remaining keyphrases. If a classification cannot be derived from the strict lexicons, the document is labeled based on its distances from both sets of centroids.

12.1 Introduction

Anomaly detection methodology is commonly used for identifying criminal activity on the web. One of the major problems is designing an efficient algorithm for labeling an incoming web document as either a normal or a terrorist one. We assume having two training collections of labeled normal and anomalous documents, downloaded from normal and terrorist web sites respectively. Each document is represented by a vector of a variable or a fixed size consisting of weighted terms, often referred to as *key phrases*, which are short expressions built from one or several words. As shown in our previous work, an arbitrary clustering method can represent the two collections by two sets of centroids, which provide a simple tool for labeling a new incoming document: the distances of the representing vector from the two sets of centroids are calculated and the document is labeled by the shorter distance. In this paper, we propose a new algorithm for detecting the document's category by comparing its list of key phrases with three lexicons: two *strict lexicons* which are the disjoint sets of key phrases used in the normal and terrorist documents respectively and the *common* lexicon, where each key phrase appears at least once in either set of labeled documents.

The key phrases of each incoming document are divided into four subsets: *strictly normal* – key phrases that appear only in the previously labeled normal documents, *strictly terrorist* – key phrases that appear only in previously labeled terrorist documents, *common* – key phrases which already appeared in both types of documents and *new* – key phrases that never occurred in the corpus before. If the strictly normal subset is nonempty and the terrorist subset is empty or vice versa, the document is classified as normal or terrorist respectively. Otherwise the sizes of the two first subsets are compared using some threshold criteria. If a definite conclusion cannot be derived based on the two strict lexicons, the distances of the *whole* vector from both sets of centroids are calculated to reach the final decision. In this manuscript, the two sets of centroids are generated by the previously introduced Fuzzy Global Clustering method (FGC) (see e.g. Friedman, Schneider, Last, Zaafrany and Kandel 2004). The Strict Lexicon Detection algorithm (SLD – see below) is not limited to terror – related data but can be applied to an arbitrary domain whose elements are labeled "normal" and "abnormal" vectors.

The military pressure put on the al-Qaeda leadership in Afghanistan after 9/11 has dramatically increased the role of the Internet in the infrastructure of the Global Terror Network. Beyond propaganda and ideology, jihadist sites seem to be heavily used for practical training in kidnapping, explosive preparation, and other "core" terrorist activities, which were once taught in Afghan training camps. According to a recent estimate, the total number of jihadi websites has increased from only 12 on September 10, 2001 to close to 5000 in 2006 (Debat 2006).

There is increasing evidence that terrorists are using the Web to distribute tactical orders to their sympathizers. The direct link between the Islamist cell, which carried out the terrorist attack in Madrid in March 2004, and an earlier

Internet posting in Arabic was emphasized by the Spanish court ruling (Harding, 2006). The July 7, 2005 bombings in London are also believed to have much stronger connections to the Internet than to any specific terrorist organization (Lyall, 2006).

The best way to monitor terrorist activity on the Web is to collect and analyze the content of Web sites and forums associated with extremist organizations. Unfortunately, such Web sites do not use fixed web domains and URLs, while the geographical locations of Web servers hosting those sites also change frequently in order to prevent effective eavesdropping. Moreover, terrorist web sites often try to conceal their real identity, e.g., by masquerading themselves as news portals or religious forums. Consequently, there is a need to develop *automated methods* for identifying terrorist content in the massive amounts of regular web traffic (Reid *et al*, 2005).

In this paper the ultimate goal is to detect terrorist documents with maximum accuracy and simultaneously recognize each incoming *normal* document and assign it to one of the existing normal clusters. Previous works (Elovici, Shapira, Last, Zaafrany, Friedman, Schneider and Kandel 2005; Friedman, Schneider, Last, Zaafrany and Kandel July 2004; Zaafrany, Shapira, Elovici, Last, Friedman, Schneider and Kandel UK, June 2004; Friedman, Schneider, Last, Shapira, Elovici, Zaafrany and Kandel June 2004) were based on the anomaly detection approach, which assumed a single large corpus of normal documents which after being clustered, was represented by a set of cluster centroids. Then, every incoming document was tested for its membership in one of the normal clusters. Otherwise, it was labeled as anomalous and suspected to contain terrorist content. The main disadvantage of this procedure is that an anomalous document may actually be a normal document representing a new area not yet considered. In this work, we reduce this effect by considering two separate sets of normal and terrorist documents rather than a single set of normal vectors. In addition we use two *strict lexicons* which are the words used only in *one* of the training sets. The complete outline of the new procedure, referred to as Strict Lexicon Detection (SLD), is given in Section 2 where we also briefly discuss the elements of the Fuzzy Global Clustering method (FGC) used for clustering both document collections. We end this section with a comment related to the *desired* number of clusters.

Most popular clustering methods such as *k-means*, ISODATA and *fuzzy c-means* (see e.g. Bezdek 1981) assume a fixed number or at least a *desired* number of clusters based on some previous knowledge of the data. If indeed the number of cluster centroids can be kept to a minimum it would mean reduction of computing costs when starting to classify the vast collection of incoming documents. However, this is not the case with an extremely large collection of documents related to many areas which cover most walks of life (Last, Shapira, Elovici, Zaafrany and Kandel 2003). Various experiments showed (see e.g.

Friedman, Last, Makover and Kandel 2007) that for this particular application, the number of clusters should not be limited except by the algorithm tuning parameters such as the distance threshold which determines whether an arbitrary vector belongs to a given cluster. An artificial reduction of the number of clusters would usually significantly decrease the classification quality of the incoming documents.

Implementation, experimental results and comparison with a Support Vector Machine (SVM) method are given in Section 3 followed by summary in Section 4.

12.2 The Model

The purpose of this study is to design a system that given an arbitrary web document should be able to determine with high accuracy whether this document was downloaded from a *terrorist* website or from a *normal* website – defined as *any* web site which is not labeled 'terrorist' by experts[1]. Each collection is clustered and represented by cluster centroids (cluster centers). Once generated, the two sets of centroids are used to detect and identify an arbitrary incoming terrorist or normal document. However, if the document has no common key phrases with any of the original collections, it is not classified as either normal or terrorist but left to be analyzed by an expert.

We are using the supervised learning approach based on two labelled sets S_N and S_T containing n_N and n_T variable-length vectors representing the given collections of normal and terrorist documents respectively. The maximum length of all vectors is m. Each vector represents a whole or a part of a web document by k components called *key phrases*, where $1 \le k \le m$. By a 'key phrase' we usually mean a single word or an expression composed of a *small* number of words extracted by a key phrase extraction algorithm (Turney 2000), which selects the most important key phrases in a document. To each key phrase t_j of an arbitrary vector $x = (t_1, t_2, K, t_k)^T$ we assign a score (or weight) ω_j which is a positive number often referred to as *importance weight*, and usually calculated by a frequency-based indexing model (Salton 1989) or by a key phrase extraction algorithm (Turney 2000). A good key phrase extractor is expected to produce a relatively small number of key words and these key words and their associated weights (generated by the extractor as well) are expected to represent the real nature of the document.

---

[1] An up-to-date list of terrorist web sites is available from the SITE Institute (http://www.siteinstitute.org/) and similar organizations

Using any given clustering method we cluster S_N and S_T with no limit on the number of clusters as stated above, and obtain two sets of cluster centroids C_N and C_T respectively. Removing the restriction on the final number of clusters increases the computing costs, but at the same time improves the classification performance on new incoming documents – whenever needed. Next we form two lexicons. The first, L_N, consists of all the key phrases shared only by the labeled normal documents, while the second, L_T, consists of all the key phrases which appear only in the labeled terrorist documents. These lexicons and the two sets of centroids provide the Strict Lexicon Detection (SLD) algorithm for detecting incoming terrorist and normal documents.

12.2.1 The SLD Algorithm

Step 1. Input: an incoming vector x representing an arbitrary incoming document with N_x key phrases in L_N, T_x key phrases in L_T, M_x key phrases common to the vectors in both sets S_N and S_T, and K_x new key phrases which did not occur so far; a terror threshold α; two sets of cluster centroids C_N and C_T.

Step 2.

$$N_x > 0\,, T_x = 0 \Rightarrow x \; normal$$
$$N_x = 0\,, T_x > 0 \Rightarrow x \; terrorist \qquad\qquad (1)$$
$$N_x, T_x > 0\,, T_x > \alpha N_x \Rightarrow x \; terrorist$$

Go to Step 5.

Step 3. If none of the conditions in Eq. (1) holds, we calculate the minimum distances d_N, d_T of x from C_N, C_T respectively and classify

$$d_N < d_T \Rightarrow normal$$
$$d_T \le d_N \Rightarrow terrorist$$

(2)

Go to Step 5.

Step 4. If $N_x = T_x = M_x = 0$, $K_x > 0$ the incoming vector is labeled *undetermined*.

Step 5. Output: classification of x.

The elements of the clustering algorithm implemented in this work are given in the next sub-section (based on Friedman *et al.* 2004).

Example 1.

Let
$$L_N = (1,2,3,4,5,6,7,8) \, , \, L_T = (6,7,8,9,10,11,12,13) \, , \, x = (3,6,7,10,11) \, .$$
Then, $N_x = 1, T_x = 2$. For $\alpha = 1$ the vector is labeled terrorist while for $\alpha = 2$ there is no final conclusion and the document's type will be determined by the vector distances from the two sets of centroids C_N and C_T.

12.2.2 Vector Pre-processing

Each key phrase t in an incoming vector x, whose possible membership in a given cluster C is examined, may have appeared already several times in C and is therefore attached to some distribution function. This function enables to assign the key phrase a *grade of membership* $\chi(t)$, $0 \le \chi(t) \le 1$ within x, with respect to 'membership in C'. The distance between x and C is defined as the fraction

$$d(x,C) = \frac{\sum w(t) \cdot [|\chi_x(t) - \chi_C(t)|]^r}{\sum w(t) \cdot [\min(\chi_x(t), \chi_C(t))]^r}$$

(3)

where t is an arbitrary key phrase in *either* x or C. The number $w(t)$ is the average weight of t if this key phrase is already within C. Otherwise, it is its specific weight in x. The quantities $\chi_x(t)$, $\chi_C(t)$ are the grades of membership of t within x and within C respectively. If a key phrase t appears in C but not in x we take $\chi_x(t) = 0$, $\chi_C(t) = 1$. If it appears x but not in C, we take $\chi_x(t) = 1$, $\chi_C(t) = 0$. If t appears in both x and C we take $\chi_C(t) = 1$ and define $\chi_x(t)$ as follows. Let $\overline{w}$ denote the average in C of the weights $w(t)$ collected from all the vectors which already belong in C and let w_0 denote the weight of t in x. Then, for some given $p > 0$ we define

$$\chi_x(t) = \begin{cases} (w_0 / \overline{w})^p \,, w_0 < \overline{w} \\ \qquad 1, w_0 \geq \overline{w} \end{cases}$$

(4)

This definition is somewhat simpler than the one given in (Friedman *et al.* 2004) but just as successful. The parameter r in Eq. (3) is a positive number chosen empirically to optimize the algorithm's performance.

Let w denote the average importance weight of an arbitrary key phrase in C. Then, implementing Eq. (3) increases the denominator by $w[\chi_x t)]^r$ and the numerator by $w[1 - \chi_x t)]^r$. This procedure is referred to as Fuzzy Global Clustering (FGC).

12.3 Experimental results and comparison with SVM methods

We applied our model to a set of 21,528 normal documents and 582 terrorist documents. The terrorist documents were downloaded from various Jihadist Web sites in English, while the normal documents were collected by passive and anonymous eavesdropping on a small network of university computers used by students from the same department. We used 21,328 normal documents and 382 terrorist documents for training obtaining two sets of cluster centroids to be used whenever the strict lexicons test of Eq. (1) failed to derive a conclusion. The terror threshold parameter α of Eq. (1) varied in our experiments from 0.25 to 2. There was no point for decreasing α beyond 0.25 since around this value there was no further improvement in the detection rate of the terrorist vectors classified by Eq. (2). Clearly, when this parameter increases there will be more vectors upon which one has to apply the test of Eq. (2) which classifies the vector to the closer set of centroids. The validation process included 200 normal documents and 200 terrorist documents. We chose randomly the validation and training sets as well as the order of their vectors and averaged the results over 10 runs. We also applied the FGC method with three distance threshold distances

$d_0 = 5$, 10, 20 called in the chart high, medium and low resolution clustering respectively. The smaller d_0 the more clusters we get and the accuracy of the detection procedure increases. However, as previously stated, the larger α becomes more vectors must be tested for their distances from the cluster centroids and the detection accuracy naturally somewhat drops.

The results given in Fig. 1 clearly support these conclusions. We did not plot normal vectors identification rate since it came to 99.5% for all α, which is equivalent to a false positive (FP) rate of 0.5%.

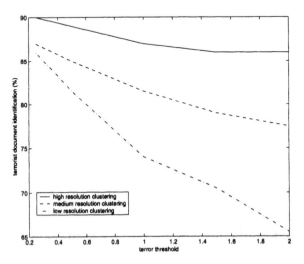

Fig 1. The Strict Lexicon Detection (SLD) performance
for three pairs of clustering sets.

It is quite clear that for high resolution clustering which provides 5642 normal clusters and 240 terrorist clusters, one gets excellent terrorist document detection rate which varies from 90% TP (True Positive) for small α to 86% TP for large α. The worst case occurred for low resolution clustering where the accuracy dropped from 86% TP (small α) to 66% TP (large α). The rate of the FP (False Positive), i.e., the number of normal documents identified as terrorist ones was always about 0.5%.

We compared our results with those obtained by using the Support Vector Machine (SVM) methodology (see Han and Kamber, 2006). Support Vector Machines are supervised learning algorithms used for classification and regression, which belong to a larger family of generalized linear classifiers. A special property of SVM is that they simultaneously minimize the empirical classification error and maximize the separation margin between classes. Hence they are also known as maximum margin classifiers.

The parameters of the maximum-margin hyperplane are derived by solving an optimization problem. There exist several specialized algorithms for quickly solving the quadratic programming (QP) problem that arises from using SVM methodology. A common method for solving the QP problem is the sequential minimal optimization (SMO) algorithm (Platt 1998) for training a support vector classifier, which breaks the problem into 2-D sub-problems that may be solved analytically, eliminating the need for a numerical optimization procedure such as the conjugate gradient method. We applied the SMO method having 21,710 documents for training and 400 documents for validation, with two different kernels. The first choice, the Radial Basis Function (RBF) kernel with $\gamma=1$ provided the detection accuracy of 50%, i.e., 50% of the 200 terrorist documents used for validation were identified as such. The second kernel of polynomial type with exponent = 1 produced the detection accuracy of 52%, significantly lower than our model for all α's between 0.25 and 2. Similar to our method, the FP (False Positive) rate was about 0.5% with both kernels, i.e. only 0.5% of normal documents were wrongly labeled as 'terrorist'.

12.4 Summary

In this work, we introduced and tested a new method for detecting a small amount of terrorist documents in a massive collection of normal documents. It is based on a procedure which combines the use of strict normal and terrorist lexicons generated from available labeled collections of normal and terrorist web documents along with sets of cluster centroids obtained by clustering the two collections, using the Fuzzy Global Clustering method. The results which outperformed the popular SVM classification algorithm, demonstrated the method applicability, particularly when the clustering is a high resolution one.

Finally, the best choice of the terror-threshold α which needs to consider the rate of detection accuracy vs. computing costs, i.e., the desire not to overuse the two sets of centroids, will be the subject for future work.

References

Bezdek, J.C.(1981) Pattern Recognition with Fuzzy Objectives Function Algorithms, Plenum Press, New York.

Debat, A. (March 10, 2006) "Al Qaeda's Web of Terror", ABC News.

Elovici, Y., Shaqpira, B., Last, M., Zaafrany, O., Friedman, M., Schneider, M. and Kandel, A. (2005) Content-based detection of terrorist browsing the web using an advanced terror detection system (ATDS). IEEE International Conference on Intelligence and Security Informatics, Atlanta, Georgia, USA.

Friedman, M., Schneider, M., Last, M., Zaafrany, O. and Kandel, A. (2004) A new approach for fuzzy clustering of web documents. Proceedings of 2004 IEEE International Conference on Fuzzy Systems, 377-381.

Friedman, M., Schneider, M., Last, M., Shapira, B., Elovici, Y., Zaafrany, O. and Kandel, A (2004) A fuzzy-based algorithm for web document Clustering. Proceedings of NAPIPS-04, Banff, Alberta, Canada, 524-527.

Friedman, M., Last, M., Makover, Y. and Kandel, A. (2007) Anomaly detection in Web documents using crisp and fuzzy-based cosine clustering methodology. Information Sciences, Special Issue on Advances in Fuzzy Logic, 177 No. 2, 467-475.

Friedman, M., Schneider, M., Last, M., Zaafrany, O. and Kandel, A. (2006) Anomaly detection in web documents using computationally intelligent methods of fuzzy-based clustering. In: A. Vasilakos and W. Pedrycz (Eds). *Ambient Intelligence, wireless networking, Ubiquitous Computing.* Artech House, Boston, pp. 401-415.

Han, J. and Kamber, M., *Data Mining: Concepts and Techniques*, 2nd Edition, Morgan Kaufmann, 2006.

Harding, B. (2006) 29 charged in Madrid train bombings. New York Times, April 11, 2006.

Last, M., Shapira, B., Elovici, Y., Zaafrany, O. and Kandel, A. (2003) Content-based methodology for anomaly detection on the web. In: E. Menasalvas et al. (Eds). *Advances in Web Intelligence.* Springer-Verlag, Lecture Notes in Artificial Intelligence 2663, pp. 113-123.

Lyall S. (2006) London Bombers Tied to Internet, Not Al Qaeda, Newspaper Says. New York Times, April 11, 2006.

Platt, J. (1998) Fast training of support vector machines using sequential minimal optimization. In: B. Schoelkopf, C. Burges and A. Smola (EDS). *Advances in Kernel Methods – Support Vector Learning.* MIT Press.

E. Reid, J. Qin, Y. Zhou, G. Lai, M. Sageman, G. Weimann, and H. Chen, Collecting and Analyzing the Presence of Terrorists on the Web: A Case Study of Jihad Websites, *Proceedings of the IEEE International Conference on Intelligence and Security Informatics, ISI 2005,* Atlanta, Georgia, May 2005, Lecture Notes in Computer Science (LNCS 3495), pp. 402-411, Springer-Verlag, 2005.

Salton G. (1989) Automatic Text Processing: the Transformation, Analysis, and Retrieval of Information by Computer. Addison-Wesley, Reading.

Turney, P.D. (2000) Learning algorithms for keyphrase extraction. Information Retrieval 2, No. 4, 303-336.

Zaafrany, O., B. Shapira, Elovici, Y., Last, M., Friedman, M., Schneider, M. and Kandel, A. (2004) OHT-online-HTML tracer for detecting terrorist activities on the web. Proceedings of the 3-rd European Conference on Information Warfare and Security. University of London, UK, 371-378.

13 A Neural Network Approach for Multifont and Size-Independent Recognition of Ethiopic Characters

Yaregal Assabie[1] and Josef Bigun[2]

School of Information Science, Computer and Electrical Engineering
Halmstad University, Sweden
[1]yaregal.assabie@ide.hh.se , [2]josef.bigun@ide.hh.se

Abstract. Artificial neural networks are one of the most commonly used tools for character recognition problems, and usually they take gray values of 2D character images as inputs. In this paper, we propose a novel neural network classifier whose input is 1D string patterns generated from the spatial relationships of primitive structures of Ethiopic characters. The spatial relationships of primitives are modeled by a special tree structure from which a unique set of string patterns are generated for each character. Training the neural network with string patterns of different font types and styles enables the classifier to handle variations in font types, sizes, and styles. We use a pair of directional filters for extracting primitives and their spatial relationships. The robustness of the proposed recognition system is tested by real life documents and experimental results are reported.

13.1 Introduction

Ethiopic script is a writing system used mainly in Ethiopia by several languages like Geez, Amharic, Tigrigna, Guragegna, etc. The recently standardized alphabet has a total of 435 characters. However, the most commonly used alphabet has 34 base characters and six other orders conveniently written as shown in Table 1. The first column represents the base character and others are modifications of the base character representing vocalized sounds.

Table 1. Part of the Ethiopic alphabet

	Base Sound	Orders						
		1st (ä)	2nd (u)	3rd (i)	4th (a)	5th (e)	6th (ə)	7th (o)
1	h	ሀ	ሁ	ሂ	ሃ	ሄ	ህ	ሆ
2	l	ለ	ሉ	ሊ	ላ	ሌ	ል	ሎ
3	h	ሐ	ሑ	ሒ	ሓ	ሔ	ሕ	ሖ
.	.	.	.	.	.	.	.	.
.	.	.	.	.	.	.	.	.
34	v	ፐ	ፑ	ፒ	ፓ	ፔ	ፕ	ፖ

Character recognition has been an area of research and development since 1950s (Suen, Mori, Kim, and Leung 2003). Unlike Latin and Asian scripts, the recognition of Ethiopic script is at its early stage, with the first published work appearing only recently in (Cowell and Hussain 2003). Moreover, Ethiopic script is a modification-based script having structurally complex characters with similar shapes posing an additional difficulty for classifiers. Artificial neural networks have been commonly used as classifiers in many pattern recognition problems, especially in handwritten character recognition. The traditional approach is to design a neural network classifier that takes the gray values of 2D document images as inputs (Dreyfus 2005). In this paper, we present a neural network classifier that takes 1D string patterns as inputs. The string patterns are generated from the primitive structures of Ethiopic character and their spatial relationships. We use a structural and syntactic model to generate patterns of primitives and their spatial relationships out of the structurally complex Ethiopic characters. The structural and syntactic model is described below and further exposed in detail in (Assabie and Bigun 2006***a***).

13.2 The Structural and Syntactic Model

13.2.1 Structural analysis of Ethiopic characters

Ethiopic characters are characterized by thick vertical and diagonal structures, and thin horizontal lines. The thick horizontal and diagonal structures are prominent structural features which give the general shape of the characters, and they form a set of *seven* primitive structures. The primitives differ from each other by their relative length, orientation, spatial position and structure. The classes of primitive structures (with example characters) are: *long vertical line* (ዘ), *medium vertical line*(በ), *short vertical line* (ሐ), *long forward slash* (ገ), *medium forward slash* (ፉ), *backslash* (ለ), and *appendages* (ቺ). By extracting the relative size of each primitive structure, we are able to develop size-independent recognition system that doesn't need size normalization of document images.

Horizontal lines connect two or more of these primitive structures to form the overall complex structure of characters. Connections between primitives occur at one or more of the following three connection regions: *top (t)*, *middle (m)*, and *bottom (b)*. The first connection detected as one goes from top to bottom is considered as *principal* and the other connections, if there exist, are *supplemental* connections. A total of 18 connection types are identified between primitives of the Ethiopic characters and a summary is given in Table 2. The principal connection is used to determine the spatial relationships between two primitives. Two connected primitives α and β are represented by the pattern $\alpha \mathbf{z} \beta$, where **z** is an ordered pair (x,y) of the connection regions *t*, *m*, or *b*. In this pattern, α is connected to β at region x of α, and β is connected to α at region y of β.

Table 2. Connection types between primitives

Principal Connection	Supplementary Connections					
	None	(m,b)	(b,m)	(b,b)	(m,m)+(b,m)	(m,m)+(b,b)
(t,t)	Π	P	٩	◻	٩	ፀ
(t,m)	rl		๔			
(t,b)	r					
(m,t)	h	Þ	৭	b		
(m,m)	H					
(m,b)	Ψ					
(b,t)	Ⴑ					
(b,m)	Ч					
(b,b)	U					

The spatial relationships of primitives representing a character are modeled by a special tree structure as shown in Fig. 1a. Each node in the tree stores data about the primitive and its connection type with its parent node. The child nodes correspond to the possible number of primitives (three to the left and four to the right) connected to the parent primitive. Primitive tree for a character is built first by selecting the left top primitive of a character as the root primitive. Then, based on their spatial positions, other primitives are appended to the tree recursively in the order of {**left**{top, middle, bottom}, **parent**, **right** {bottom, middle1, middle2, top}}. An example of a primitive tree is shown in Fig. 1b.

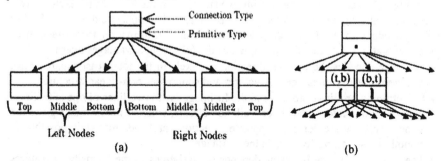

Figure 1. (a) General tree structure of characters, (b) primitive tree for the character ∩

13.2.2 Extraction of structural features

Structural features are extracted by making use of a pair of directional filters both of which are computed from direction field tensor. Direction field tensor, also called the structure tensor, is discussed in detail in (Bigun 2006) and its computation is presented in (Assabie and Bigun 2006*b*). Since the directional features are observed along lines, the local direction is also called Linear Symmetry (LS). The LS property of a local neighborhood of an image can be estimated by eigenvalue analysis of the direction field tensor using complex moments formulated as:

$$I_{mn} = \iint ((D_x + iD_y)f)^m ((D_x - iD_y)f)^n \, dxdy \tag{1}$$

where m and n are non-negative integers, and D_x and D_y Gaussian derivative operators. Among other orders, of interest to us are I_{10}, I_{11}, and I_{20} which are derived as follows.

$$I_{10} = \iint ((D_x + iD_y)f) dxdy \tag{2}$$

$$I_{11} = \iint |(D_x + iD_y)f|^2 \, dxdy \tag{3}$$

$$I_{20} = \iint ((D_x + iD_y)f)^2 dxdy \tag{4}$$

I_{10} is equivalent to the ordinary gradient field in which the angle shows the direction of intensity differences and the magnitude shows the average change in intensity. I_{11} measures the optimal amount of gray value changes in a local neighborhood. I_{20} is complex valued where its argument is the optimal local direction of pixels (the direction of major eigenvector of S) in double angle representation and its magnitude is measure of the local LS strength (the difference of eigenvalues of S). Fig. 2 shows I_{10} and I_{20} images displayed in color where the hue represents direction of pixels with the red color corresponding to the direction of zero degree.

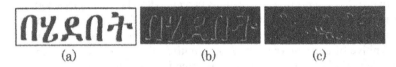

(a)   (b)   (c)

Figure 2. (a) Ethiopic text, (b) I_{10} of a, (c) I_{20} of a

In Fig. 2, it can be seen that a primitive structure in the text image results in two lines (at left and right edges) in the I_{10} and I_{20} images. The opposite directions for left and right edges in the I_{10} image provide convenient information for extraction of structural features. On the other hand, I_{20} has the following advantages over I_{10}:

- I_{20} image encodes the optimal direction of pixels in the total least square sense, and therefore amplifies linear structures and suppresses non-linear structures.
- Smoothing a primitive structure in the I_{10} image (with two lines of opposite directions) over a window leads to cancellation effects, whereas the I_{20} image gives the same result for gradients of opposite directions and therefore it is possible to smooth the structural features in the I_{20} image.
- The magnitude in the I_{10} image depends on variations in the intensity of features against the background, whereas this kind of variation in the I_{20} image can be normalized by using the magnitude of $\frac{I_{20}}{I_{11}}$.

Therefore, we use the synergy effect of I_{10} and I_{20} to extract structural features. Extraction of the structural features is done on segmented characters. The horizontal area that lacks LS in the I_{20} image segments text lines, and the vertical area that lacks LS segments individual characters within each text line. The I_{20} image is used to group pixels into parts of primitives and connectors based on the direction information. After converting the double angle of I_{20} into a simple angle representation (by halving the argument of I_{20}), pixels of linear structures with directions of [0..60] degrees are considered as parts of primitives and those with directions of (60..90]

degrees are considered as parts of connectors. The extracted linear structures in the
I_{20} image are mapped onto the I_{10} image to classify them into left and right edges of
primitives. A primitive is then formed from the matching left and right edges, as
shown in Fig. 3.

(a)   (b)

Figure 3. (a) Ethiopic text, (b) extraction of primitives

13.3 Neural Network Classifier

Neural networks are classification techniques inspired by neuronal operations in
biological systems. Artificial neurons are typically organized into three layers: input,
hidden and output. The input layer takes data of the unknown pattern whereas the
output layer provides an interface for generating the recognition result. The hidden
layer contains many of the neurons in various interconnected structures hidden from
the outside view (Bishop 1995). Neural networks have been used for character recognition problems, and specifically widely used for recognition of handwritten text.
Usually, the inputs to the neural network systems are pixel intensity values in two-
dimensional space (Dreyfus 2005).

13.3.1 The neural network model

In Section 1, we introduced the design of the neural network model as a classifier
system whose inputs are 1D string patterns of primitives and their spatial relationships. Data stored in the primitive tree of a character is converted into 1D string by
recursively traversing the tree in the order of {**left**{top, middle, bottom}, **parent**,
right{bottom, middle1, middle2, top}}. This is similar to *in-order* traversal of binary search trees and produces a unique string pattern for each primitive tree.

Since neural networks take numerical data as inputs, we assigned numbers to
primitives and their spatial relationships. Three-digit and five-digit binary numbers
are sufficient to represent the seven primitives and the eighteen spatial relationships,
respectively. The longest string pattern generated from the primitive tree is for the
character ሯ which has 9 primitives (3x9 binary digits) and 9 spatial relationships
(5x9 binary digits) generating a total string size of 72 binary digits. Each Ethiopic
character in the alphabet is also encoded with a nine-digit binary number which is
sufficient to represent all the 435 characters. Therefore, the neural network model
has 72 input nodes and 9 output nodes. The hidden layer also has 72 nodes which is
set optimally through experiments. Fig. 4 shows the diagram of the neural network
model.

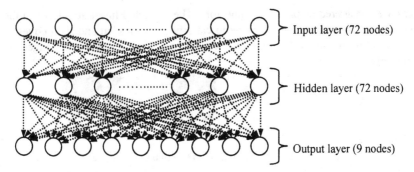

Figure 4. The neural network model

13.3.2. Training the network

The general structures of primitives and their spatial relationships remain similar under variations in fonts and their sizes. For example, irrespective of variations in font type and size, the character *U* is represented as two *Long Vertical Line* primitives both connected at the bottom, i.e., {ₗ (b,b), ₎} . Its italicized version (*U*) is represented as two *Forward Slash* primitives both connected at the bottom, i.e., {/, (b,b), /}. Thus, the set of patterns {{ₗ (b,b), ₎}, {/, (b,b), /}} represents the character *U* for various font types, styles and sizes. Such possibly occurring patterns of primitives and their spatial relationships are prepared for each character. The neural network is trained with such patterns of primitives and their relationships. For each Ethiopic character, possibly occurring 1D strings of primitives and their spatial are used as training samples. Table 3 shows training data created from the string patterns using NetMaker which is a data processing component in BrainMaker neural network tool.

Table 3. Training data

	Pattern	Pattern	Pattern	Pattern	Pattern	Pattern	Pattern	Pattern	Pattern	Input	Input	Input	Input	Input	...
	A	B	C	D	E	F	G	H	I	J	K	L	M	N	
308	0	1	0	0	1	1	0	1	1	0	0	0	0	0	...
309	0	1	0	0	1	1	0	1	1	0	0	0	0	0	...
310	0	1	0	0	1	1	1	0	0	0	0	0	0	0	...
311	0	1	0	0	1	1	1	0	0	0	0	0	0	0	...
312	0	1	0	0	1	1	1	0	1	0	0	0	0	0	...
313	0	1	0	0	1	1	1	1	0	0	0	0	0	0	...
314	0	1	0	0	1	1	1	1	0	0	0	0	0	0	...
315	0	1	0	0	1	1	1	1	0	0	0	0	0	0	...
316	0	1	0	0	1	1	1	1	0	0	0	0	0	0	...
317	0	1	0	0	1	1	1	1	1	0	0	0	0	0	...
318	0	1	0	0	1	1	1	1	1	0	0	0	0	0	...
319	0	1	0	1	0	0	0	0	0	0	0	0	0	0	...
320	0	1	0	1	0	0	0	0	0	0	0	0	0	0	...
321	0	1	0	1	0	0	0	0	1	0	0	0	0	0	...

Output data (9 values)   Input data (72 values)

A back propagation algorithm, which is one of the most commonly used supervised learning techniques, was used to train the neural network. The non-linear sigmoid function was used as a transfer function for the multilayer network architecture. Fig. 5 shows the first runs of the training progress using BrainMaker neural network tool. The graph depicts that the average error is declining over the course of training, which is a desired property of a good neural network model.

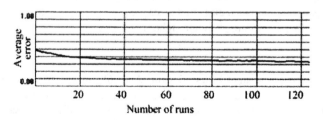

Figure 5. Progress of training

13.4 Experiments

13.4.1 Database development

Experiments are done using documents from Ethiopic Document Image Database (EDIDB) that we develop for testing the recognition system with different real life documents. The database consists of 1,204 images of documents (scanned with a resolution of 300dpi) taken from a wide range of document types such as books, newspapers, magazines, and printouts with various font types, sizes and styles. Sample documents from EDIDB are shown in Fig. 6.

Figure 6. Sample documents with (a) VG2000 Main font, (b) VG2000 Agazian font, (c) VG Unicode italic font (d) book, (e) newspaper, (f) magazine

13.4.2 Recognition process

The only parameter that is changed during the recognition process is the size of Gaussian window which must be optimized according to font sizes and document types. For clean documents, we used a window of 3x3 pixels for texts with font sizes of less than or equal to 12, a window of 5x5 pixels for font sizes of 16, and a window of 7x7 pixels for font sizes of 20. On the other hand, for most documents taken from books, newspapers, and magazines (font sizes are equivalent to about 12), a window of 5x5 pixels was used because of their higher level of noise.

13.5 Result

The robustness of the system is tested with about 68 images of documents taken from EDIDB. Each image consists of an average number of 1,400 characters. For books, newspapers and magazines an average accuracy of 89% was achieved. The recognition system also tolerates documents with skewness of up to 10°. For clean printouts with Visual Geez Unicode font type and with 8, 10, 12, 16, and 20 font sizes, we obtained recognition rates of 93%, 93%, 94%, 95% and 95%, respectively. For printout documents with Visual Geez Unicode font type and 12 font size, recognition rates of 94%, 92% and 95% were achieved for normal, italic and bold font styles, respectively. The recognition system is also tested with various font types, each with 12 font size and the result is summarized in Table 4.

Table 4. Recognition results for different fonts

Font Type	Recognition (%)
Visual Geez Unicode	94
Visual Geez 2000 Main	94
Visual Geez 2000 Agazian	96
Power Geez	93
Geez Type	92

13.6 Discussion and Conclusion

It is quite common to see real life documents with varying font types, styles, and sizes. Thus, it has become important that recognition systems should be able to recognize documents irrespective of the variations in the characteristics of the text. To this effect, we have designed a structural and syntactic analyser that easily represents complex structures of characters using the spatial relationships of primitives which are easier to extract. Since we encode only the relative length of primitives, the structural and syntactic component of the system handles variations in font sizes without resizing the image. By training the neural network with primitive patterns of characters with different font types and styles, the network classifier is able to recognize the characters. The common errors in the recognition process arise from extraction of primitive structures and segmentation of characters. The recognition accuracy can be further improved by additional studies of these algorithms. The use of spell checker and parts of speech analyser can also help to increase the recognition result.

References

Assabie, Y. and Bigun, J. (2006*a*) Structural and syntactic techniques for recognition of Ethiopic characters. In: *Structural, Syntactic, and Statistical Pattern Recognition*, volume LNCS-4109. Springer, Heidelberg, pp. 118-126.

Assabie, Y. and Bigun, J. (2006*b*) Ethiopic character recognition using direction field tensor. In: *Proc. of the 18th Int'l Conf. Pattern Recognition-ICPR2006*. IEEE Computer Society, Piscataway, NJ, pp. 284-287.

Bigun, J. (2006) *Vision with Direction: A Systematic Introduction to Image Processing and Vision*. Springer, Heidelberg.

Bishop, C. M. (1995) *Neural Networks for Pattern Recognition*. Oxford University Press, USA.

Cowell, J. and Hussain, F. (2003) Amharic Character Recognition Using a Fast Signature Based Algorithm. In: *Proc. of the 7th Int'l Conf. Information Visualization*. pp. 384-389.

Dreyfus, G. (2005) *Neural Networks: Methodology and Applications*, Springer, Heidelberg.

Suen, C. Y., Mori, S., Kim, S. H., and Leung, C. H. (2003) Analysis and Recognition of Asian Scripts-The State of the Art. In: *Proc. ICDAR2003*, vol. 2, Edinburgh, pp. 866-878.

14 Automated Classification of Affective States using Facial Thermal Features

Masood Mehmood Khan[1], Robert D. Ward[2] and Michael Ingleby[3]

[1] American University of Sharjah, SA&D-Multimedia Group, mkhan@aus.edu
[2] University of Huddersfield, Department of Behavioral Sciences, r.d.ward@hud.ac.uk
[3] University of Huddersfield, School of Computing and Engineering, m.ingleby@hud.ac.uk

Abstract. We propose a novel feature extraction and pattern representation approach to develop classification rules for affect recognition using bio-physiological data from a training sample of individuals asked to express various emotions by natural facial gesture. Thermal imaging features at corresponding facial locations were shown to follow a multivariate normal distribution, with clustering at different centres in feature space for different positive or negative affective states. A multivariate analysis of variance was used to represent thermal images as vectors with components along principal components (PCs) of a covariance matrix. Derived PCs were ranked in order of their effectiveness in the between-cluster separation of affective states, and only the most effective PCs were retained in an optimized subspace for affect recognition purposes. A set of Mahalanobis distance based rules was constructed to classify the simulated affective states in a person-independent manner. Results suggest that an optimized subspace allows better between-cluster separation, and hence better emotion detection by, for example, a robot, than standard reduction to PCs contributing most of the training sample variance.

14.1 Introduction

Earlier researchers have reduced the problem of classifying facial expressions and affective states to the classification of measurements taken at equivalent points on visible-spectrum or thermal images of different faces. Hence, automated classification of affects using such measurements has been made possible (Dubuisson et al. 2002; Fasel and Luettin 2003). Several computational approaches have been proposed to develop suitable discriminant functions for AFEC and AAR systems (Choi 1972; Gupta and Logan 1990; Jolliffe 2002). However, the data sets formed by equivalent point sampling are of high dimensionality and present challenging problems of data modeling and pattern representation. Researchers have found that Principal Component Analysis (PCA) and Linear Discriminant Analysis (LDA) can helpfully reduce the complexity of this problem (Jolliffe 2002; McLachlan 2004).

Building upon the classical PCA-LDA combination, we propose a novel approach for classifying the training data sets. Our approach begins with PCA to obtain independent linear combinations of equivalent point data, 'eigenfaces'. We then select the eigenfaces that account for the greatest between-cluster variance of clusters grouped for the same intensional affect by different donors in our training samples, and use these to define a decision space for affect representation. The decision space is partitioned using linear discriminants that separate each affect cluster from others, and points in the same class of the partition are assigned to a nearest cluster using the standard Mahalanobis distance (point to cluster centre in units of within-cluster variance).

We compared performance of the resulting classifier with that of a classifier based solely on PCA techniques for data reduction. Our decision functions result in many fewer affect-recognition errors than standard PCA when tested using thermal images of faces excluded from the training sample used to establish clusters, decision spaces and Mahalanobis distances. Thus, our proposed approach would allow detecting emotional changes using repeated measurements of bio-physiological signals, notably, the facial skin temperature measurements. Such functionality might be of use when interrogating criminal suspects or when assessing user response to software interfaces.

14.2 Thermal Data Acquisition and Analyses

This work is based on the scientific findings suggesting that a change in affective state would cause thermo-muscular changes under the facial skin. Consequently, the facial skin surface would experience temperature variations. Researchers were able to extract information about the affective states from the measurements of skin temperature variation along the major facial muscles. Previous studies discovered that the thermal infrared image of a "neutral" face, with all muscles in their natural position, was thermally different from the one expressing an affective state (Garbey et al. 2004; Khan et al. 2005; Khan et al. 2006; Klein et al., 2002; Pavlidis 2000; Sugimoto et al. 2000; Yoshitomi et al. 2000).

In this and previous studies, we used a Cantronic IR 860 thermal infrared camera to capture thermal images of 16 undergraduate students, 12 boys and 4 girls, whose self-reported mean age was 20 years 9 months. Guidelines for protecting the human participants' of biomedical and behavioral research, provided in the Belmont report (Belmont Report 1979) were followed during the image acquisition. 320x240 pixel thermal and digital visible-spectrum images of participants' normal faces were captured first. The process was repeated when participants pretended happiness, positive surprise, sadness, disgust and anger.

We pre-processed the infrared images to reduce the built-in noise and improve the possibility of extracting most effective thermal features. A thermal analysis software, CMView Plus, comes bundled with several noise reduction algorithms was used for infrared image processing. The "median smoothing filter" recognized as one of the most effective best order-statistic filter (Gonzalez and Woods 2002), was invoked on the infrared images for noise reduction. In a following step, Sobel operator-based edge detection algorithm was invoked for extracting the contours within the TIRIs.

Regions of interest were manually selected along the major facial muscles for discovering the temporal thermal information. The analysis was repeated several times. After analyzing 112 infrared images, significant thermal variations were discovered at 75 physical locations along the major facial muscles. Variations in the Thermal Intensity Values (TIVs) on the faces with a change in facial expression were measured with the objectives of maintaining the minimum correlation among the TIV data and maximum between-group variance. Having achieved these two objectives, each infrared image could be represented as a vector in a 75-dimensional thermal feature space. Figure 1 shows the 75 Facial Thermal Feature Points (FTFPs) on a human face. The TIV data were tested for multivariate normality. Results suggested that the data were normally distributed, vector x having a vector mean μ with p components and a $p \times p$ covariance matrix Σ, that is $x \sim N (\mu, \Sigma)$ (Chatfield and Collins 1995).

14.3 Computational Approach

Based on an extensive literature review, a computational approach (exhibited in Figure 2) was developed. Our approach required deriving the PCs first to reduce the complexity of the feature space. The optimal PCs were then discovered from within the derived PCs and only those PCs that contributed most to between-affect variance were retained in the decision subspace. The classification of new faces was based on a distance in decision space from cluster centres located using training data. Distances were measured using the Mahalanobis distance. Algorithmic details of each implementation step are given in the following paragraphs.

Singular Value Decomposition based Principal Component Analysis: The Singular Value Decomposition (SVD) based PCA was invoked for deriving the principal components (PCs) as eigenvectors of a training sample covariance matrix Σ (Jolliffe 2002; McLachlan 2004; Rencher 1995; Sharma 1996). When the PCs are used as basis vectors, Σ becomes diagonal D, with Eigenvalues decreasing down the leading diagonal. In the subspaces spanned by selected sets of PCs, affects were represented as more or less separated clusters and the restriction of D to a subspace encoded different amounts of within-cluster and between-cluster variance in the sample faces. In such subspaces, the statistical model of the sampled data takes the form

$$x_{ijk} = \mu_i + \tau_{ij} + \varepsilon_{ijk} \qquad\qquad (1)$$

where x_{ijk} is the ith observation for a face simulating expression j in the kth such face with this expression, μ_i is the mean value of all observations at point i, τ_{ij} the offset of the centre of the jth cluster from μ_i and ε_{ijk} is a residual to be minimized when estimating the other model parameters from a training sample of faces. One could generalize the model to allow an affect to be represented by two or more clusters if donors had various ways of expressing certain affects facially, but our data does not show such variety in the relatively small sample used.

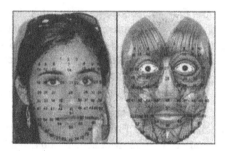

Fig. 1. Facial Thermal Feature Points on a human face and along the facial muscles

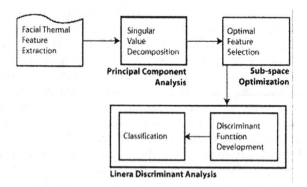

Fig. 2. Algorithmic implementation of the system

Estimates of model parameters from a training sample with p-dimensional observation vectors, N_j instances of faces with expression j, and J different expressions are $\hat{\mu}_i = (1/\sum_j N_j)\sum_{ijk} x_{ijk}$ and $\hat{\tau}_i = (1/N_j)\sum_k x_{ijk}$.

Subspace optimization: We propose using an iterative process to discover a subset of M best discriminating PCs from within the set $\{\zeta^{(l)} | l = 1,...,p\}$ of PCs. The method is based on the stepwise test process in which less effective PCs are eliminated step by step and only the best discriminating PCs are retained in an optimized subspace. The process begins with all PCs ranked by size of a Fisher ratio for the distribution of components $x_{ijk} \cdot \zeta^{(l)}$ of training sample observations projected along the $\zeta^{(l)}$ direction. These distributions have variances $S^{(l)}$, which are sums of a between-cluster part S_W^l, and a within-cluster part S_B^l. The Fisher ratio for $\zeta^{(l)}$ is given by $F^{(l)} = S_B^{(l)}/S_W^{(l)}$ and is greater for the PCs that better discriminate between the clusters. A similar ratio can be defined for subspaces E spanned by several PCs, except that the variances $S^{(E)}$, $S_W^{(E)}$, and $S_B^{(E)}$ generalize to square matrices. For such an E, the Fisher ratio, $F^{(E)}$, can be defined as the ratio of determinants S_B^l and S_W^l of these variance matrices. Then the optimized subspace that our procedure seeks out can be expressed as $M = \arg\max_E \{F^{(E)}\}$, where E varies over all possible spans of two, three or more PCs, and M is the argument of function $F^{(E)}$ that corresponds to the maximum value of the function. Our procedure approaches this subspace via a sequence M_1, M_2, M_3,... M_n starting with the 1-dimensional space spanned by the most discriminating PCs. Having reached, using at least the n most discriminating PCs to span an n-dimensional M_n with Fisher ratio F_n , the next space M_{n+1} is formed by considering the next-most discriminating PC, $\zeta^{(l)}$, and the test span T formed by this and M_n. If $F^{(T)}$ exceeds F_n , then T is a better approximation to optimal M than M_n and we take $M_{n+1} = T$; otherwise we retain M_n and take a new $\zeta^{(l)}$ and form a new test span T. Finding optimal PCs using Fisher's criterion is an established and well-tested approach (Dubuisson et al. 2002; McLachlan 2004), and we adapt it here to the classification problem in hand.

Classifier construction: After PCA of a training sample, the use of linear discriminants (LDA) has been successful in several related investigations. Typically, a linear discriminant is a hyperplane that separates optimally a cluster of the training sample from the rest of the sample (Jolliffe 2002). With J affect clusters, the resulting J hyperplanes partition the observation space into 2^J regions bounded by hyperplanes, of which J contain only one cluster centre, $^JC_2$ contain 2 centres, $^JC_3$ contain 3, and so on. A new thermal image vector can be 'classified' by assigning it to one region, but if the region contains several centres the classification is ambiguous. To lift the ambiguity, a distance or similarity criterion is needed: it must assign the new vector to the nearest or most similar cluster centre in the region. In this work we used the Mahalanobis distance, defined in terms of the pooled within-cluster variance matrix, W, of a training sample. If the x-x_j is the vector joining new image vector to the centre of cluster j, then the Euclidean length $\|(x\text{-}x_j)W^{-1}\|$ defines the Mahalanobis distance from x to cluster j. Thus, the nearest cluster to x in a region containing several cluster centres is given by $argmax_j \{\|(x\text{-}x_j)W^{-1}\|\}$. This way of developing the discriminant rules in a classification problem has a long history (Everitt and Dunn 1991; McLachlan 2004). We implemented it as a critical foil to our optimized subspace method, operating in a subspace spanned by all the PCs of training samples that contribute more than 1% to total variance measured by the trace of D. Test results were not encouraging: in an experiment using only three intentional affects ('happy', 'sad' and 'neutral'), and training samples with one face of known intentional affect excluded from our total data set, only 46% of excluded faces were assigned to the correct class (see Table 1 below).

14.4 Results

In addition to the test experiments on LDA classification described in section 3, the same test procedure was carried out using the optimal subspace M spanned by only the most discriminating PCs. The result of such 'leave one out' experimentation improved the classification accuracy dramatically to about 84%, as shown in Table 1

The experiments were repeated using 4 non-neutral facial expressions ('happy', 'disgusted', 'surprised' and 'angry'). The results in Table 2 show that the accuracy of both types of classifier deteriorated, but the classifiers based on optimally discriminating PCs remained at an acceptable 67% success rate. Their worst performance was in detection of disgust (56%), and their best performance was in the detection of positive surprise (88%). This suggests that the kind of Gaussian mixture model with one cluster per intentional affect works better for some affects than others, and motivates further investigation with more complex Gaussian mixture models.

Table 1. 3-facial expression classification success results with general and optimal PCs

Classification		Group	Predicted Group Membership			Total
			Normal	*Happy*	*Sad*	
Higher Eigenvalued PCs. Cross-Validated results [a]	%	Neutral	62.5	25.0	12.5	100.0
		Happy	43.8	25.0	31.3	100.0
		Sad	25.0	25.0	50.0	100.0
[a] 45.8 % of cross-validated group cases correctly classified						
Optimal PCs. Cross-Validated results [b]	%	Neutral	81.3	6.3	12.5	100.0
		Happy	0	87.5	12.5	100.0
		Sad	6.3	12.5	81.3	100.0
[b] 83.8 % of cross-validated group cases correctly classified						

Table 2. 4-facial expression classification success rate with general and optimal PCs

Classification		Group	Predicted Group Membership				Total
			Happy	*Disgust*	*Surprise*	*Angry*	
Higher Eigenvalued PCs. Cross-Validated results [a]	%	Happy	31.3	18.8	31.3	18.8	100.0
		Disgusted	31.3	37.5	6.3	25.0	100.0
		Surprised	12.5	18.8	50	18.8	100.0
		Angry	25.0	37.5	6.3	31.3	100.0
[b] 37.5 % of cross-validated group cases correctly classified							
Optimal PCs. Cross-Validated results [b]	%	Happy	62.5	6.3	31.3	0	100.0
		Disgusted	6.3	56.3	18.8	18.8	100.0
		Surprised	6.3	6.3	87.5	0	100.0
		Angry	6.3	18.8	12.5	62.5	100.0
[b] 67.2 % of cross-validated group cases correctly classified							

14.5 Conclusion

This work proposed a novel feature extraction and pattern representation approach to classify the facial expression of affective states using bio-physiological data in a sample group of donors. The proposed computational approach using an optimized subspace of input vectors allowed better between-group separation than the classical PC selection approaches such as Kaiser's rule, which simply reduce data complexity by eliminating PCs that contribute little to total variance. The work is based on a fairly simplistic model of intentional expressions in which each affect is supposed to define a single, donor-independent cluster of TIVs. The results suggest that this simplicity is more valid for some affects than others, and motivates experimentation on more sophisticated models that acknowledge gross individual differences between the ways distinct donors portray the same emotion. More generally, it raises questions about intentional expression that call for investigation of possible differences between a donor's intentional expressions and those evoked involuntarily (by canonically emotive stimuli exciting disgust, sadness and other types of emotion).

References

Belmont Report. 1979. *Ethical principles and guidelines for the protection of human subjects of research*, available online: http://ohsr.od.nih.gov/guidelines/belmont.html, United States Government, National Institute of Health, Washington D.C.

Chatfield, C., and Collins, A.J. 1995. *Introduction to Multivariate Analysis*, London, Chapman & Hall.

Choi, S.C. 1972. "Classification of multiple observed data," *Biomedical Journal*, vol. 14, pp. 8-11.

Dubuisson, S., Davoine F., and Masson, M. 2002. "A solution for facial expression representation and recognition," *Signal Processing: Image Communication*," vol. 17, pp. 657-673.

Everitt B.S., and Dunn, G. 1991. *Applied Multivariate Data Analysis*, London: John Wiley and Sons.

Fasel B., and Luettin, J. 2003. "Automatic facial expression analysis: a survey," *Pattern Recognition*, vol. 36, pp. 259-275.

Garbey, M., Merla, A. and Pavlidis, I. 2004. "Estimation of blood flow speed and vessel location from thermal video," *In the Proceedings of CVRP 2004, IEEE 2004 Conference on Computer Vision and Pattern Recognition*, vol. 1, pp. 1356-1363, Washington DC.

Gonzalez, R. C., and Woods, R.E. 2002. *Digital Image Processing*, New Jersey: Prentice-Hall.

Gupta, A.K., and Logan, T.P. 1990. "On a multiple observations model in discriminant analysis," *Journal of Statistics and Computer Simulation*, vol. 34, pp. 119–132.

Jolliffe, I.T. 2002. *Principal Component Analysis*, New York, Springer-Verlag.

Khan, M.M., Ingleby, M. and Ward, R.D. 2006 "Automated facial expression classification and affect interpretation using infrared measurement of facial skin temperature variation," *ACM Transactions on Autonomous and Adaptive Systems*, Vol. 1, No. 1, pp. 91-113, ISSN: 1556-4665.

Khan, M.M., Ward, R.D., and Ingleby, M. 2005. "Distinguishing facial expressions by thermal imaging using facial thermal feature points," *In the Proceedings of 19th British HCI Group Annual Conference HCI 2005*, vol. 2, September 2005, Edinburgh, UK, L. MacKinnon, O. Bertelsen and N. Bryan-Kinns (Eds.), British Computer Society, Scotland, pp. 10-14.

Klein, J., Moon, Y., Picard, R.W. 2002. "This computer responds to user frustration: Theory, design and results," *Interacting with computers*, vol. 14, no. 2, pp. 119-140.

McLachlan, G. J., 2004. *Discriminant Analysis and Statistical Pattern Recognition*, New Jersey, Wiley.

Pavlidis, I. 2000. "Lie detection using thermal imaging," *In Thermal facial screening: Proceedings of SPIE – Thermosense XXVI, Annual conference of the International Society for Optical Engineering*, April 2004, Bellingham, USA, pp. 270-279.

Rencher, A.C. 1995. *Methods of multivariate analysis*, New York: Wiley and Sons.

Sharma, S. 1996. *Applied Multivariate Techniques*. New York: Wiley.

Sugimoto, Y., Yoshitomi Y., and Tomita, S. 2000. "A method of detecting transitions of emotional states using a thermal facial image based on a synthesis of facial expressions," *Robotics and Autonomous Systems*, no. 31, pp. 147-160.

Yoshitomi, Y., Kim, S-I., Kawano T., and Kitazoe, T. 2000. "Effects of sensor fusion for recognition of emotional states using voice, face image and thermal image of face," *In the Proceedings of the IEEE International workshop on Robotics and Human Interactive Communication*, Osaka, Japan, September 2000, pp. 178-183.

15 On-line One Stroke Character Recognition Using Directional Features

Murad Al Haj[1], Ariel Amato[1], Gemma Sánchez[1], Jordi González[2]

[1] Computer Vision Centre & Departament Informàtica, Universitat Autònoma de Barcelona , 08193 Cerdanyola, Spain. Corresponding Author: malhaj@cvc.uab.es

[2] Institut de Robòtica i Informàtica Industrial (UPC-CSIC), Edifici U, Parc Tecnològic de Barcelona. C/ Llorens i Artigas 4-6, 08028 Barcelona, Spain

Abstract. This paper presents a method based on directional features for recognizing on-line characters represented by one-stroke. A new alphabet is proposed, and each character is represented as a vector of directional angles. The novelty of this method, as compared with other chain code methods, relies on the feature extraction approach and the use of the directional vector as a path in the decision tree.

15.1 Introduction

Handwriting recognition has many applications in different fields. These applications include reading hand-written notes on PDAs, bank cheques, postal addresses, and other fields on different forms. The persistent use of handwriting, in the era of digital computers, as the natural mean for storing data and information explains its convenience for numerous daily activities [1]. This extensive use of handwriting raises the importance of developing handwriting recognition systems.

When talking about handwriting recognition, one has to differentiate between two kinds of handwritten data: on-line and off-line. The former is obtained by writing with a special device such as a digital pen or on a special surface such as a PDA screen, while the lateral is obtained through an image of an already written document, through scanning for example. In the on-line case, spatio-temporal information of the input data is available, while in the off-line case only spatio-luminance information of the image is available [1]. In other words, the on-line case provides the pen trajectory while the off-line case provides only the image of the written data; however, due to sampling, some of the information is lost. Figure 1 shows the difference between the two cases for the same character written with a digital pen. In Fig. 1.(a), the actual written pattern is shown, while Fig. 1.(b) shows the sampled version of this character which is reconstructed from the information obtained by the digital pen. A survey for on-line graphics recognition is presented in [2]. A sketch-based interface for inputting graphics on small screen devices was developed in [3].

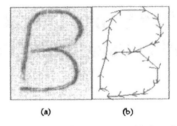

Fig. 1. (a) Off-line data (b) On-line data: Red arrows are added to show direction information

With the development of ink-aware modules, the concept of digital ink was introduced and a standard called Digital Ink Markup Language (InkML) was developed by the W3C as a format for representing ink that is entered by an input device [4]. Therefore, off-line processing of on-line data is now available. We believe that soon the distinction will no longer be on-line data and off-line data, but rather between on-line processing and off-line processing.

In this paper, we propose a method for on-line one stroke character recognition through directional features. The advantage of this method over previously existing ones [5,6,7] is its simplicity in extracting a compact robust feature for each character, in addition to the computational efficiency of recognition that does not depend on the concept of minimum distance, where each character has to be compared with all the alphabet. The directional features extracted are used for path selection on the decision tree.

This paper is organized as follows. Section 2 introduces the framework in which we developed our method. Section 3 presents the feature extraction method while section 4 presents the recognition method. In section 5, experimental results are shown. Concluding remarks are discussed in section 6.

15.2 Framework Overview

To obtain on-line information of the character strokes, a digital pen and a paper enabled with the Anoto functionality were used. The Anoto paper is a standard paper with a special pattern of dots printed on it. These dots are invisible to the human eye and they are 0.3 mm apart and are slightly shifted from a grid structure to form the proprietary Anoto patten [8].

When writing with a digital pen on an Anoto paper, the movement of the pen is recorded through snapshots taken by a tiny camera inside the pen. The pattern of dots allows dynamic information coming from the digital camera in the pen to be processed into signals representing writing and drawing. This information is recorded on a memory chip found also inside the pen.

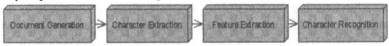

Fig. 2. System overview

In Fig. 2, an overview of the system is shown. The document is generated from the information saved inside the digital pen. Extracting the characters from the document is simple, since we are assuming that the document contains only strokes that represent alphabet characters. Thereafter, the term character refers only to an alphabet character. The feature extraction step is discussed in section 3 while the character recognition step is discussed in section 4.

15.3 Features Extraction

The feature used in recognizing different characters is the directional feature. This method tries to encode the pen trajectory into a vector of directional angles. The advantages of such a method are its robustness and its ability to extract general representative information from a given pattern.

15.3.1 Alphabet

For representing each character in one stroke, a slightly modified version of the Graffiti Alphabet and the Graffiti 2 Alphabet, both designed by Palm Inc., is proposed, see Fig. 3. Our modification aims at a more robust representation by further differentiating the characters. For example, it can be seen, in Graffiti and Graffiti 2, that the stroke representations for B, P, and R are similar for a long period of the sketching time. In other words, to sketch B, P, or R one has to follow the same pen trajectory for a long time. Thus, our proposed alphabet is shown in Fig. 4.

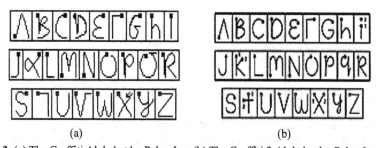

(a)   (b)

Fig. 3. (a) The Graffiti Alphabet by Palm, Inc. (b) The Graffiti 2 Alphabet by Palm, Inc.

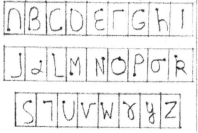

Fig. 4. Our proposed Alphabet

15.3.2 Discrete Directional Features

For recognition, each character is represented by a vector of normalized discrete directional angle values. These values are -90, 0, 90, and 180. The angle value represents the normalized movement of the pen from the recorded points. Each character stroke is then represented by a vector of these values. For example, a stroke representing the character "A" will be recorded as the vector (90, 0, -90).

15.3.3 Filtering

Due to the way humans write, one expects noise while obtaining the angles vector. Also, since the normalization is in big proportions, more noise is introduced. Thus, filtering is necessary in order to obtain a representative vector that will be used in recognition. The filtering is based on the length of segment having the angular direction and the number of sampled points obtained from that direction. The idea here is that a sub-stroke (having a constant angular direction) is representative if it has a significant relative length or if the writer spent significant time writing it (a lot of sampled points were obtained), or both. For example, the angular vector obtained for one "A" stroke is (180, 0, 90, 0, -90, 90). The relative length of each sub-stroke having these angles is shown in Fig. 5 (a), while the number of points forming each sub-stroke is shown in Fig. 5 (b).

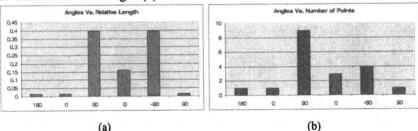

(a)   (b)

Fig. 5. (a) Relative Length of the sub-strokes (b) Number of points of the sub-strokes

It can be easily seen from Fig. 7 that the representative vector is (90, 0, -90). The algorithm used to generate the representative vector is the following:

Given a vector of angles $(a_1, a_2, ..., a_n)$ representing sub-strokes with the following set of relative lengths $(r_1, r_2, ..., r_n)$ and the following number of points $(p_1, p_2, ..., p_n)$
For every angle a_i in the vecor
    If $r_i > T_r$ or $p_i > T_p$
        Keep a_i in the vector
    Else if $r_i > T'_r$ and $p_i > T'_p$
        Keep a_i in the vector
    Else
        Remove a_i from the vector

where T_r is the threshold for the relative length and T_p is the threshold for the number of points. T'_r & T'_p are lower thresholds for the relative length and the number of points respectively.

15.4 Character Recognition

After the vector of representative angles is obtained, it is considered as a path in the decision tree to reach a character. The decision tree is shown in Fig. 6, and it is constructed by considering the vectors of angles that are used to form each character.

15.4.1 Multiple Paths

In most cases, there is more than one path to reach a character. For example, the path {90, 0, -90, 180} and the path {90, -90, 180} lead both to the character P. The purpose of having multiple paths is an attempt to cover all the possible generated vectors of representative angles in order to make the recognition more robust.

15.4.2 Robustness and Efficiency

It should be noted that the minimal and the most representative vector of angles is obtained; thus, the probability of this information being erroneous is extremely low.

The main advantage of this method is its computational efficiency: unlike other methods, it does not require comparing the obtained character with the rest of the alphabet for recognition. Moreover, size variation problems are automatically solved because only the relative length and the number of points for each sub-stroke are considered, and slant problems are solved by the big normalization interval.

15.4.3 Differentiating between G, O, and Q

The characters G, O, and Q have the same sequence of angles in the decision tree. However, noting that the initial sub-stroke (with 180° angle) in Q is longer than that of G and O, Q can be separated from the rest. Moreover, the differentiation between G and O is done based on the fact that the 90° sub-stroke is shorter in G than in O.

15.5 Experimental Results

Our testing revealed impressive results. We have obtained 354 samples representing all the alphabet from 8 different subjects. With the threshold set experimentally, T_r to 0.07, T_p set to 3, T'_r set to 0.04, and T'_p set to 2, we were able to achieve a recognition rate of 99.15%: only 3 characters out of the 354 were not correctly recognized.

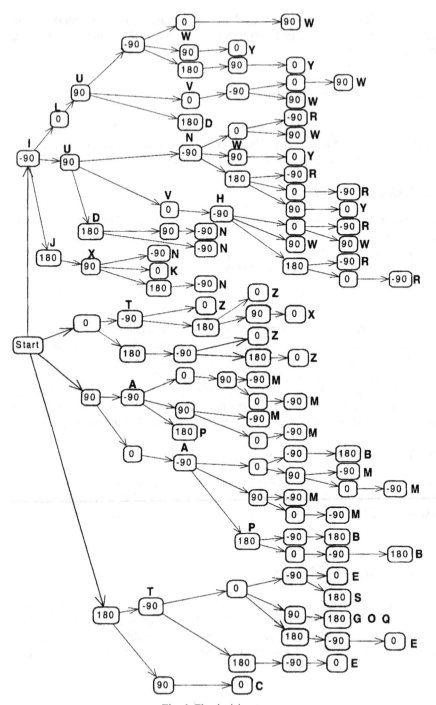

Fig. 6. The decision tree

15.6 Conclusions

In this paper, we present an on-line one stroke character recognition method that is based on directional features. The novelty of this method is that it uses the directional vector as a path in the decision tree. Therefore, there is no need to compare each character with the rest of the alphabet. This method is computationally efficient and robust to noise. The experimental results are promising. In the future, this method will be explored further and dynamic approaches to allocate the thresholds for obtaining the vector of angles will be considered.

Acknowledgements

This work has been supported by EC grants IST-027110 for the HERMES project and IST-045547 for the VIDI-Video project, and by the Spanish MEC under projects TIN2006-14606, DPI-2004-5414 and TIN2006-15694-C02-02. Jordi Gonzàlez also acknowledges the support of a Juan de la Cierva Postdoctoral fellowship from the Spanish MEC.

References

[1] Plamondon, R. and Srihari, S. N., "On-line and Off-line Handwriting Recognition: A Comprehensive Survey", *IEEE Transcations on Pattern Analysis and Machine Intelligence*, vol. 22, no.1, pp. 63-84, January 2000.

[2] Wenyin, L., "On-line Graphics Recognition: State-of-the-Art", *5th IAPR Workshop on Graphics Recognition (GREC03), CVC, UAB*, LNCS, vol. 3088, pp. 291-304, Springer, 2004.

[3] Weyin, L., Jin, X., Sun, Z., "Sketch-Based User Interface for Inputting Graphic Objects on Small Screen Devices", *3rd IAPR Workshop on Graphics Recognition (GREC01), LNCS*, vol. 2390, pp. 67-80, Springer, 2002.

[4] W3C Multi-modal Interaction Working Group. Ink markup language (inkml). *http://www.w3.org/2002/mmi/ink*, 2007.

[5] Long, T., Jin, L.W., Zen, L.X. and Huang, J.C., "One Stroke Cursive Character Recognition Using Combination of Directional and Positional Features", *IEEE International Conference on Acoustics, Speech, and Signal Processing*, vol. 5, pp. 449-452, March 2005.

[6] Ozer, O.F., Ozun, O., Tuzel, C.O., Atalay, V. and Cetin, A.E., "Vision-Based Single-Stroke Character Recognition for Wearable Computing", *IEEE Intelligent Systems*, vol. 16, issue 3, pp.33-37, May-June 2001.

[7] Haluptzok, P., Revow, M., Abdulkader, A., "Personalization of an Online Handwriting Recognition System", *10th International Workshop on Frontiers in Handwriting Recognition*, inria-00104782 - version 1, 2006.

[8] Kolberg, M., Magil, E.H., Wilson, M., Birstwistle, P. and Ohlstenius,O., "Controlling Appliances with Pen and Paper", *Second IEEE Consumer Communications and Networking Conference*, pp. 156-160, January 2005.

16 Comparison of SVMs in Number Plate Recognition

Lihong Zheng, Xiangjian He and Tom Hintz

University of Technology, Sydney, Department of Computer Systems,
{lzheng, sean, hintz}@it.uts.edu.au

Abstract. High accuracy and high speed are two key issues to consider in automatic number plate recognition (ANPR). In this paper, we construct a recognition method based on Support Vector Machines (SVMs) for ANPR. Firstly, we briefly review some knowledge of SVMs. Then, the number plate recognition algorithm is proposed. The algorithm starts from a collection of samples of characters. The characters in the number plates are divided into two kinds, namely digits and letters. Each character is recognized by an SVM, which is trained by some known samples in advance. In order to improve recognition accuracy, two approaches of SVMs are applied and compared. Experimental results based on two algorithms of SVMs are given. From the experimental results, we can make the conclusion that 'one against one' method based on RBF kernel is better than others such as inductive learning-based or 'one against all' method for automatic number plate recognition.

16.1 Introduction

Number recognition is playing an important role in image processing field. For example, there are thousands of containers and trucks need to be registered every day at container terminals and depots. Normally, this registration will be done manually. However, this is not only prone to error but also slow to meet the increasing volume of containers and trucks. Hence, an automatic, fast and precise number recognition process is required.

The fundamental issues in number plate recognition are the requirements of high accuracy and high recognition speed. Since last two decades, various commercial ANPR products (Zheng, He and Li 2005) around the world are available, such as SeeCar in Israel, VECON in Hongkong, LPR in USA, the ANPR in UK, IMPS in Singapore, and the CARINA in Hungary (Zheng 2005). Even though there have been so many successful ANPR systems, there are still several problems for character recognition of number plates. The following three problems are the most critical. Firstly, the recognition system must be able to handle various sizes, fonts, spaces and alignments of the characters in the number plates. Secondly, the recognition system must be robust to changes in illumination and colors used. Thirdly, the recognition system must be able to distinguish the obscured characters in real-life images due to rust, mud, peeling paint, and fading color. To resolve the problems above, an effective method must have a general adaptability to different conditions. It should have good tolerance for noise and classify and recognize the characters in number plate accurately and credibly.

In order to improve the performance of recognition, an algorithm on number recognition was proposed in (Aksoy, Cagil and Turker 2000) based on RULES-3 induction theory. This algorithm trains character samples and obtains the rules that are used to recognize the numbers on number plates. One advantage of using this method is that the recognition speed is much quicker in number recognition. But it is not robust to image rotation, translation and scaling. However, it cannot distinguish digits 6 and 9 without additional observation.

In order to improve the recognition performance, we propose another algorithm to number recognition (Zheng and He 2006). This technique uses a Support Vector Machine (SVM) to train character samples and obtain the rules that are used to recognize the numbers on number plates. SVM (Cristianini 2000; Vapnik 1999) is forcefully competing with many methods for pattern classification. An SVM is a supervised learning technique first discussed by Vapnik (Vapnik 1999). SVM takes Statistical Learning Theory (SLT) as its theoretical foundation, and the structural risk minimization as its optimal object to realize the best generalization. They are based on some simple ideas and provide a clear intuition of what learning from examples is all about. More importantly, they possess the feature of high performance in practical applications. From 1960s to present, SVMs become more and more important in the field of pattern recognition.

The organization of this paper is as follows. We first introduce some basic knowledge of SVMs in Section 2. In Section 3, multi-class classifier model and 'one against all' and 'one against one' strategy are briefly introduced. The algorithm of number plate recognition is done in Section 4. The experimental results for number recognition are demonstrated in Section 5. We conclude in Section 6.

16.2 Principles of SVMs

In 2000, SVM was defined by Cristianini & Taylor (Cristianini and Shawe-Taylor 2000) as 'a system for efficiently training linear learning machines in kernel-induced feature spaces, while respecting the insights of generalization theory and exploiting optimization theory'. An SVM is a pattern recognizer that classifies data without making any assumptions about the underlying process by which the observations were granted. The SVMs use hyperplanes to separate the different classes. Many hyperplanes are fitted to separate the classes, but there is only one optimal separating hyperplane. The optimal one is expected to generalize well in comparison to the others. The optimal hyperplane is determined only by support vectors, which are ideally distributed near class boundaries. The hyperplane is constructed so as to maximize a measure of the 'margin' between classes. A new data sample is classified by the SVM according to the decision boundary defined by the hyperplane.

An SVM corresponds to a linear method in a very high dimensional feature space. The feature space is nonlinearly related to the input space. Classification is achieved by realizing a linear or non-linear separation surface in the feature space (Vapnik 1999).

We briefly describe general knowledge of SVMs as follows (Zheng and He 2006).

Given a two-class classification problem, separating hyperplanes can be defined as:

$$H_{\tilde{w},b} : \tilde{w}^T \tilde{x} + b = 0 ,$$

where w is a normal vector, the input is denoted by x and b is an offset. SVM tries to find the optimal hyperplane via maximizing the margin between the positive input vectors, $\{x_i$ when $y_i=+1$, for $i=1, ..., n\}$, and negative input vectors, $\{x_i$ when $y_i=-1$, for $i=1, ..., n\}$.

In the linear case, this is equivalent to maximize $2/\| \tilde{w} \|$ ($\|.\|$ is norm of $\tilde{w}$) that is regarded as a canonical representation of the separating hyperplane, i.e.,

$$\begin{cases} \min \quad \dfrac{1}{2} \| \tilde{w} \|^2 \\ s.t. \quad y_i (< \tilde{w}, \tilde{x}_i > +b) \geq 1, \quad \forall i \end{cases} \quad (1)$$

Here $\tilde{w}$ can be solved as follows by applying the Lagrangian multiplier α.

$$\tilde{w} = \sum_{i=1}^{n} \alpha_i y_i \phi(x_i)$$

where $\alpha_i \geq 0$, $(i = 1, 2, ..., n)$, is the Lagrangian multiplier, and ϕ is the kernel function.

For a new input, its classified label is according to the result of:

$$f_{H_{\tilde{w},b}}(x) = \mathrm{sgn}(\tilde{w}^T \phi(x) + b) = \mathrm{sgn}(\sum_{i=}^{n} \alpha_i y_i K(x, x_i) + b) ,$$

where $K(x, x_i) = \phi(x)^T \phi(x_i)$.

In the case that the set is not linearly separable or does not satisfy the inequality constraint $y_i (< \tilde{w}, x_i > +b) \geq 1$, for all i, a slack and nonnegative variable ξ is added into Eq. 1 as shown by

$$\begin{cases} \min \quad \dfrac{1}{2} \| \tilde{w} \|^2 + C \sum_{i=1}^{n} \xi_i \\ s.t. \quad y_i (\tilde{w}^T \phi(x_i) + b) \geq 1 - \xi_i, \xi_i \geq 0, \quad i = 1, ..., n \end{cases} \quad (2)$$

The term $\sum_{i=1}^{n} \xi_i$ is an upper bound on the number of misclassification in the training set. It indicates the distance that the training point from the optimal hyperplane and the amount of violation of the constraints. Furthermore, C is the penalty term for misclassifications. C controls the trade-off between maximizing the margin and minimizing the training error, and between a better generalization and an efficient computation.

16.3 Multi-class Model of SVMs

Among many classification methods, SVM has demonstrated superior performance. It has been successfully utilized in handwritten numeral recognition. However, SVM was originally designed for binary classification, and its extension to solve multi-class problems is not straightforward. The popular methods for applying SVM to multi-class problems decompose a multi-class problem into many binary-class problems and incorporate many binary-class SVMs.

Two main approaches have been suggested for applying SVMs for multi-class classification (Foody and Mathur 2004). In each approach, the underlying basis has been to reduce the multi-class problem to a set of binary problems, and to enable the use of basic SVM.

The first approach, called 'one against all' (Foody and Mathur 2004; Dong, Suen and Krzyzak 2005), uses a set of binary classifiers, each trained to separate one class from the rest. For a given input x_i, there are k decision functions. x_i is classified to be in the one of k classes that gives the largest decision value.

The second approach is called 'one against one'. In this approach, a series of classifiers are applied to each pair of classes, and only the label of the most commonly computed class is kept for each case. The application of this method requires $k(k-1)/2$ classifiers or machines be applied to each pair of classes, and a strategy to handle instances in which an equal number of votes are derived for more than one class for a case. Once all $k(k-1)/2$ classifiers have been undertaken, the max-win strategy is followed.

The multi-class model can be described as follows.

Given n training data

$$\Omega = \{(x_1, y_1), (x_2, y_2), \ldots, (x_n, y_n) |$$
$$x_i \in R^n, (i=1,2,\ldots,n)\}, \text{ and } y_i \in \{1,2,3,\ldots,k\},$$

where k is the number of classes. The classification function is as:

$$\begin{cases} \min_{w^i,b^i,\xi^i} \quad \dfrac{1}{2}\|w_j^i\|^2 + C\sum_{j=1}^{n}\xi_j^i \\ (w^i)^T\phi(x_i)+b^i \geq 1-\xi_j^i, if \quad y_j = i, \\ (w^i)^T\phi(x_i)+b^i \leq -1+\xi_j^i, if \quad y_j \neq i, \\ \xi_j^i \geq 0, \quad j=1,...,n \end{cases} \text{s.t.}$$

where $K(x,x_i) = \phi(x)^T\phi(x_i)$

In APRN, k is 36, which includes 10 for digits and 26 for letters. The above formula implies the following 36 decision functions for all 36 digits and letters:

$$(w^1)^T\phi(x)+b^1,$$

...

$$(w^{36})^T\phi(x)+b^{36}.$$

An x is classified to be the digit or letter a if its decision function gives the maximum value in the SVM for a, i.e.,

$$\text{Class of } x \equiv \arg\max_{i=1,...,36}((w^i)^T\phi(x)+b^i).$$

Fig.1. The number plate samples

16.4 Number Plate Classifier Design

The car number plate at the New South Wales state of Australia has up to six characters as shown in Fig. 1. Usually, the number plate consists of two main sections. The upper section contains main information of the number plate, and the lower part is for the name of the state. The upper part is more important, and is separated into two groups of characters. The first group usually consists of three or four letters of A to Z and the second group consists of three or two digits of 0 to 9. In order to speed up the process, two sets of SVMs are designed according to these two groups of characters. One set of SVMs is designed for recognizing digital numbers and the other one is designed for letters. The details of our algorithms are described as follows. For comparison, the 'one against all' and 'one against one' methods are both adopted.

In the first approach using 'one against all' method, for recognizing the digits in a number plate, ten SVMs are designed for the ten digits from 0 to 9. Each SVM has one digital number sample as one label and all or some of the other samples are as another label. After training, each SVM gets its own values of parameters. The decision value of the testing sample will be calculated based on the values of parameters obtained. The final recognition result will be achieved according to the class that gives the maximum decision value. The procedure for recognizing the letters in a number plate is the same as that for digits except that the total number of SVMs is 26 for 26 letters.

In the second approach using 'one against one' method, SVM has one digital number sample as one label and any one of the other samples is taken as another label. Therefore, 45 SVMs are designed for the ten digits from 0 to 9, and 325 SVMs are for letter A to Z.

We summarize the SVM based algorithm for number recognition in this paper as follows. In order to recognize a number plate, we go through the following steps.

Step 1. Pre-process the image of number plate.

Step 2. Segment the image into several parts of which each contains only a single character.

Step 3. Normalize each letter or digit on the number plate.

Step 4. Extract the feature vector of each normalized candidate

Step 5. Recognizes the single character (a digit or a letter) by the set of SVMs trained in advance.

Step 6. If there are no more unclassified samples, then STOP. Otherwise, go to Step 5.

Step 7. Add these test samples into their corresponding database for further training.

Step 8. Recognize number plate by bringing all characters used together.

When a number plate region is located and extracted, the histogram projection methods are applied for character segmentation. The number plate is segmented and the sub-images containing individual characters (digits and letters) forming the number plate are obtained. In the pre-processing step, each sub-image of a character is normalized into a certain size which is 20 pixels in width and 36 pixels in length. Then the sub-image is binarized into range of $[-1, +1]$ for enhancing the character from background. The support vectors are calculated directly from the binarized sub-images. The high dimensional feature vectors are stored into two kinds of database, one is for digital numbers, and the other is for letters. The above feature vectors are used to train SVMs with RBF kernel (see Section 5). In our experiments, 720 dimensional feature vectors are input into SVMs, which have been trained successfully. Then, which character that a given candidate should be can be obtained in according to the outputs of SVMs.

When all digits and letters on a number plate are recognized (or classified), the recognition of the number plate is complete.

16.5 Experimental Results

Support vector machines in our experiments are trained using algorithms as shown in (Gunn 1997). Based on the approach we described above, we did experiments for digital numbers of 0 to 9 and letters of A to Z. In our database, there are average 768 training samples for character which are segmented from real images of number plates. Figure 2 presents some of example of characters in number plates. We selected randomly one third of them for training and the rest samples were used for testing.

Fig.2. Segmented characters

The experimental results are based on two methods, namely 'one against all' and 'one against one'. Two kernel functions that are linear kernel and RBF kernel are used and shown below.

Linear: $K(x, x_i) = \langle x \cdot x_i \rangle$

RBF: $K(x, x_i) = \exp\left(-\|x - x_i\|^2 / 2\sigma^2\right)$

Tables 1 and 2 show a comparison of using the two methods. Also, we estimate the matching rate using different kernel parameters σ and cost parameters C. Matching rate = Number of recognized characters correctly/Number of all testing characters.

Table 1 The experimental results of characters (Digits and Letters) of number plate (One against all)

	Digital Numbers		Letters	
	RBF kernel $(C=10^{-2}\sim10^{4}$, $\sigma=.1\sim1.0)$	Linear Kernel $(C=10^{-2}\sim10^{4})$	RBF kernel $(C=10^{-2}\sim10^{4}$, $\sigma=.1\sim1.0)$	Linear Kernel $(C=10^{-2}\sim10^{4})$
Matching rate	83.8%	75.7%	80.7%	65.3%
Percentage of SV	98%	14.3%	98.8%	11.5%
Training Time(seconds)	0.46	0.5	6.1	7.2
Testing time	0.6	1.88	0.31	0.56

We also report the training time, testing time and the percentage of support vectors in the tables. All the experiments are performed on a Pentium 4 PC with 2.0GHz CPU. The training time and testing time increase with the number of training samples. However, the classification accuracy does not change much. For further comparison, we also give the experimental results as shown in Table 3 obtained from well-known database iris and UCI (UCI).

Table 2 The experimental results of characters (Digits and Letters) of number plate (One against one)

	Digital Numbers		Letters
	RBF kernel $(C=10^{-2}\sim10^4, \sigma=.1\sim1.0)$	Linear Kernel $(C=10^{-2}\sim10^4)$	RBF kernel $(C=10^2\sim10^2, \sigma=.5\sim1.0)$
Matching rate	68.8%	70.6%	63%
Percentage of SV	98%	14.3%	98.8%
Training Time(seconds)	0.02	0.01	4.3
Testing time	1.88	0.5	0.5

Table 3. The experimental results of iris and UCI database (RBF) (One against all)

Cases	Test matching rate $C=(500\sim10^2) \sigma=.5\sim1$	Percentage of SV	Training Time(s)	Testing time
Iris	97.8%	16%	0.1	0.01
UCI	89.86%	29.3%	63.8	0.4

16.6 Discussion and Conclusions

The major advantages of SVMs are that each SVM is a maximal margin hyperplane in a feature space built using a Kernel function, and each SVM is based on firm statistical and mathematical foundations concerning generalization and optimization theory. The training for SVMs is relatively easy. From the experimental results, it is obvious that SVMs based on RBF kernel function perform better due to its properties described in above section. The algorithm based on 'one against all' gets higher matching rate than method of one again one.

Due to noise contained in the image of real number plates, the recognition rate is lower than what obtained in some standard database such as *iris* (Gunn 1997) and UCI (UCI). But the following conclusion still holds. In 'one against one method', each classifier must give a label to a candidate no matter if it is correct or not. Therefore, in many cases, error label information is given and data are mistrained. The parameters after training have lower credit. On the contrary, however, 'one against all' method shows better performance.

For the failed cases in our experiment, we notice that the amounts of every character's samples are not evenly in our database. For example, character 'A' owned much more samples than other characters. Characters 'H' and 'L' have smaller number of samples in our database. The parameters obtained through training are less powerful than others which were trained using a big amount of samples. Another reason is that the images of these characters are much more blurred or distorted than the training samples. These characters are misclassified into other similar classes. However, compared with earlier results using inductive Rule3 (Zheng, He, Wu and Hintz 2006) where the recognition accuracy rate is 71%, accuracy rates obtained using SVM is competitive and better.

Having said all above, SVMs can be applied in number plate recognition successfully especially for heavier noisy characters. Since SVM has the highest classification accuracy as a binary classifier, for further improvement of matching rate, we should combine some other classifiers together to make the number of characters in a group as small as possible. Therefore, the overall matching rate will be definitely higher than other methods for number plate recognition.

References

Aksoy, M. S., Cagil, G. and Turker, A. K. (2000) Number-plate recognition using inductive learning. *Robotics and Autonomous Systems*, Elsevier, Vol.33, pp.149-153.

Cristianini, N.and Shawe-Taylor, J. (2000) An introduction to support vector machines and other kernel-based learning methods. *Cambridge University Press.*

Dong, J., Suen, CY. and Krzyzak, A. (2005) Algorithms of fast SVM evaluation based on subspace projection. *2005 IEEE International Joint Conference on Neural Networks,* Vol. 2(31), pp.865-870.

Foody, G.M. and Mathur, A. (2004) A relative evaluation of multiclass image classification by support vector machines. *IEEE Transactions on Geoscience and Remote Sensing,* Vol.42(6), pp.1335–1343.

Gunn, S. R. (1997) Support vector machines for classification and regression. *Technical report.* Image Speech and Intelligent Systems Research Group, University of Southampton.

UCI www.kernel machines\data\UCI.html

Vapnik, V. N. (1999) The nature of statistical learning theory. New York: *Springer.*

Zheng, L., He, X. and Li, Y. (2005) A comparison of methods for character recognition of car number plates. *Proc. of International Conference on Computer Vision (VISION'05),* Las Vegas, pp.33-39.

Zheng, L. and He, X. (2006) Number plate recognition based on support vector machines. *Proceeding of IEEE AVSS 2006 conference.* ISBN-13: 978-0-7695-2688-1.

Zheng, L., He, X., Wu, Q. and Hintz, T. (2006) Learning-based number recognition on Spiral Architecture. *Proceeding of IEEE ICARCV2006.* Singapore, pp.897-901.

17 Three Different Models for Named Entity Recognition in Bengali

Asif Ekbal*, Sivaji Bandyopadhyay and Amitava Das
Department of Computer Science and Engineering,
Jadavpur University, Kolkata, India-700032
* corresponding author, Email:asif.ekbal@gmail.com

Abstract. The paper reports about the development of a Named Entity Recognition (NER) system in Bengali using a portion of the tagged Bengali news corpus, developed from the archive of a leading Bengali newspaper available in the web. Three different models of the NER system have been developed. A semi-supervised learning method has been adopted to develop the first two models, one without linguistic features (Model A) and the other with linguistic features (Model B). The third one, i.e., Model C, is based on the statistical Hidden Markov Model, where more contextual information has been considered. All the models have been trained with a training corpus of 62,280 wordforms. Evaluation results of the six-fold cross-validation tests yield 72.48%, 77.01% and 83.63% average F-Score values for models A, B and C, respectively. The NER system has demonstrated the highest average Recall, Precision and F-Score values of 89.62%, 78.47% and 83.63%, respectively, in Model C.

Keywords: Bengali corpus, Named Entity (NE), Named Entity Recognition (NER), Hidden Markov Model (HMM), Semi-supervised learning, Cross-validation.

17.1 Introduction

Named Entity Recognition (NER) is an important tool in almost all Natural Language Process-ing (NLP) application areas. The objective of named entity recognition is to identify and classify every word/term in a document into some predefined categories like person name, location name, organization name, miscellaneous name (date, time, percentage and monetary expressions) and "none-of-the-above". The challenge in de-tection of named entities is that such expressions are hard to analyze using traditional NLP because they belong to the open class of expressions, i.e., there is an infinite variety and new expressions are constantly being invented.

The level of ambiguity in NER makes it difficult to attain human performance. There has been a considerable amount of work on NER problem, which aims to address many of these ambiguities, robustness and portability issues. There are two kinds of evidences that can be used in NER to solve the ambiguity, robustness and portability problems involved in NER. The first is the internal evidences found within the word and/or word string itself while the second is the external evidence gathered from its context. During the last decade, NER has drawn more and more attention from the named entity (NE) tasks [11] [12] in Message Understanding Conferences (MUCs) [MUC6; MUC7]. The problem of correct identification of named entities is specifically addressed and benchmarked by the developers of Information Extraction System, such as the GATE system [13]. NER also finds application in question-answering systems [17] and machine translation [1].

The current trend in NER is to use the machine learning approach, which is more attractive in that it is trainable and adoptable and the maintenance of a machine learning system is much cheaper than that of a rule based one. The representative machine learning approaches used in NER are HMM (BBN's IdentiFinder in [16] [3], Maximum Entropy (New York University's MEME in [4] [5]), Decision Tree (New York University's system in [18] and SRA's system in [2] and Conditional Random Fields [15]. NER can also be treated as a tagging problem where each word in a sentence is assigned a label indicating whether it is part of a named entity and the entity type. Thus methods used for part of speech (POS) tagging can also be used for NER. The papers from the CoNLL-2002 shared task, which used such methods (e.g., [14]; [7]) show results significantly lower than the best system [8]. However, Zhou and Su [20] have reported state of the art results on the MUC-6 and MUC-7 data using an HMM-based tagger.

Among the machine learning approaches, the evaluation performance of the HMM is higher than those of others. The main reason may be due to its better ability of capturing the locality of phenomena, which indicates names in text. Moreover, HMM seems more and more used in NER because of the efficiency of the Viterbi algorithm [19] used in decoding the NE-class states sequence. However, the performance of a machine learning system is always poorer than that of a rule based one. This may be because current machine learning approaches capture important evidence behind NER problem much less effectively than human experts who handcraft the rules, although machine learning approaches always provide important statistical information that is not available to the human experts.

All the works, carried out already in the area of NER, are in non-Indian languages. India is a multilingual country with a lot of cultural diversities. In the present work, we present a NER system, first two models (A and B) of which are based on semi-supervised pattern directed shallow parsing approach. The third model, i.e., Model C, is developed with the help of statistical Hidden Markov Model (HMM). These models have been developed and tested on the Bengali news corpus.

The rest of the paper is organized as follows. The three different models of the named entity recognition system have been described in Section 2. Experimental results with the six-fold cross-validation tests for all the NER models along with the evaluation methods are presented in Section 3. Finally, Section 4 concludes the paper.

17.2 Named Entity Recognition in Bengali

Bengali is one of the widely used languages all over the world. It is the seventh popular language in the world, second in India and the national language of Bangladesh. Named Entity (NE) identification in Indian languages in general and in Bengali in particular is difficult and challenging. In English, the NE always appears with capitalized letter but there is no concept of capitalization in Bengali. A tagged Bengali news corpus [9] has been developed from the archive of a widely read Bengali newspaper available in the web. At present, the corpus contains around 34 million word forms in ISCII (Indian Script Code for Information Interchange) and UTF-8 format. A portion of this tagged corpus has been used for the Named Entity Recognition (NER) task. The location, reporter, agency and different date tags in the tagged corpus [9] help to identify the location, person, organization and miscellaneous names respectively. The objective of all the NER models, developed here, is to identify the NEs from a Bengali text and classify them into person name, location name, organization name, miscellaneous name and "none-of-the-above". Miscellaneous names include date, time, percentage and monetary expressions.

17.2.1 Model A and Model B of the NER System

Initially, the NER system has been developed using only the lexical contextual patterns learned (Model A) from the training corpus and then linguistic features have been included along with the same set of lexical contextual patterns (Model B). Model A is used as the *baseline* for the named entity recognition systems i.e., models, in the present study. Block diagrams of Model A and Model B are shown in Fig. 1 and Fig. 2, respectively. It is evident from the block diagrams (Fig. 1 and Fig. 2) that Model B follows the same structure as the *baseline* model, Model A, except the second component, i.e., " Tagging with linguistic features". The addition of the second component in Model B makes it more powerful than Model A and this is also experimentally established.

Creation of Seed Data

Three different seed lists of person names, location names and organization names have been created to train the models of the NER system. The words automatically extracted from the reporter, location and agency tags of the tagged corpus [9] are treated as the initial seed data and put into the appropriate seed lists. In addition to these extracted words, most frequently occurring person names, location names and organization names have been collected from the different domains of the newspaper and kept in the corresponding seed lists. At present the person, location and organization seed lists contain 253, 215 and 146 entries respectively. The date expressions have some fixed patterns and so these can be recognized by some handcrafted rules.

Tagging with Seed Lists and Clue Words

The tagger places the left and right tags around each occurrence of the named entities of the seed lists in the corpus. For the *baseline* model, the training corpus is tagged only with the help of different seed lists. In case of Model B, after tagging the entire training corpus with the NEs from the seed lists, the algorithm starts tagging with the help of different internal and external evidences that help to identify different NEs. It uses the clue words like surname, middle name, prefix word and suffix word for person names. A list of common words has been kept that often determines the presence of person names. It considers the different affixes that may occur with location names. The system also considers the several clue words that are helpful in detecting organization names. Tagging algorithm also uses the list of words that may appear as part of NE as well as the common words. The clue words and linguistic rules are used to tag more and more NEs during the training of the system. As a result, more potential patterns are generated in the lexical pattern generation phase.

Lexical Seed Patterns Generation from the Training Corpus

For each tag T inserted in the training corpus, the algorithm generates a lexical pattern p using a context window of maximum width 4 (excluding the tagged NE) around the left and the right tags, e.g., $P = [l_{-2}l_{-1} < T > l_{+1}l_{+2}]$, Where $l_{\pm i}$ are the context of p. Any of $l_{\pm i}$ may be a punctuation symbol. In such cases, the width of the lexical patterns will vary. These lexical patterns are generalized by replacing the tagged NE $< T > \dots < /T >$ by $< T >$ itself. These different types of patterns form the set of potential seed patterns, denoted by P. All these patterns, derived from the different tags of the tagged training corpus, are stored in a *Seed Pattern table* which has four different fields namely: pattern *id* (identifies any particular pattern), pattern *type* (Person name/ Location name/ Organization name) and *relative frequency* (indicates the number of times any particular pattern appears in the entire training corpus relative to the total number of patterns generated).

Generation of New Patterns through Bootstrapping

Every pattern p in the set P is matched against the entire training corpus. In a place, where the context of p matches, p predicts where one boundary of a name in text would occur. The system considers all possible noun, verb and adjective inflections during pattern matching. At present, there are 27 different noun inflections and 214 different verb inflections in the system. Three different forms of adjectives have been considered.

During pattern matching, the maximum length of a named entity is considered to be six words. Each named entity so obtained in the training corpus is manually checked for correctness. The training corpus is further tagged with these newly acquired named entities to identify further lexical patterns. The bootstrapping is applied on the training corpus until no new patterns can be generated. The patterns are added to the pattern set P with the *type* and *relative frequency* fields set properly, if they are not already in the pattern set P with the same *type*. Any particular pattern in the set of potential patterns P may occur many times but with different *type* and with equal or different *relative frequency* values. For each pattern of the set P, the *relative frequencies* of its occurrences as person, location and organization names are calculated.

For the candidate patterns acquisition, a particular threshold value of relative frequency is chosen. If the *relative frequency* for a particular pattern (along with the *type*) is less than this threshold value then this pattern (only for that *type*) is discarded otherwise it is retained in the pattern table. All these patterns form the set of *accepted* patterns that is denoted by *Accept Pattern*. A particular pattern may appear more than once with different *type* in this set. So, while testing the NER models, some identified NEs may be assigned more than one NE categories (*type*) that needs classification disambiguation. Model A cannot deal with this NE-classification disambiguation problem. The different linguistic features, used in Model B during tagging, can deal with this NE-classification disambiguation problem.

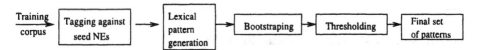

Fig. 1. Block Diagram of Model A of the NER System

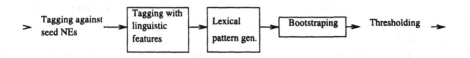

Fig. 2. Block Diagram of Model B of the NER System

17.2.2 Model C of the NER System

A HMM based NE tagger has been used in this work to identify NEs in Bengali and classify them into the predefined five major categories. Block diagram of this model is shown in Fig. 3. To apply HMM in named entity tagging task, the following NE tags have been defined:

PER (Single-word person name), LOC (Single-word location name), ORG (Single-word organization name), MISC (Single-word miscellaneous name), B-PER (Beginning i.e., the first word of a multi-word person name), B-LOC (Beginning i.e., the first word of a multi-word location name), B-ORG (Beginning i.e., the first word of a multi-word organization name), B-MISC (Beginning i.e., the first word of a multi-word miscellaneous name), E-PER (End i.e., the last word of a multi-word person name),

E-LOC (End i.e., the last word of a multi-word location name), E-ORG (End i.e., the last word of a multi-word organization name), E-MISC (End i.e., the last word of a multi-word miscellaneous name), I-PER (Internal part of person name of more than two words), I-LOC (Internal part of location name of more than two words), I-ORG (Internal part of organization name of more than two words), I-MISC (Internal part of miscellaneous name of more than two words) and NNE (Words that are not named entities).

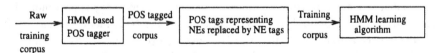

Fig. 3. Block Diagram of Model C of the NER System

Hidden Markov Model based Named Entity Tagging

The goal of NER is to find a stochastic optimal tag sequence $T = t_1, t_2, t_3, \ldots t_n$ that is optimal for a word sequence $W = w_1, w_2, w_3 \ldots w_n$. Generally, the most probable tag sequence is assigned to each sentence following the Viterbi algorithm [19]. The named entity tagging problem becomes equivalent to searching for $argmax_T P(T) * P(W|T)$, by the application of Bayes' law ($P(W)$ is constant).

We have used trigram model, i.e., the probability of a tag depends on two previous tags, and then we have, $P(T) = P(t_1) \times P(t_2|t_1) \times P(t_3|t_1, t_2) \times P(t_4|t_2, t_3) \times \ldots \times P(t_n|t_{n-2}, t_{n-1})$.

An additional tag '$' (dummy tag) has been introduced in this work to represent the beginning of a sentence. So, the previous probability equation can be slightly modified as: $P(T) = P(t_1|\$) \times P(t_2|\$, t_1) \times P(t_3|t_1, t_2) \times P(t_4|t_2, t_3) \times \ldots \times P(t_n|t_{n-2}, t_{n-1})$.

Due to sparse data problem, the linear interpolation method has been used to smooth the trigram probabilities as follows:
$P'(t_n|t_{n-2}, t_{n-1}) = \lambda_1 P(t_n) + \lambda_2 P(t_n|t_{n-1}) + \lambda_3 P(t_n|t_{n-2}, t_{n-1})$, such that the λs sum to 1. The values of λs have been calculated by the following method given in [6]:

1. set $\lambda_1 = \lambda_2 = \lambda_3 = 0$
2. for each trigram (t_1, t_2, t_3) with $freq(t_1, t_2, t_3) > 0$ depending on the maximum of the following three values:
   - case: $\frac{(freq(t_1, t_2, t_3) - 1)}{(freq(t_1, t_2) - 1)}$: increment λ_3 by $freq(t_1, t_2, t_3)$
   - case: $\frac{(freq(t_2, t_3) - 1)}{(freq(t_2) - 1)}$: increment λ_2 by $freq(t_1, t_2, t_3)$
   - case: $\frac{(freq(t_3) - 1)}{(N - 1)}$: increment λ_1 by $freq(t_1, t_2, t_3)$
3. normalize $\lambda_1, \lambda_2, \lambda_3$.

Here, N is the corpus size, i.e., the number of tokens present in the training corpus. If the denominator in one of the expression is 0, then the result of that expression is defined to be 0. The -1 in both the numerator and denominator has been considered for taking unseen data into account.

By making the simplifying assumption that the relation between a word and its tag is independent of context, we can simplify $P(W|T)$ as the following equation:
$P(W|T) \approx P(w_1|t_1) \times P(w_2|t_2) \times \ldots \times P(w_n|t_n)$.
The emission probabilities in the above equation can be calculated from the training set as, Emission Probability: $P(w_i|t_i) = \frac{freq(w_i|t_i)}{freq(t_i)}$.

Context Dependency

To make the Markov model more powerful, *additional context dependent feature* has been introduced to the emission probability that specifies the probability of the current word depends on the tag of the previous word and the tag to be assigned to the current word. Now, $P(W|T)$ is calculated by the following equation:
$P(W|T) \approx P(w_1|\$, t_1) \times P(w_2|t_1, t_2) \times \ldots \times P(w_n|t_{n-1}, t_n)$.

So, the emission probability can be calculated as: $P(w_i|t_{i-1}, t_i) = \frac{freq(t_{i-1}, t_i, w_i)}{freq(t_{i-1}, t_i)}$.
Here, also the smoothing technique is applied rather than using the emission probability directly. The emission probability is calculated as: $P'(w_i|t_{i-1}, t_i) = \theta_1 P(w_i|t_i) + \theta_2 P(w_i|t_{i-1}, t_i)$, where θ_1, θ_2 are two constants such that all θs sum to 1. The values of θs should be different for different words. But the calculation of θs for every word takes a considerable amount of time and hence θs are calculated for the entire training corpus. In general, the values of θs can be calculated by the same method that was adopted in calculating λs.

Handling the Unknown Words

Handling of unknown words is an important issue in NE tagging. Viterbi algorithm [19] attempts to assign a tag to the unknown words.

For words, which have not been seen in the training set, $P(w_i|t_i)$ is estimated based on features of the unknown words, such as whether the word contains a particular suffix. The list of suffixes has been prepared for Bengali. At present there are 435 suffixes; many of them usually appear at the end of different named entities (NEs) and non-NEs. A null suffix is also kept for those words that have none of the suffixes in the list. The probability distribution of a particular suffix with respect to specific tag is generated from all words in the training set that share the same suffix. Two additional features that cover the numbers and symbols have been considered also. To handle the unknown words further, a lexicon has been developed in an unsupervised way from the tagged Bengali news corpus. Lexicon contains the root words and their basic part of speech information such as: noun, verb, adjective, adverb, pronoun and indeclinable. At present, lexicon contains approximately 100,000 entries. If an unknown word is found in the lexicon, then most likely it is not a named entity.

17.3 Experimental Results of the NER System

Three different models of the NER system have been trained with the help of a training set of 62,280 wordforms. The training set is initially distributed into 6 subsets of equal size. In the open test, one subset is withheld for testing while the remaining 5 subsets are used as the training sets. This process is repeated 6 times to yield an average result, which is called the 6-fold open test or cross-validation test.

For HMM-based NER, the training set is run through a HMM-based part of speech (POS) tagger [10] to tag the training set with the 26 different POS tags [1], defined for the Indian languages. This POS-tagged training set is searched for some specific POS tags (NNPC [compound proper noun], NNP [proper noun] and QFNUM [cardinals and ordinals numbers]) that represent NEs. These POS tags are replaced by the appropriate NE tags as defined in Section 2.2. The confusion matrix obtained from our POS tagger suggests that most ambiguities occur between the proper nouns and the common nouns. So, additionally the POS tags (e.g., NNC [compound common noun], NN [common noun]) representing common nouns are checked for the correctness and replaced by the appropriate NE tags in the training set, if necessary. The training set thus obtained is a corpus, tagged with the sixteen NE tags (not NNE) and POS tags (not representing NEs). In the output, the POS tags are replaced by the NNE tag.

17.3.1 Evaluation Method

The Bengali NER system is evaluated in terms of Recall, Precision and F-Score. The three evaluation parameters are defined as follows:

$$\text{Recall (R)} = \frac{\text{No. of tagged NEs}}{\text{Total no. of NEs present in the corpus}} \times 100\ \%$$

$$\text{Precision (P)} = \frac{\text{No. of correctly tagged NEs}}{\text{No. of tagged NEs}} \times 100\%$$

$$\text{F-Score (FS)} = \frac{2 \times \text{Recall} \times \text{Precision}}{\text{Recall} + \text{Precision}} \times 100\%.$$

To evaluate Model A and Model B, each pattern of the *Accept Pattern* set is matched against the test set and the identified NEs are stored in the appropriate tables. One identified NE may be assigned more than one NE categories, i.e., the NE needs classification disambiguation. Model A cannot cope with this NE-classification disambiguation problem. Linguistic features, used in Model B, can tackle this problem. Once the actual category of a particular NE is established, it is removed from the other NE category tables. Some person, location, organization and miscellaneous names can be identified from the appropriate tags in the test set. A 6-fold cross-validation scheme is applied to evaluate Model C.

17.3.2 Discussion of Results

Results of the three different models have been represented in Table 1. It is observed from the results that Model C performs best with an average Recall, Precision and F-Score values of 89.62%, 78.47% and 83.63%, respectively. The reason behind the high

[1] http://shiva.iiit.ac.in/SPSAL2007/iiit_tagset_guidelines.pdf

Table 1. Results of six-fold cross-validation tests for three different NER models

Test Set	Model A			Model B			Model C		
	R	P	FS	R	P	FS	R	P	FS
Set1	75.50	66.50	70.71	77.50	73.50	75.45	88.10	77.90	82.69
Set2	76.40	68.30	72.12	79.40	76.30	77.82	89.80	78.30	83.66
Set3	74.98	69.40	72.08	80.98	75.40	78.09	90.43	79.40	84.56
Set4	77.67	69.80	73.52	79.90	73.80	76.73	90.19	77.90	83.60
Set5	76.50	70.40	73.32	81.30	75.40	78.24	90.80	78.40	83.90
Set6	76.30	70.20	73.12	78.80	73.90	76.27	88.40	78.90	83.38
Average	76.22	69.10	72.48	79.65	74.72	77.01	89.62	78.47	83.63

values of Recall, Precision and F-score parameters in Model C compared to Model A and Model B is that unlike models A and B, model C is not dependent on the context word. It has been observed that person names are surrounded by more contextual clues followed by organization and location names. The NEs appearing in the test set may not be identified by either the models A or B, if their contexts words do not match with any member of the *Accept Pattern* set. On the other hand, HMM-based NER calculates the tag of any word probabilistically during testing. These facts are reflected in the experimental results that show Model C performs uniformly for all NE types while Models A and B do not perform well for organization, location and miscellaneous names. Furthermore, Model C captures more generalization in terms of POS tags rather than Models A and B. The performance of this HMM-based NER system can further be improved by checking the POS-tagged training set manually, as POS tagging errors often lower the performance of this model. The use of linguistic NE features in Model B improves its performance over the *baseline* model, i.e., Model A.

17.4 Conclusion

We have presented a named entity recognizer for Bengali that uses three different approaches. A portion of the tagged Bengali news corpus, developed from the archive of a leading Bengali newspaper available in the web, has been used for the development of the NER models. We have shown that the NER system has high recall and good F-Score values with Hidden Markov Model framework.

Future works include investigating other methods to boost precision of the NER system. Building NER systems for Bengali using other statistical techniques like Maximum Entropy Markov Model (MEMM), Conditional Random Field (CRF) and analyzing the performance of these systems is another interesting task.

References

Babych, Bogdan, Hartley, A. (2003) Improving machine translation quality with automatic named entity recognition. In Proceedings of EAMT/EACL 2003 Workshop on MT and other language technology tools. pp. 1–8.

Bennet, Scott W., Aone, C., Lovell C. (1997) Learning to Tag Multilingual Texts Through Observation. In Proceedings of EMNLP. Providence, Rhode Island, pp. 109-116.

Bikel, Daniel M., Schwartz, R., Weischedel, Ralph, M. (1999) An Algorithm that Learns What's in Name. Machine Learning (Special Issue on NLP).1–20.

Borthwick, Andrew, Sterling, J., Agichtein, E., Grishman, R. (1998) NYU: Description of the MENE Named Entity System as Used in MUC-7. MUC-7. Fairfax, Virginia.

Borthwick, Andrew. (1999) A Maximum Entropy Approach to Named Entity Recognition. Ph.D. Thesis. New York University.

Brants, T. (2000) TnT: a statistical parts-of-speech tagger. In Proceedings of the sixth international conference on Applied Natural Language Processing, Seattle, WA, pp. 224–231.

Burger, John D., Henderson John C., Morgan, T. (2002) Statistical Named Entity Recognizer Adaption. In Proceedings of the CoNLL Workshop, Taiwan, pp. 163–166.

Carrears, Xavier, Marquez, Liuis, Padro, Liuis. (2002) Named Entity Recognition using AdaBoost. In Proceedings of the CoNLL Workshop, Taiwan, pp. 167–170.

Ekbal, A., Bandyopadhyay, S. (2006) A Web-based Tagged Bengali News Corpus. In Language Resources and Evaluation (Accepted).

Ekbal, A., Mandal, S., Bandyopadhyay, S. (2007) POS Tagging Using HMM and Rule Based Chunking. In Proceedings of the Workshop on Shallow Parsing for South Asian Languages (SPSAL), IJCAI 07, Hyderabad, India, pp. 31–34.

Chinchor, Nancy (1995) MUC-6 Named Entity Task Definition (Version 2.1). MUC-6, Columbia, Maryland.

Chinchor, Nancy (1998) MUC-7 Named Entity Task Definition (Version 3.5). MUC-", Fair fax, Virginia.

Cunningham, H. (2001) GATE: A general architecture for text engineering. Comput. Humanit. 36, 223–254.

Malouf, Robert. (2002) Markov models for language independent named entity recognition. In Proceed-ings of the CoNLL Workshop, Taipei, Taiwan, pp. 187–190.

McCallum, A., Li., W. (2003) Early Results for Named Entity Recognition with Conditional Random Fields, Feature Induction and Web-Enhanced Lexicons. In Proceedings of Seventh Conference on Natural Language Learning (CoNLL), Edmonton, Canada.

Miller, S., Crystal, M., Fox, H., Ramshaw, L., Schawartz, R., Stone, R., Weischedel, R., the Annotation Group. (1998) BBN: Description of the SIFT System as Used for MUC-7. MUC-7, Fairfax, Virginia.

Moldovan, Dan I., Harabagiu, Sanda M., Girju, Roxana, Morarescu, P., Lacatusu, V. F., Novischi, A., Badulescu, A., Bolohan, O. (2002) LCC Tools for Question Answering. In TREC, Maryland, pp. 1–10.

Sekine, Satoshi. (1998) Description of the Japanese NE System Used for MET-2. MUC-7, Fairfax, Virginia.

Viterbi, A. J. (1967) Error Bounds for Convolution Codes and an Asymptotically Optimum Decoding Algorithm. IEEE Transactions on Information Theory. 13, pp. 260–269.

Zhou, GuoDong, Su, Jian (2002) Named Entity Recognition using an HMM-based Chunk Tagger. In Proceedings of ACL, Philadelphia, pp. 473–480.

18 Comparison of Local and Global Thresholding for Binarization of Cheque Images

Narges Marashi[1], Jamshid Shanbezadeh[2]

[1]Islamic Azad University-Science and Research Branch, Tehran, Iran
N.marashi@seiau.ir
[2]Tarbiat Moalem University, Tehran, Iran
Jamshid@saba.tmu.ac.ir

Abstract: Binarization is the most important step in cheque processing. In most cases, cheques have complex background or low contrast. Therefore, we need to employ sophisticated algorithm to eliminate background of cheque and binarize it. There are two techniques for cheque binarization: global and local. This paper presents a novel binarization algorithm based on histogram modification and physical structure of cheques. This novel algorithm has been compared with two well known algorithms: Otsu and Background Subtraction. The comparison is based on the speed and precision of these three algorithms. The quality and precision of algorithm is measured by calculating the precision and recall of words in foreground. Simulations are performed on a database of cheque images obtained from 5 banks of Persian language. The simulation results show speed and precision improvement of novel algorithm in comparison with local and global algorithms.

Keywords: cheque processing, local thresholding, global thresholding, background elimination, binarization.

18.1 Introduction

Billions of cheques are processed every year. Cheque processing is a repetitive task that needs to be performed automatically. This process saves time and cost. The first step of cheque processing is segmentation. This step consists of background elimination and binarization (BEB), skew detection and correction, baseline detection and correction, restoration of lost data during the last steps, noise removal, detection of text blocks and separating printed words of handwritten words. BEB heavily affect the other steps involving cheque processing.

Two popular BEB techniques are thresholding and image subtraction. Most of BEB techniques of bank cheques are based on thresholding (a simple method of binarization). There are two thresholding strategies: local and global. In global thresholding, there is only one threshold value for the whole image but in local thresholding, image is partitioned and a threshold value is considered for each image partition.

In [1], Image Subtraction is found by subtracting the template image from the original image and the output image from the subtraction step is binarized by a threshold. The other method in global thresholding is called QIR (Quadratic Integral Ratio) which is done through two steps. First, there are three classes: background, foreground, and the other class is the fuzzy class that is not obvious as to which class it belongs. Next Step is for finding final threshold of this fuzzy region [2]. Yanowitz and Bruckstein detect threshold by grey level values and high gradient regions [3].

One of the best global thresholding techniques is Otsu's method that is based on histogram of grey level and maximizing variance between classes [4]. Some techniques work on optimization of Otsu's method. One of them uses Otsu's technique recursively. In every loop threshold (evaluated by Otsu's method) and separability factor (SF) are calculated. SF shows the probability of class separation with the lowest intensity. The loop will be finished provided that it is greater than a constant amount. [5].

There is a local thresholding that uses Otsu's method. In this algorithm window with an approximation size of a word is defined. It is a foreground pixel if local contrast is greater than threshold of Otsu's method and the pixel value is less than local mean [6]. One of the well-known local thresholding is Nibalck's method [7]. In this method local threshold is evaluated by local deviation multiplied with a constant and added with local mean. It is obvious that global thresholding has a high speed and local thresholding has a precise result. Purpose of this article is to introduce new thresholding technique that works well on both speed and accuracy.

18.2 Thresholding Method

We chose a global and local well known algorithm named as Otsu and Background subtraction to evaluate, compare our algorithm. Our test is focused on both speed and precision of three algorithms.

18.2.1 Binarization with Otsu's Method

In this method, there are two classes, background and foreground. Threshold is found by minimizing variance within classes and maximizing variance between classes. σ^2_w, σ^2_B and σ^2_T are variance of each class, variance between classes and variance of whole image.

$$\sigma^2_B + \sigma^2_W = \sigma^2_T \qquad (1)$$

σ^2_B and σ^2_W are dependent on threshold. If the number of pixels in gray level i is n_i and n is the number of pixels in image, Pi is the likelihood of occurrence gray level i and is defined as:

$$P_i = n_i / n \qquad (2)$$

ω_1 and ω_2 are the probability of two classes c_1 and c_2, μ_1 and μ_2 are the mean of these classes. l is the number of grey levels and t is threshold of image and is defined by maximizing σ^2_B (Equation 9)[4].

$$\omega_1(t) = \Sigma P_i \quad , i = 1{:}t \qquad (3)$$
$$\omega_2(t) = \Sigma P_i \quad , i = t{+}1{:}l \qquad (4)$$
$$\mu_1 = \Sigma\, i\, P_i / \omega_1(t) \ , i = 1{:}t \qquad (5)$$
$$\mu_2 = \Sigma\, i\, P_i / \omega_2(t) \ , i = 1{:}t{+}1{:}l \qquad (6)$$
$$\mu_T = \mu_1\, \omega_1 + \mu_2\, \omega_2 \ , \omega_1 + \omega_2 = 1 \qquad (7)$$
$$\sigma^2_B = \omega_1 (\mu_1 - \mu_T)2 + \omega_2 (\mu_2 - \mu_T)\,2 \qquad (8)$$
$$t^* = \text{Arg Max } \{\sigma^2_B(t)\} \ , 1{<}{=}t{<}l \qquad (9)$$

18.2.2 Background Subtraction (BS)

BS [11] is a good local thresholding technique for cheque images. This method is performed in several steps. First, important areas such as printed and handwritten words will be removed by using a morphological closing with a small disk structure element [9]. Then the image extracted from the pervious step is subtracted by the original image. Finally the threshold of the subtracted image will be evaluated by Otsu's method.

18.2.3 Proposed Method for Global Threshold

The proposed algorithm is used for optimization of thresholding. In this method we try to make use of structure of cheque. Our algorithm focused on the approximation number of pixels in foreground that is estimated through consideration of physical structure. This method consists of training and testing steps.

18.2.3.1. Training

3 cheque images of each bank cheque are applied for training step. It is better to choose images with high quality for training step in response of acquire the best result. Purpose of training is to find the percentage of pixels in foreground (PPF).

First, we try to find PPF that is capable of segmenting foreground and background pixels. Images are binarized by Otsu's method. It is better to find threshold by Background Subtraction if our cheques have complex background. Then numbers of pixels in foreground (NPF) are defined by summing foreground pixels (Value of foreground pixels in binary images with a white background are 0). It is easy to identify PPF from NPF (Equation 10).

$$PPF = NPF/\ Size\ of\ Image \qquad\qquad\qquad (10)$$

PPFs for 3 cheque images with the same structures are calculated. Mean of PPF (MPPF) is saved for testing step.

18.2.3.2 Testing

The reverse process of training is going to find threshold in the testing step. NPF is evaluated by equation 10 (PPF is replaced by MPPF that is saved from previous step). Optimized threshold is estimated during the histogram and cumsum calcula-tion steps. The final step is to find max of cumsum (I) that is equal or less than NPF (Equation 11). This equation can put up with changes in handwritten pixels because threshold will be optimized when cumsum (I) is less than NPF, cumsum (I) is not a constant and it varies in different cheques.

%Training
1) Find threshold by Background Subtraction method for 3 bank cheques with same physical structures
2) Numbers of pixels in foreground (NPF) of binarized images are found
3) Percentage of foreground pixels (PPF) is found with equation 10
4) Mean of PPF (MPPF) is evaluated

%Testing (Reverse of Training Step)
1) Estimate NPF with Equation 10 by replacing PPF with MPPF achieved of prior step
2) Threshold = max (find (cumsum (I) <NPF))

18.3 Experimental Results and Discussion

Our database consists of 150 cheque images on 5 different banks using Persian lan-guage. Cheque images are of different resolutions, sizes, and also of different con-trast in handwritings. Our Language programming is Matlab and all tests have been performed in the same condition (on a same computer). The standard criteria, preci-sion and recall [10], were used to compare the performance of the proposed method. Precision and Recall are defined as:

$$Pr\,ecision = \frac{Correctly\ Detected\ Words}{Totally\ Detected\ Words}$$

$$Re\,call = \frac{Correctly\ Detected\ Words}{Total\ Words}$$

Table1- Comparison speed of three algorithms on 150 cheque images on 5 different banks

	Background Subtraction	Otsu	Proposed Method
Refah	1.750444	0.07	0.031
Tejarat	1.8268	0.073	0.0357143
Mellat	1.855643	0.250375	0.04262
Keshaarzi	1.76125	0.05875	0.03
Melli	1.737214	0.036285	0.0365

Image No	1	2	3	4	5

Table2 -Recall and Precision of 10 cheque images

A1 – Otsu
A2 - Proposed Global Thresholding
A3 – Background subtraction

Pre ----- Precision
Rec ----- Recall

	Rec	Pre	Rec	Pre	Rec	Pre	Rec	Pre	Rec	Pre
A1	100	100	78	78	100	100	100	100	50	75
A2	100	100	78	78	100	100	100	100	100	100
A3	100	100	100	100	100	100	100	100	100	100

6		7		8		9		10		Average	
Rec	Pre	Rec	Pre	Rec	Pre	Rec	Pre	Rec	Pre	Rec	Pre
63	83	100	100	100	100	100	100	100	100	89	94
100	100	100	100	100	100	100	100	100	100	98	98
100	100	100	100	100	100	43	43	100	100	94	94

Table3 – Comparison of Precision and Recall of
Background subtraction and proposed method in database

	Averge Preci-sion1	Averge Rcall 1	Average Preci-sion2	Average Recall2	Final Average Precision	Final Average Recall
Background Subtraction	0.96	0.95	0.79	0.79	0.88	0.87
Proposed Global Alg	0.92	0.86	0.96	0.96	0.94	0.9

18.4 Conclusion

Using of histogram is a common step in both proposed algorithm and Otsu's method. In our method the calculation of histogram takes almost 95% of the time of processing whereas there are too many parameters to evaluate in Otsu's method (μ, ω, σ^2_B). Therefore Our method is performed faster than a fast method like Otsu (Table1).On the other hand Otsu can not distinguish the background from fore-ground in a cheque with complex background (figure 1.1 and 1.2), But our method is capable of dealing with this type of cheques (Figure 3). BS is compared with 4 well known algorithm: Niblack [7], Mean_Gradient [11], Quadratic Integral Ratio [8], Yanowitz and Bruckstein [3]. BS operates satisfactorily in comparison with these 4 methods especially in binarizaion of cheques [11]. Results indicate that our method is superior in both speed and precision against BS and Otsu's algorithm (Table 1~3).

Speed of 3 algorithms has identified in Table1. Images of 5 different banks with dissimilar background are produced for database. Refah, Tejarat, Mellat, Keshavarzi and Melli are the banks that made our database. We can find from table1 that local thresholding technique (BS) has a low speed. Low speed is relevant to local thresh-olding nature. The strength of our method is related with training. The proposed technique has ability to understand the structure of cheques by training step, But the two methods (BS an Otsu's) have no idea about construction of image. They are all_ purposed methods.

Images used in table2 are 10 cheque images that have been selected randomly from database to evaluate accuracy of algorithms. As it is observable Background Subtraction has a better precision in compare with Otsu's method. The proposed algorithm is dependent to structure and consequently low resolution or quality are not affected to this type of method. BS and specially Otsu's method do not have a wide view point of organization of images, as a result if the resolution or quality of image is not prepared properly, it will be a bad reflection on algorithms.

Precision and recall of two accurate methods, Background Subtraction and proposed algorithm are calculated in table 3.Database used in this part is consisting of two databases of cheque images from two different bank cheques.

References

[1] Alessandro L. Koerich, Lee Luan Ling (1998) A System for Automatic Extraction of the User–Entered Data from Bank checks in International Symposium on Computer Graphics, Vision and Image Processing (SIBIGRAPI), Rio de Janeiro, Brazil, pp.270-277

[2] Y.Solihin, C.G.Leedham(1999) Integral Ratio: A New class of Global Thresholding Techniques for Handwriting Images in IEEE Trans. PAMI, vol.21, no. 8, pp. 761-768, August.

[3] S.D. Yanowitz and A.M. Bruckstein (1989) A new method for image segmentation in Computer Vision, Graphics and Image Processing, vol. 46, no. 1, pp. 82-95, Apr

[4] N. Otsu. (1978) A threshold selection method from gray-scale histogram in IEEE Trans. on Systems Man & Cybern., volume SMC-8, pages 62-66.

[5] Zheng Lee(2001) A fast way to locate the item regions of grey level images of cheques in A thesis presented partial fulfillment of the requirements for the degree of master of Computer Science Concordia University Montreal, Quebec, Canada

[6] Xiangyun Ye, Mohamed Cheriet, Ching Y. Suen1, Ke Liu, (1999) Extraction of bank-check items by mathematical morphology in IJDAR International Journal on Document Analysis and Recognition, 2: 53{66

[7] W. Niblack (1986) An Introduction to Digital Image Processing, pp. 115-116, Prentice Hall.

[8] Ping-Sung liao, Tse-Sheng Chen, Pau-Choo Chung (2001) A Fast Algorithm for Multi-level Thresholding in Journal of Information Science and Engineering 17, 713-727

[9] R.C. Gonzalez, and R.E. Woods (2002) Digital Image Processing, pp 554-555 in Prentice-Hall, New Jersey.

[10] M. Junker, R. Hoch (1999) On the Evaluation of Document Analysis Components by Recall, Precision, and Accuracy in Proc. Of 5th ICDAR, India, pp. 713-716.

[11] Graham Leedham, Chen Yan, Kalyan Takru, Joie Hadi Nata Tan and Li Mian (2003) Comparison of Some Thresholding Algorithms for Text/Background Segmentation in Difficult Document Images in Seventh International Conference on Document Analysis and Recognition (ICDAR 2003) 0-7695-1960-1/03, IEEE

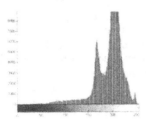

Fig 1-2. cheque Image with simple background

Fig 1-1. cheque Image with complex background

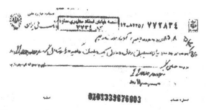

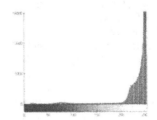

Fig 2-1. Histogram of cheque image with complex background(image 1.1)

Fig. 2-2. Histogram of cheque image with simple background(image 1.2)

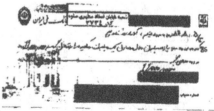

Fig. 3-1. proposed method

Fig. 3-2. Otsu's method

Fig. 4-1. proposed method

Fig. 4-2. Background Subtraction method

19 Reading out 2D Barcode PDF417

Michael Trummer[1] and Joachim Denzler[2]

[1] Friedrich Schiller University of Jena, Chair for Computer Vision, Ernst-Abbe-Platz 2, 07743 Jena, Germany, trummer@informatik.uni-jena.de
[2] Friedrich Schiller University of Jena, Chair for Computer Vision, Ernst-Abbe-Platz 2, 07743 Jena, Germany, denzler@informatik.uni-jena.de

Abstract. Reading devices for 2D barcodes based on laser scanning hardware are widely spread. But for certain applications it is necessary to detect and read out such a barcode by means of an CCD camera. When reading a barcode from an image, special problems, caused by poor printing quality, document condition or reflections, must be handled. This paper shows possibilities to overcome these problems and proposes a clear hierarchical procedure to robustly read out a 2D barcode PDF417 from an adequate camera image.

19.1 Introduction

Two-dimensional barcodes as PDF417 have gained importance in many applications like identification and data management tasks. One such symbol offers a data capacity up to 2710 digits, 1850 text characters or 1108 bytes, respectively, and allows various error correction levels (cf. specification (AIM 2001)). Since the use of such code symbols is obligatory for certain identification documents (covered by specification (ICAO 2005)), a method has been developed to read out these kind of symbols in cooperation with the Cross Match Technologies GmbH. In the context of this paper, reading out means the image processing task to establish the binary matrix belonging to a barcode symbol, and not to decode the contained information. The source images are taken with a three megapixel CCD camera installed inside of a document reading device with controlled illumination.

Searching publications for relevant previous work points out lots of patents protecting reading devices as well as many commercial homepages offering black-box solutions. (Ottaviani, Pavan, Bottazzi, Brunelli, Caselli, and Guerrero 1999) show a general framework for the image processing task. But, regarding actual procedures for reading out barcode PDF417 from digital images, there is no literature, yet.

The remainder of this paper is organized as follows. Section 2 shows the architecture of a PDF417 symbol in a comprehensive manner. The actual reading procedure is being described in section 3. Practical results are demonstrated in section 4. Section 5 gives a summary of the proposed procedure and of the results.

19.2 Code Architecture

This sections shows the structure of a PDF417 symbol and introduces necessary terminology. In accordance to (AIM 2001), barcode *symbol* means the whole barcode as shown in Fig. 1.

A PDF417 symbol can be seen as a matrix of *codewords* (Fig. 1 (b)). Each codeword consists of 17 binary elements, the *modules*. Within a codeword, the 17 modules are arranged in four bars (black parts) and four spaces (white parts). Each bar and each space contains one to six modules. A PDF417 symbol is composed of defined *start* and *stop patterns* and the *data region* in between. For illustration of the components see Fig. 1. The last barcode column is always blinded out for privacy purposes.

Fig. 1. Example for PDF417 symbol. Start and stop pattern (a,c) and one codeword (b).

The marked codeword (b) in Fig. 1 indicates, what *rows* and *columns* are in a PDF417 barcode symbol (since it is the crossing of a row and a column). The first module of each codeword is black, the last one is white, whereby column separation is guaranteed. To ensure separability of rows, codewords of consecutive rows belong to different disjoint subsets of all possible codewords. Thus, it is impossible to have two identical codewords among each other within a PDF417 symbol.

The next section shows how this knowledge about the symbol structure can be used to establish the symbol reader and improve its robustness.

19.3 Reading Procedure

The characteristics of a symbol's architecture are incorporated into the reading procedure in the following, hierarchical manner. The overall target is to transform the data region into a grid of appropriate dimensions in order to decide for each module by integrating within the respective grid field. Thus, the approach uses the matrix structure of the code symbol.

First, the barcode symbol has to be located within the source image containing at most one barcode symbol. This is achieved by contour analysis aiming at the start and stop pattern. Within the cut image region (containing the whole barcode symbol), a rectification is performed to yield the rows horizontal and the columns vertical. These properties can then be utilized to analyze the numbers of rows and columns as well as the positions by x- and y-histograms. Finally, this information allows to establish the desired grid within the rectified symbol image and to decide for each grid field, if the underlying module is black or white.

19.3.1 Finding the Barcode Symbol

The first step performs a contour search and analysis in order to find the start and stop pattern of a PDF417 symbol that consist of two kinds of elements. These are wide (see Fig. 2, a) and thin (Fig. 2, b) rectangles. With respect to runtime efficiency, candidate contours are rated hierarchically. A contour is classified as an element of the start or stop pattern only if the contour has the following features: it is closed; contour length and area are within certain boundaries (depending on resolution parameters); the height-width-ratio is not wider than square; the corresponding region has the overall shape of a rectangle, considering noise and distortion. This last feature is being checked by a fitting method using region moments (Voss and Suesse 1997).

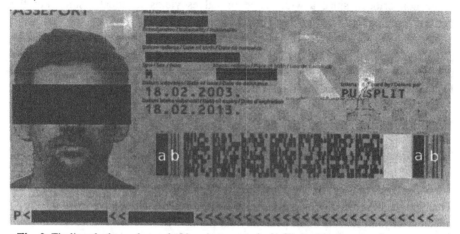

Fig. 2. Finding the barcode symbol by contour analysis. Elements of start and stop pattern marked, wide (a) and thin (b) rectangles.

With the known positions of the start and the stop pattern, the image region containing the barcode symbol can be extracted accurately. Thus, the cut barcode region endows a new image. An interesting characteristic of this approach is that only one element of the start and the stop pattern, respectively, needs to be found to ensure the correct extraction of the symbol region.

19.3.2 Rectification

The barcode frequently appears slightly rotated in the source image. Further distorting effects can be non-linear distortions caused by some bending of the document, a lamination sheet or poor printing quality. By performing a projective transformation of the actual barcode corners to the image corners of the cut image, rotation can be balanced and the other disturbing effects can be smoothed. This transformation (homography) is calculated from the mappings of four image points (actual corner points of the barcode symbol mapped to image corners) by singular value decomposition as described in (Hartley and Zisserman 2002). Here, the crucial task is to find the actual corner points of the symbol. To do so, at first the convex contour of the barcode symbol is computed. This contour shows a rectangular shape, where corners can be identified by a local corner measure. Given one contour point, the coordinates of the next i points in both directions are observed, and the x- and y-intervals covered by this part of the contour. The size of these intervals is denoted by dx_1, dy_1 for the next contour points in one direction of x, and dx_2, dy_2 for the next points in the other direction. The local corner measure m_x in point x is given by

$$m_x = |dx_1 - dx_2| + |dy_1 - dy_2|. \tag{1}$$

This measure reaches its maximum, if the two contour tails at point x are perpendicular to each other and parallel to the image axes. Evaluating the corner measure from Equation 1 for each contour point yields four clear local maxima along the contour indicating the barcode corners. The number i of contour points to be considered on each side surely depends on the image resolution. But this parameter has proven to be non critical, since a wide range of values yields identical results. For the present application, $i = 25$ has been chosen.

Once the barcode symbol corners are located, it is possible to calculate and to apply a homography mapping the barcode corners to the image corners of the cut barcode image. This yields a new image of the barcode symbol without margins, ideally, and with axially parallel rows and columns of the barcode matrix.

19.3.3 Detecting Barcode Rows

The rectified image of the PDF417 symbol shows the barcode rows in horizontal orientation. This fact is utilized for detecting the barcode rows.

The main idea is not to detect barcode rows, but the transitions between the rows. This approach is induced by the fact that codewords of consecutive rows belong to different disjoint subsets of all possible codewords. Thus, codewords of one column and consecutive rows differ in at least one module. If we consider a vertical scan line leading through these differing modules, the transition between the two rows is being detected as an alternation between black and white (object and background). In order to achieve robust detection, the vertical scan line is moved through the image, and detected alternations are cumulated in an y-histogram (see Fig. 3).

Fig. 3. Y-histogram of detected vertical alternations (left). Detected row transitions (right).

The histogram in Fig. 3 shows clear peaks indicating row transitions. The non zero values between the peaks are due to image noise and interpolation effects associated with the homography. The peak identification is solved by using the method of (Otsu 1979), that is applied to the y-histogram of the histogram in Fig. 3.

After this step, the number of barcode rows is known as well as the positions of the upper and lower borders of each row.

19.3.4 Detecting Barcode Columns

The information about column number and positions defines the second dimension of the desired grid for reading out the barcode symbol. The column detection regards the fact that each codeword starts with a black module and ends with white one. For barcode columns follows that each has a stack of black modules on the left and of white modules on the right side. Consequently, the beginning of a barcode column can be identified uniquely. This yields an easy decision rule based on the x-histogram of object pixels (see Fig. 4).

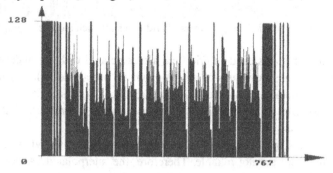

Fig. 4. X-histogram of object pixels.

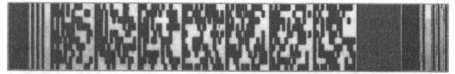

Fig. 5. Candidate positions for starting barcode columns (light) and detected columns (dark).

Exploring the histogram from Fig. 4, each peak preceded by a zero value is a candidate position for a starting column. In practice, the criteria (peak height, "zero" value, distance between "zero" and peak position) have to be softened in order to handle noisy and distorted images. From the list of candidate positions, the actual column positions need to be chosen. First, the maximum distance between two consecutive candidate positions is computed. In accordance to the code architecture, this maximum distance is equal to the column width of the barcode symbol. Starting in the list at the position of this first column found, the further column positions to the left and to the right are computed. The result is shown in Fig.5. The start and stop patterns can be identified as non valid columns (not inside the data region) by the large rectangles.

At this point, column number and positions are available.

19.3.5 Reading out the Barcode Symbol

At this stage of processing, all the necessary information for aligning a grid with the barcode data region is given. In fact, the borders of each single module can be calculated using the information yielded in former processing steps. Upper and lower module borders are given by the respective row borders. Left and right borders can be calculated from the respective column borders, whereby each column is divided into 17 equal sub-columns (the module stacks). For the example image, the center of each grid field is highlighted in Fig. 6. Each grid field is used to determine the state (black/white) of one module.

Fig. 6. Rectified barcode image. Centers of grid fields for each module highlighted.

Now, the image pixels inside a grid field are associated with the underlying barcode module. For this, the values of all the pixels within a grid field are taken into account. The intermediate result is a double-value matrix containing the mean values of the grid fields. Due to the mentioned distortions and to discretization, this matrix is in general not binary.

The conclusive step could be a simple binarization. But it is obvious that values close to the threshold are not reliable. Therefore, the interpolated value of the grid field center (cf. Fig. 6) is assigned to grid fields with a mean value close to the binarization threshold. Within the application, grid fields with mean values within 10% above or below interval mean are treated in this way. Afterwards, the final result is given as a binary matrix like in Fig. 7.

Fig. 7. Final result as binary matrix.

In comprehension, an orthogonal grid is established using information computed from the source image (rows, columns). The barcode image is transformed into this grid, and the state of each module is estimated by integrating within each grid field and by deciding with the help of extended binarization (see preceding paragraph).

The next section will give information about testing results.

19.4 Practical Results

A database of hundreds of real-world barcode images was available for testing and visual inspection. But since this database lacks ground-truth data and since manual labeling is still under construction, this collection does not allow comprehensive tests, yet. Therefore, *module recognition rate r* (rate of correctly classified binary elements) against image noise has been tested systematically by means of a synthetic barcode image (20 rows, 10 columns, module resolution 3x12 pixels). The image noise on the 8-bit gray values has been modeled as *Gaussian noise with standard deviation* σ . For some images the procedure was unable to detect the correct dimensions (rows, columns) of the barcode symbol. The *percentage of rejected images e* and the recognition results of images not rejected are presented in Table 1 (30 images generated and tested for each value of σ).

σ	10	20	30	40	50	60	70	80	90	100
e (%)	0	0	0	0	0	0	6.67	3.34	13.34	16.67
r (%)	100.00	100.00	100.00	99.97	99.86	99.77	99.58	99.02	98.73	97.68

Table 1. Test Results. Percentage e of rejected barcodes. Module recognition rate r (within the barcode images not rejected) against Gaussian noise, standard deviation σ.

As a further hint at the procedure's performance, Fig. 8 gives an example of a low quality barcode image and the achieved recognition rate. The processing time of this image is about 300 msec on a 3 GHz PentiumIV.

Fig. 8. Example with low contrast, geometric distortions and low resolution. $r = 97.7\%$

In conclusion, not only the impressions from visual inspection and from the practical application, but the results of systematic tests and of worst case analysis underline the procedure's robustness against the mentioned kinds of distortions.

19.5 Summary

This paper proposed a procedure that solves the image processing task of reading out a 2D barcode symbol PDF417. It has been demonstrated, how the special knowledge about the code architecture can be used to yield a robust hierarchical solution for this problem. Practical experiments have been carried out to prove the procedure's capability to handle noticeable amounts of image noise, distortions and other inhibiting circumstances. The according software has already been installed on commercial document reading devices.

References

AIM Association for Automatic Identification and Mobility, Uniform Symbology Specification PDF417, ISO/IEC 15438:2001

ICAO International Civil Aviation Organization (2005), Machine Readable Travel Documents, Sixth Edition, ISO/IEC 7501:2005

Ottaviani, E., Pavan, A., Bottazzi, M., Brunelli, E., Caselli, F. and Guerrero, M. (1999) A common image processing framework for 2D barcode reading, *Proc. of 7th International Conference on Image Processing and Its Applications*, vol. 2, pp. 652-655

Voss, K. and Suesse, H. (1997) Invariant Fitting of Planar Objects by Primitives, *IEEE Trans. on Pattern Analysis and Machine Intelligence*, vol. 19, no. 1, pp. 80-84

Hartley, R. and Zisserman, A. (2002), Multiple View Geometry in Computer Vision, Second Edition, *Cambridge University Press*, Cambridge, p. 91

Otsu, N. (1979) A threshold selection method from grey level histograms, *IEEE Trans on Systems, Man, and Cybernetics*, vol. 9, pp. 62-66

20 Off-Line Hand-Written Farsi/Arabic Word Segmentation into Subword under Overlapped or Connected Conditions

Maryam Rastegarpour[1], Jamshid Shanbezadeh[2]

[1]Islamic Azad University-Science and Research Branch, Tehran, Iran,
Rastegarpour@iau-saveh.ac.ir
[2]Tarbiat Moalem University, Tehran, Iran
Jamshid@saba.tmu.ac.ir

Abstract: Segmentation is a fundamental step in character recognition, since it affects recognition accuracy, speed, and dictionary size. A critical problem in segmenting handwritten text is the recognition of overlapping or connecting characters that comes from handwriting style rather than the language grammar. Up to now, no solution has been proposed for these conditions and, this paper presents a simple, fast and accurate solution based on modification of the Projection Profile. This scheme partitions a handwritten word into subwords under one or two conditions: connected, overlapped or both conditions simultaneously. Simulations have been performed on a set containing 700 words from standard IFN/ENIT database. The simulation results show 92.56 percents accuracy and a reasonable speed when compared with the Connected Components method.

Keywords: Optical Character Recognition, Segmentation, Farsi/Arabic text Recognition, Handwritten Text Recognition, Projection Profile

20.1 Introduction

The progress of information technology and, the increased call for information result in high demand for text documents containing information. Despite the use of electronic documents, the amount of printed or handwritten documents has never been decreased. It is very complicated and expensive to store and retrieve the ever increasing documents. On the other hand, electronic documents have several advantages in storage, retrieval, search and updating. Text Document Image Analysis (TDIA) covers the algorithms to transform text documents into electronic format. Every language has its own characteristics and this affects TDIA. The important characteristics of Farsi/Arabic language words, that make its text recognition difficult, include character connectivity and different shape for characters depending on their locations in the word (Khorsheed 2002; Lorigo and Govindaraju 2006; Safabakhsh and Adibi 2005).

Text recognition can be online or offline and performed for handwritten or machine printed texts. Offline Handwritten Text Recognition (OHTR) has more applications including bank check processing, office automation, form processing and similar ones. These wide ranges of applications necessitate the implementation of systems for OHTR, which is the most difficult one, since handwriting depends on the writer, font, text line direction, words' and subwords' connectivity and overlapping. All these problems should be overcome during preprocessing via segmentation algorithms (Al-Rashaideh 2006; Boushofa and Spann 1997; Hamid and Harati 2001; Mansour, Benkhadda, and Benyettou 2005; Lorigo and Govindaraju 2006; Olivier, Miled, Romeo, and Lecourtier 1996; Safabakhsh and Adibi 2005; Sari, Souici, and Sellami 2002; Touj, Amara, and Amiri 2002; Zahour, Taconet, Mercy, and Ramdane 2001).

Figure 1 illustrates the block diagram of an OHTR system. The first step is obtaining an image of a document from the text with a scanner. The second step is the pre-processing to remove the artifacts from the scanned image. The third step segments the document into basic elements. The basic elements can be subwords or characters depending on the employed approach, which is analytical or holistic. We have to segment a word into characters where there are infinite numbers of words for recognition. Otherwise, we can segment the words into subwords. After segmentation, we have to extract features from the basic elements. The extracted features are the inputs of the recognition section.

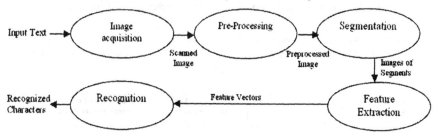

Fig. 1. Text Document Recognition System

The focus of this paper is on segmenting words into subwords. Here for simplicity, we assume that the required pre-processing step has been performed successfully and all we need is to segment words into subwords. Figure 2 illustrates three situations of two adjacent subwords: separated, overlapped or connected. The simultaneous occurrence of the last two situations is an unsolved problem for Farsi/Arabic text recognition system.

The segmentation consists of two phases: the horizontal and the vertical one. The roles of these two are partitioning text into rows and rows into words and then subwords respectively. The horizontal projection is employed in horizontal segmentation (Elgammal and Ismail 2001; Lorigo and Govindaraju 2005; Sari, Souici, and Sellami 2002; Sarfraz, Nawaz, and Al-Khuraidly 2003; Zheng, Hassin, and Tang 2004). There are two approaches for vertical segmentation: statistical and structural (Khorsheed 2002; Lorigo and Govindaraju 2006). While using the vertical projection, the two most difficult parts of segmentation are facing overlapped subwords or connected subwords as shown in Fig. 2. Up to now, there has been no solution for connectivity situations. Table 1 presents an example where the vertical Projection Profile and the Connected Component analyses fail in recognizing segmentation points of adjacent subwords. This paper focuses on these and solves the overlapping and connectivity problems.

The rest of this paper is as follows: next section explains the new segmentation algorithm, section 4 and 5 present the results and conclusion, section 6 talks about future research, and the final section is acknowledgments.

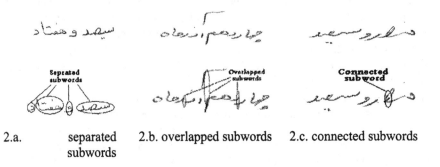

2.a.   separated   2.b. overlapped subwords   2.c. connected subwords
              subwords

Fig. 2. Three types of subwords: separated, overlapped, and connected.

Table 1. The vertical Projection Profile and the Connected Component analyses fail to find segmentation points facing with overlapped or connected adjacent subwords shown with indicators.

Words' conditions	Input image	Output based on vertical projection profile	Output based on component analysis
1. Without overlapped and connected subwords			
2. With overlapped subwords without connected subwords			
3. With overlapped and connected subwords			
Results	---	Fails in the second and third types of words	Fails in the third types of words

20.2 Modified Projection Profile

Every Farsi/Arabic word may consist of one to several subwords. Figure 3 shows three words. The wide dark line shows the boundary between words and the dashed lines separate the subwords. The modified Projection Profile will solve the segmentation problem facing with adjacent overlapped or connected subwords. A modification of the Projection Profile has been successfully applied to remove the text skewness (Al-Rashaideh 2006). Here, for the first time we employ it for word segmentation.

Fig. 3. Three words and their corresponding subwords. The wide lines separate words and the dashed lines separate the subwords of one word.

We start rotating each line of words and generating the vertical Projection after each rotation and, mark those places with amplitude less than a threshold. Our experiments show that the best threshold, the rotation degree, and the final rotation degree are 5 pixels, 5 and 70 degrees respectively. The rotation is performed counter clock wise. After finding the segmentation points, we segment the word and rotate the segments in reverse direction to obtain the original form of segments. Figure 4 presents the pseudo code of new algorithm and, Figure 5 illustrates the output of algorithm on a sample word.

```
For each subword do
 Begin
    T1=0;
    T2=70;
    Threshold=5
    theta=T1;
    While (theta<=T2) do
       Begin
       Rotate the image with the theta angle in a counterclockwise direction;
       Obtain the vertical Projection for the rotated image;
          Search for a point with an amplitude less than Threshold in
       the vertical Projection as a segmentation point.
       If the segmentation point is found then
          The employed theta for that rotation is optimal.
          /* the optimum theta is found */
          Segment the input image to reach the segmentation point;
          Break;
       Else
          Enlarge theta five degrees to obtain optimal theta i.e.:
          theta = theta+5;
    End; /*while*/
    If previous loop doesn't segment
       Repeat again loop with a clockwise direction;
 End; /*for*/
```

Fig. 4. Pseudo code of new algorithm

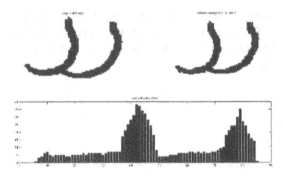

Fig. 5. The output of segmentation algorithm on a sample word after a 5 degree rotation

In situations where we can not find the segmentation points in the counterclockwise direction, we have to perform the algorithm in the clockwise direction to find the segmentation point. See fig.6.

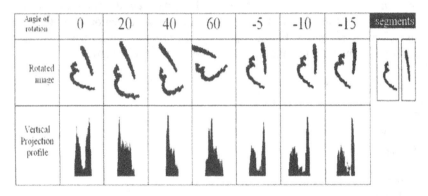

Fig. 6. Runs of the simulation of the proposed algorithm until the segments are obtained

This algorithm works well under these conditions: words containing dot, noisy words, and askew words. Figure 7 shows examples of these conditions. Figure 7.a shows that a word with dots has been successfully partitioned into subwords. Figure 7.b shows the same word contaminated with noise and the extracted subwords are the same as the noise-free image. Figure 7.c shows the rotated version of the image in Figure 7.a and, the same result as shown in Fig. 7.a is obtained.

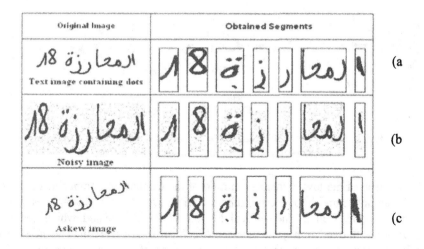

Fig. 7. Application of new algorithm on the images with dots, noise and skewness

20.3 Results

We have performed our experiments on the standard database IFN/ENIT (Pechwitz, Maddouri, Maergner, Ellouze, and Amiri 2002). This database contains about 26400 handwritten Arabic words containing more than 210000 characters written by 411 people on forms and includes the name of cities, villages, and streets of Tunisia. It is designed for training and testing recognition systems for handwritten Arabic words and is available for the purpose of research.

We have chosen 700 word images that consist of overlapped or connected subwords (or both of them) with all possible orientations between 10 to 70 degrees that are difficult to segment. These images are different in size and skewness. They are pre-processed in advance, so there is no need to do some operations from pre-processing stage such as size normalisation and noise removal. You can see a sample of this database in fig. 8 that has both overlapped and connected subword shown with dashed circles.

This algorithm has been implemented in Matlab environment and tested on 700 words chosen from IFN/ENIT database. The average accuracy rate is about 92.56. Table 2 shows the results of proposed algorithm under four conditions; noise, skew, secondary strokes, and without these conditions. In simulations, we employed salt and pepper noise with 0.06 probabilities. Secondary strokes are those parts of alphabetical characters which are apart from the main body such as dots, diacritics, and so on. Figure 8 shows examples of secondary strokes with normal circles.

Secondary
strokes

Overlapped
subwords

Connected
subwords

Fig. 8. A sample of IFN/ENIT database with connected and overlapped subwords in dashed circles, and secondary strokes in normal circles

The reason of the low segmentation ratio of the Connected Components method is it can not segment connecting subwords (however it can segment overlapping subwords), as well as the vertical Projection Profile method which can not segment both overlapping and connecting subwords. For more understanding see table 1 again. It must be mentioned that the reason of the non-segmentation ratio of the Connected Components method in facing the noise is it declares a noise point as a segment. It is independent on skewness and secondary strokes, so it can segment about half of subword images (i.e. overlapping subwords) of employed database.

Table 2. Results of the proposed algorithm under four conditions and comparison between it and the other algorithms

Condition / Algorithm	Noise	skew	Secondary strokes	Without these conditions
New algorithm	90.73	92.23	87.45	92.56
vertical Projection Profile	none	none	none	none
Connected Components	Almost nothing	50.00	50.00	50.00

20.4 Conclusion

This paper presents a novel algorithm in order to segment words into subwords under conditions in which adjacent subwords are overlapped and connected. This algorithm is robust under noisy condition and askew words. The accuracy of this algorithm has been measured on standard database IFN/ENIT and shows about 92.56 percents accuracy. The other segmentation algorithms, the vertical Projection Profile and the Connected Component analyses, are unable to perform segmentation.

20.5 Future research

We would like to test the algorithm and improve the algorithm under more complicated conditions and find methods for optimum threshold values. Meanwhile, constructing a standard database for Farsi words will extend the area of our algorithm's applications.

20.6 Acknowledgments

We would like to appreciate the managers of IFN/ENIT database, for their cooperation in providing us with the database and the relevant papers, and Dr. Ali Broumandnia for his help during testing the algorithm.

References

Al-Rashaideh, H. (2006) Preprocessing phase for Arabic Word Handwritten Recognition. Tom. 6, no. 1, Cmp. pp. 11-19.

Bushofa, B.M.F. and Spann, M. (1997) SEGMENTATION OF ARABIC CHARACTERS USING THEIR CONTOUR INFORMATION. Proc. of 13th International Conference on Digital Signal Processing, DSP 97. Vol. 2, pp. 683-686.

Elgammal, A.M. and Ismail, M.A. (2001) A Graph-Based Segmentation and Feature Extraction Framework for Arabic Text Recognition. Proc. of Sixth International Conference on Document Analysis and Recognition, IEEE, pp. 622-626.

Hamid, A. and Haraty, R. (2001) A Neuro-Heuristic Approach for Segmenting Handwritten Arabic Text. ACS/IEEE International Conference on Computer Systems and Applications (AICCSA'01), pp. 110-113.

Khorsheed, M.S. (2002) Off-Line Arabic Character Recognition – A Review. Pattern Analysis & Applications, Springer London, vol. 5, num. 1, pp. 31-45.

Lorigo, L.M. and Govindaraju,V. (2006) Off-line Arabic Handwriting Recognition: A Survey. IEEE transaction on pattern analysis and machine intelligence, Vol. 28, Issue 5, pp. 712- 724.

Lorigo, L. and Govindaraju, V. (2005) Segmentation and Pre-Recognition of Arabic Handwriting. In Proc. Eighth International Conference on Document Analysis and Recognition (ICDAR'05), Seoul, Korea, vol. 2, pp. 605-609.

Mansour, M., Benkhadda, M. and Benyettou, A. (2005) Optimized Segmentation Techniques for Handwritten Arabic Word and Numbers Character Recognition. IEEE SITIS, pp. 96-101.

Olivier, G., Miled, H., Romeo K. and Lecourtier, Y. (1996) Segmentation and Coding of Arabic Handwritten Words. In Proc. 13th International Conference on Pattern Recognition (ICPR '96), vol. 3, pp. 264-268.

Pechwitz, M.S., Maddouri, S., Maergner, V., Ellouze, N. and H. Amiri (2002) IFN/ENIT – database of handwritten Arabic words. In Proc. of CIFED 2002, Hammamet, Tunisia, pp. 129-136.

Safabakhsh, R. and Adibi, P. (2005) NASTAALIGH HAND WRITTEN WORD RECOGNITION USING A CONTINUOUS-DENSITY VARIABLE-DURATION HMM. The Arabian Journal for Science and Engineering, Volume 30, Number 1B, pp. 95-118.

Sarfraz, M., Nawaz S.N. and Al-Khuraidly, A. (2003) Offline Arabic Text Recognition system. Proc. of the 2003 International Conference on Geometric Modeling and Graphics (GMAG'03), pp. 30-35.

SARI, T., SOUICI, L. and SELLAMI, M. (2002) Off-line Handwritten Arabic Character Segmentation Algorithm: ACSA. Proc. of the Eighth International Workshop on Frontiers in Handwriting Recognition (IWFHR'02), Niagara-on-the-lake Ontario, Canada, pp. 452-457.

Touj, S.M. Ben Amara, N. Amiri, H. (2002) Segmentation stage of PHMM-based model for off-line recognition of arabic handwritten city names. International Conference on Systems, Man and Cybernetics, 2002 IEEE, vol. 4, pp. 5-9.

Zahour, A., Taconet, B., Mercy, P. and Ramdane S. (2001) Arabic Hand-Written Text-Line Extraction. In Proc. of Sixth. Int. Conference on Document Analysis and Recognition, ICDAR 2001, Seattle, USA, pp. 281-285.

Zheng, L., Hassin A.H. and Tang, X. (2004) A new algorithm for machine printed Arabic Character segmentation. Pattern Recognition Letters 25, Elsevier Science Inc., vol. 2, Issue 15, pp. 1723–1729.

21 Iris Biometrics Algorithm for Low Cost Devices

Judith Liu-Jimenez[1], Ana Ramirez-Asperilla[2], Almudena Lindoso[1], Raul Sanchez-Reillo[1]

Electronic Technology Dpt.
Universidad Carlos III de Madrid,
C/ Butarque 15
28911 Leganes, Madrid, Spain
[1]{jliu, alindoso, rsreillo}@ing.uc3m.es
[2]100025117@alumnos.uc3m.es

Abstract. One of the most emerging applications of pattern recognition is Biometrics. Security is becoming one of major concerns in many companies and daily situations. Iris Biometrics has proved to be one of the best Biometric techniques as it presents low false rates and high performance results. In this paper, an algorithm for performing Iris Identification for low cost devices is described. Results obtained demonstrate the algorithm feasibility and the possibility of implementing it in low cost devices thanks to its simplicity, which avoids the use of high performance equipment and its corresponding cost.

Keywords: Iris Biometrics, Iris Preprocessing, Feature Extraction, Log-Gabor filters, Matching.

21.1 Introduction

Biometrics is becoming one of the most used solutions for Authentication tasks. It allows remote and automatic identification without using external devices or passwords, just by a physical or behavioral characteristic [1]. Using a personal characteristic the user has problems due to possible forges or steals are highly reduced. But some of the main disadvantages of these systems are the use of high performance processors and the high security level related to them as they are managing high sensible information, i.e. user identity.

In this paper, authors propose a new algorithm for Iris Biometrics for low cost devices. To describe the implementation developed, considerations made and results and conclusions obtained, this paper is divided in different sections. The following section describes the biometric scheme. Algorithm proposed is described in section III, so in section IV some of the results obtained are shown. Finally conclusions and some of future work will be mentioned.

21.2   Iris Biometrics

One way to classify Biometric Techniques is by the characteristic studied. There are techniques based on one or several characteristics such as fingerprint or face recognition. Choosing one or another relays on the environment to be applied. For those environments where security is a major concern, Iris techniques are one of the most suitable solutions. Human Iris presents some characteristics that make it perfect to be used for identification. Several algorithms have been proposed by different authors [2],[3],[4],[5],[6]. Most algorithms are based on the scheme shown in Fig.1.

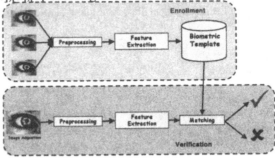

Fig.1: Biometric block diagram. Above row shows the enrollment process, where the user is first introduced in the system, after that, each access will just perform identification (below row)

In Identification, first step is acquiring an image of the Iris. This image can be taken using a photograph or video camera of high resolution, preferably using an infrared camera [3]. This preprocessing block generally consists of isolating the Iris, equalization processes, improving the quality of the image, etc. Afterwards, the image is transformed to obtain a quantifiable vector. The vector obtained is designated as feature vector. This vector should represent the image and allow to measure differences from one image to another, so similar images will lead into two similar vectors, i.e., in terms of pattern recognition, close vectors. The feature vector obtained is then compared to vectors previously stored (templates) in the system. If the distance between the sample vector and the template is below a threshold, it is considered to belong to the user whose pattern is being analyzed.

21.3   Algorithm Proposal

In this section our algorithm will be deeply described. The main aim of the algorithm proposed is to minimize the use of high performance processors or large amount of memory, i.e., developing an algorithm suitable for low cost devices.

Each algorithm, specially the pre-processing block, depends on the database used. Different databases can be found in public domain, each of them with different characteristics but one of the probably most known and used is the one provided by the National Laboratory of Pattern Recognition Institute of Automation Chinese

Academy of Sciences [8]. CASIA database, as it is named, is the biggest public domain Iris database. It consists of 756 images of 108 different eyes, collected in two sessions. The images were captured by an infrared video camera, and from each record, several frames were taken.

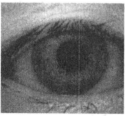

Fig.2: Iris from CASIA database [8]

21.2.1   Pre-processing Block

Main functions of this block are Iris isolation and enhancing image quality to improve feature extraction block performance. For enhancing image quality several histogram stretchings are done. Histogram stretching intention is sparing the histogram components on the whole bandwidth, so it is recommended to perform it initially and once the Iris is isolated so Iris peaks and valleys become more noticeable.

Iris Isolation

Isolating the Iris basically consists in detecting circles on an image. There are different algorithms for this purpose, but most algorithms are based on integro-differential operators [2] or the Hough transform [3],[5],[7]. These solutions are not suitable for low cost devices as they require high performance processors and large memory for temporary data. The solution proposed tries to reduce the use of these elements, searching the boundaries through luminance variations.

Inner Boundary

Due to the characteristics of database images, finding the boundary between Iris and pupil is suggested to perform first, as the difference between the pupil and the Iris is sharper than the difference between the Iris and the sclera. Therefore, the algorithm starts searching for groups of 5 or more pixels which luminance is lower than 60.

Once the pupil area is located in the image, pupil centre and radius have to be specified. The centre coordinate on each axis is set as the mean between the maximum and the minimum pixel address in the axis direction computed in previous step. Radius is, then, approximated to the mean of the possible four radii considering the centre and the borders previously detected.

Radius and centre coordinates found are used as first approach. For an inner radius reliable calculation, an area surrounding the centre of 3 times the radius approximation is more deeply studied. Several circumferences are drawn around the centre previously computed. The radius whose circumference provides maximum difference between its luminance and the luminance of its nearest circumference is chosen as the inner radius of the pupil.

Outer Boundary

For outer boundary computation the process followed before cannot be applied as sclera and Iris difference is no so sharp and eyelashes and eyelids usually occlude part of the Iris, so the whole Iris circumference cannot be observed.

Outer boundary is calculated as those pixels where the (1) reaches its maximum value.

$$D = \sum_{m} \sum_{k=1}^{5} \left(I_{n,m} - I_{n-k,m} \right) \tag{1}$$

Iris centre is not the same as the pupil centre as they are usually not concentric. Small variations are done on the pupil centre to set the real Iris centre considering outer boundaries found.

Rubber sheet

As it has been said, in most of the cases, especially in Asian eyes, eyelids and eyelashes occlude part of the Iris. For avoiding the problem of detecting them and considering the natural Iris shape [6], a polar scale change is done and the study area is reduced to two laterals cones of 60° width.

21.2.2   Feature Extraction Block

When designing the feature extraction block, Gabor filters were considered, as they are widely used in image processing, especially in texture analysis [2][6][10]. Gabor filters provide information of the texture phase, but their main disadvantage is that all of them have a DC component whenever the bandwidth is larger than one octave. However, zero DC component can be obtained for any bandwidth by using a Gabor filter which is Gaussian on a logarithmic scale, this is known as the Log-Gabor filter.

$$G(f) = \exp\left(\frac{-\left(\log\left(f/f_0 \right) \right)^2}{2\left(\log\left(\sigma/f_0 \right) \right)^2} \right) \tag{2}$$

Where f_0 is the central filter frequency and σ determines its bandwidth.

Previous authors have used Gabor filters for extracting features in two dimensions; however, in order to reduce the complexity of the algorithm we have used them in one dimension. So the feature extraction block consist in splitting the rubber sheet in several 1-dimension signals, each of them is transformed through a FFT, filter is applied and on the resulting vector the inversed FFT is carried out. Because of the FFT, resulting vector of this process is formed by complex numbers. The feature extraction codification is made as proposed in [2].

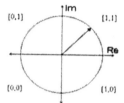

Fig. 3: Feature Extraction Codification.

21.2.3   Matching algorithm

In [6], Sanchez-Reillo et al. study different matching algorithm for two different feature extraction implementations. Although several studies have been made, best results are obtained when using Hamming distance for comparison. Some modifications have been made in Hamming distance to consider usual head turns. The resulting formula is shown in (3).

$$d_{H,J}(y,p) = \frac{1}{L} \sum_{i=1}^{L} p_i \oplus y_{i\text{-}J} \tag{3}$$

Where L is the vector length, p_i the i-th component of the template and $y_{i\text{-}j}$ the i-j-th component of the sample vector.

21.4   Tests and Results

In Biometrics, intraclass and interclass distributions have to be studied ad they show the system capability of distinguishing one user from others. For fixing system parameters decidability is used [2]. Decidability is defined as formula (4) shows.

$$d = \frac{|\mu_{IA} - \mu_{IE}|}{\sqrt{\dfrac{(\sigma_{IA}^2 + \sigma_{IE}^2)}{2}}} \tag{4}$$

Where μ_{IA} and μ_{IE} are the means, σ_{IA} and σ_{IE} the standard deviations of intraclass and interclass distributions respectively. So as high as this parameter is the separation between both distributions increases, being our algorithm more accurate.

21.4.1   Filter parameters

When talking about Log-Gabor filters two parameters have to be defined: bandwidth and central frequency. Their values have been obtained empirically.

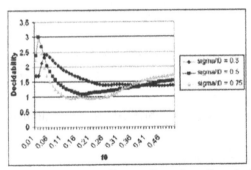

Fig. 4: Decidability results for different filter configurations. Best decidability results are obtained for low central frequencies as most representative information is situated in those frequencies.

21.4.2   Shifts

Fig. **5** shows Decidability dependence with shifts done in Hamming distance formula. Optimal value seems to appear at 8 shifts.

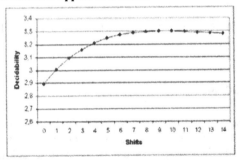

Fig. 5: Decidability vs shifts in matching algorithm

Considering best values obtained for number of shifts and filter parameters, intraclass and interclass distributions are shown in Fig. **6**

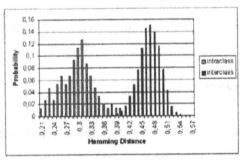

Fig. 6: Interclass and intraclass distributions

21.4.3   Performance Results

When working on Biometrics, two parameters are used for describing performance results: False Acceptance Rate (FAR) and False Rejection Rate (FRR). FRR is the number of users, who belonging to the database, are rejected, on the other hand, FAR is the probability of acceptance a non-authorized user. Table 1 shows the performance results obtained for the algorithm proposed and other author's algorithms.

Table 1: Performance comparison of Iris Recognition Algorithms Ref.

Algorithm's author	FAR/FRR	Overall % accuracy
Daugman [2]	0.01/0.09	99.90%
Li-Ma [5]	0.02/1.98	98.00%
Sanchez-Avila [6]	0.03/2.08	97.89%
Proposed Algorithm	1.45/1.33	97.24%

21.5   Conclusions and Future Work

In this paper, a low cost Iris Recognition algorithm has been introduced. The algorithm proposed relays on previous works from different authors, but introducing also mechanisms to reduce the complexity of those algorithms so allowing this algorithm to be implemented in a low cost device. Results obtained demonstrate that, in spite of its simplicity, the algorithm is suitable for being used in a verification scheme. The reduction of complexity of the algorithm, specially in the pre-processing block, allows this algorithm to be included in a identification token of low cost, as no high cost hardware is required for recognition computing.

From this algorithm much work can be done in different fields. Considering pattern recognition, pre-processing block can be adapted for other databases or quality detection algorithms can be introduced. About its implementation, also much work can be done, e.g. implementing the algorithm in different platforms for accelerating the processing time, for securing it or for reducing the cost of the equipment, through hardware sources reuses.

References

1. A. Jain, R. Bolle and S. Pankanti Eds, Biometrics: Personal Identification in a Networked Society. Norwell, MA: Kluwer, 1999.
2. J. Daugman, "High confidence visual recognition of persons by a test of Statistical independence" IEEE Trans. Pattern Analysis and Machine Intelligence, vol. 15, pp 1148-1161, Nov. 1993.
3. R. Wildes, "Iris Recognition: an emerging biometric technology" Proc. IEEE, vol. 85, pp 1348-1363, Sept. 1997.

4. W. Boles and B. Boashash, "A human identification technique using images of the Iris and wavelet transform", IEEE Trans. Signal Processing, vol. 46, pp. 1185-1188. Apr. 1998.
5. Li Ma; Yunhong Wang; Tieniu Tan , "Iris recognition using circular symmetric filters" Proceedings of 16th International Conference on Pattern Recognition, 2002, 11-15 Aug. 2002 Page(s):414 - 417 vol.2.
6. C. Sanchez-Avila, R. Sánchez-Reillo "Two different approaches for Iris Recognition using Gabor filters and multiscale zero-crossing representation". Elsevier Pattern Recognition vol. 38(2): 231-240 (2005)
7. Toennies, K. Behrens, F. Aurnhammer, M. , "Feasibility of Hough-transform-based Iris localisation for real-time-application" Proc. IEEE 16th International Conference on Pattern Recognition, 2002.
8. http://www.nlpr.ia.ac.cn/english/index.html
9. Vatsa, M.   Richa Singh   Gupta, P. "Comparison of iris recognition algorithms" Proceedings of International Conference on Intelligent Sensing and Information Processing, 2004. Page(s): 354- 358
10. Libor Masek, Peter Kovesi. MATLAB Source Code for a Biometric Identification System Based on Iris Patterns. The School of Computer Science and Software Engineering, University of Western Australia. 2003.

22 Optimization on PCA Based Face Recognition Models

D. S. Guru[1], R. Divya[1], T. N. Vikram[2],

[1] Department of Studies in Computer Science and
[2] International School of Information Management,
guruds@lycos.com, kumbledivya@yahoo.co.in, vikram@isim.ac.in

Abstract. In this paper, an optimization on principal component analysis (PCA) based subspace methods using mean and standard deviation is proposed. An image I (m×n) is transformed into a matrix S (m×2). Each row elements of the transformed matrix S(m×2) is the mean (μ) and the standard deviation (σ) of the elements of the corresponding row of the actual image I (m×n). PCA based face recognition methods are then applied on the transformed image. Representation of the facial images in μ and σ reduces the computational burden in obtaining the feature vector, which eventually decreases the recognition time. Experimentations carried out during the course of this research have revealed that the proposed optimization on the PCA based subspace methods is competent enough and has better runtime performance when compared to the conventional schemes.

Keywords: Face Recognition, PCA, Moments, Eigen-Faces

22.1 Introduction

Appearance based models consider the face images holistically and apply dimensionality reduction techniques and conduct subspace analysis. Earliest of these methodologies were based on principal component analysis (PCA) and linear discriminant analysis (LDA)/ Fisher's linear discriminant (FLD). Works of Turk and Pentland [8], Belhumeur et al. [2], and Pentland et al [7] have formed the core of the research in subspace analysis and most of the contemporary subspace techniques are inspired by these original works. A survey of subspace methodologies for face recognition can be found in Zhang et al., [12]. By and large, the ability to withstand change in poses and illumination by the variants of PCA and LDA as contrasted to the original schemes have been illustrated in the experiments carried out in [6]. It is inferred that the variants are more robust enough in handling variations in poses and illumination than the conventional PCA and LDA.

In this paper, we are motivated to deduce an optimization specifically for the PCA based subspace methods to speed up the recognition task to suit the real time recognition applications. The optimization is based on the representation of face images in a lower dimensional space using moments like mean and standard deviation before applying PCA. The remaining part of the paper is organized as follows. In Section 2 we describe the proposed scheme of optimization. The details of the experiments that were carried out are presented in Section 3. In Section 4, we carry out a discussion and thereby some conclusions are drawn.

22.2 Proposed scheme of optimization

The proposed scheme transforms an image I of size $m \times n$ onto a matrix S of size $m \times 2$. The two columns of the transformed image consists of the means and the standard deviations of the corresponding row elements of the actual image. Let I be an input image and let S be the transformed image.

Appearance based face recognition models are thus recommended to be applied on the transformed image representative matrix (S) instead of directly on the actual images (I). Since the size of S is very much smaller than that of I, the computational saddle of arriving at the feature vector is apparently reduced. Mean and standard deviation may not be unique descriptors of a sample of integers, however they have been used as unbiased estimators. If populations have identical means then they satisfy null hypotheses and are classified into the same cluster [13]. This has been exploited in k-means cluster methodology and several multivariate data analysis techniques employ mean and variance analysis to classify samples [4].

The proposed method has a better runtime performance when compared to conventional methods and thus suits real time recognition applications. However preprocessing is required before the application of the appearance based models, to find the mean and standard deviation for each row of the image matrix, which contributes to the increase in training time of the system. But since the dimension of the image representative used for further computation (eigen vectors) is much lesser as compared to the actual image, the overall training time of the system remains tractable.

$$I = \begin{bmatrix} x_{11} & x_{12} & \cdots & x_{1n-1} & x_{1n} \\ x_{21} & x_{12} & \cdots & x_{2n-1} & x_{2n} \\ . & . & . & . & . \\ . & . & . & . & . \\ x_{m1} & x_{m2} & \cdots & x_{mn-1} & x_{mn} \end{bmatrix} \longrightarrow S = \begin{bmatrix} \mu_{11} & \sigma_{12} \\ \mu_{21} & \sigma_{22} \\ . & . \\ . & . \\ \mu_{m1} & \mu_{m2} \end{bmatrix}$$

where μ_{i1} and σ_{i2} are mean and standard deviation of the ith row of the image I.

Let x be the number of images in the database and let the size of each image be m×n. Then the transformation (I→S) is of quadratic time complexity with O(xmn). The training time required for the conventional alternative 2DPCA[9] is cubic with $O(mn^2)$ and the training time required for the proposed scheme is quadratic with $O(m(2)^2+xmn) = O(4m + xmn)$, as in the transformed image n = 2.

     This infers that in case of proposed method, only the transformation of the image is of quadratic time complexity and the further computations are linear, unlike the conventional method where all the computations are of cubic time complexity. The training time complexities of variants of PCA are presented in Table. 1.

Table.1 Training time complexities of the conventional and proposed scheme for the variants of PCA.

	PCA	2DPCA [9]	Alternative 2DPCA [10]	2D²PCA [11]
Conventional	$O(x^2nm)$	$O(nm^2)$	$O(n^2m)$	$O(n^2m + nm^2)$
Proposed	$O(xnm + 2x^2m)$	$O(xnm + 2m^2)$	$O(xnm + 4m)$	$O(xnm + 2m^2 + 4m)$

Based on the data from Table. 1 it is clear that the training time required for the proposed scheme is utmost quadratic where as, in case of the conventional scheme it is sometimes cubic. The value of n in most of the applications is greater than 2. Therefore it can be inferred that the training time required for the proposed scheme is marginal as contrasted to the conventional. The detailed algorithms thus designed for the training and recognition processes are as trivial as follows.

Let A_i^j represent an image j of class i. Let p be the number training of classes. s_i represents the number of classes in class i.

Algorithm. Training scheme

Input: Training images, $\Gamma = \{ A_i^j \mid 1 \leq i \leq p, 1 \leq j \leq s_i \}$

Output: Knowledge base . $\Psi = \{ T_i^j \mid 1 \leq i \leq p, 1 \leq j \leq s_i \}$

Optimal projection axes, X.

Method:
1. Transform every image in Γ using the proposed transformation. (I➔S) to obtain $\Phi = \{ B_i^j \mid 1 \leq i \leq p, 1 \leq j \leq s_i \}$
2. Compute Average C of Γ.
3. Transform C using the proposed transformation. (I➔S) to obtain C^1.
4. Mean center Φ with C^1 as the average vector to obtain ξ.
5. Compute the covariance matrix *CM* for ξ.
6. Compute Eigen vectors and Eigen values of *CM*.
7. Let $X = (X_1, X_2,..., X_d)$, where $X_1, X_2,..., X_d$ are eigenvectors associated with the first d largest Eigen values constituting the optimal projection axes.
8. Create knowledge base Ψ by projecting Φ onto X.

Algorithm Training scheme ends.

Algorithm. Recognition scheme

Input: Knowledge base . $\Psi = \{ T_i^j \mid 1 \leq i \leq p, 1 \leq j \leq s_i \}$

X, optimal projection axes,

Q, A query image,

Output: class label of *Q*.

Method:
1. Transform *Q* using the proposed transformation. (I➔S) to obtain Q^1.
2. Obtain feature vector Z of the query image Q^1 by projecting it onto *X*
3. Find the value of $i \in I$ corresponding to min arg ($\left\| Z - T_i^j \right\|_2$).
4. Classify the query image *Q* as a member of the ith class.

Algorithm Recognition ends.

22.3 Experimental results

Experiments were conducted using Matlab 7 on Microsoft Windows XP, with a Pentium 4, 2.66Ghz processor. Experiments have been conducted on the ORL dataset, and a dataset obtained by pooling the images of ORL and UMIST databases. In all the experiments, alternate samples are considered as query and training samples.

On ORL database.
The ORL (http://www.uk.research.att.com/facedatabase.html) database consists of 400 images of 40 subjects, with each subject contributing 10 different images. Images were normalized to a size of 112×92 pixels. The optimal recognition and the runtime performance for the existing PCA based models and their corresponding optimized counterparts (proposed) are given in Table.2.

Table. 2. Runtime performance of the PCA based methodologies on ORL at optimal recognition

| Methodology | Method | Running time. | | Dimension of feature vector | Optimal recognition rate (%) |
		Training time (sec)	Recogniti on time (sec)		
PCA[8]	Existing	7.25	9.37	40	95.5
	With the proposed optimization	6.39	3.95	46	92.00
2D-PCA[9]	Existing	12.15	2.58	2×112	95.5
	With the proposed optimization	2.04	1.82	21×2	96.00
Alt. 2D-PCA[10]	Existing	11.96	4.10	9×92	94.50
	With the proposed optimization	2.03	1.98	2×112	96.50
$2D^2$-PCA[11]	Existing	12.10	1.81	4×4	92.50
	With the proposed optimization	1.87	1.73	2×5	97.00

Comparison of the recognition times for the conventional methods and their optimized counterparts are also presented in Fig.1.and it can be observed that the recognition time of the proposed optimization is much less than that of the conventional methods.

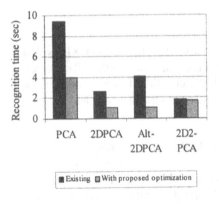 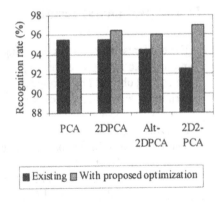

Fig. 1. Recognition time on ORL database   Fig. 2. Optimal recognition rate on ORL database

Fig.2. shows that the optimal recognition performance of the proposed scheme is as high as 97%. The conventional 2D-PCA has the optimal recognition performance of 95.5%. It is important to note that the proposed optimization scheme has better optimal performance in most of the cases in addition to a reduction in recognition time.

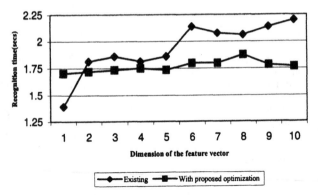

Fig.3(a) Recognition time versus varying dimension of the feature vector for ORL dataset with 2D^{2}PCA and its optimized counter part (proposed)

Fig. 3(a) shows that the run time performance of the proposed method is much less when compared to that of conventional method in case of 2D^{2}PCA on ORL dataset with varying dimensions of the feature vector. Fig. 3(b) shows that the recognition rate of the proposed optimization scheme has a consistent performance for all dimensions of the feature vector when compared to that of the conventional methods.

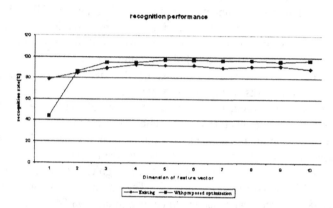

Fig.3(b) Recognition rate versus varying dimensions of the feature vector for ORL dataset with 2D²PCA and its optimized counter part (proposed).

Fig. 4 shows the training time of the conventional and proposed model with different number of images in the database. The proposed scheme has consistently less time when compared to that of the conventional method which is a clear indication that the system is not over burdened because of the preprocessing required for the proposed scheme.

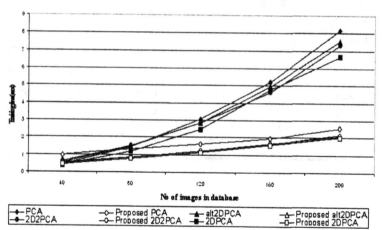

Fig. 4.

Training time versus number of images in the dataset for conventional and proposed scheme

UMIST and ORL pooled together.

We have conducted similar experiments on a dataset, which is obtained by pooling UMIST and ORL. The interest of this experiment is to store a larger face data set, which has different environmental variations in face images. UMIST and ORL are created under different conditions and constraints. Creating a single dataset by pooling these two datasets would test the robustness of the face recognition schemes. In a real life scenario, the size of the training set is large, and the subjects are photographed under varying conditions of illuminations and poses. Change in technological constraints like the camera being used to grab the image, the format in which the image is stored, resolution and the size of the image would add to the difference in the constraints that were assumed to create the standard dataset.

All the images in the pooled dataset is normalized to a size of 112×92 pixels. The performance of the conventional schemes and their optimized counterparts on the pooled dataset are described in Table. 3. The recognition times and recognition rates are given in Fig. 5 and Fig. 6 respectively. The optimal recognition for the proposed method is 98.83 percent whereas that of conventional is 98.54 percent.

Table. 3 Runtime performance of the PCA based methodologies on Pooled UMIST and ORL images at optimal recognition

Method	Method		Running time.		Dimension of feature vector	Optimal recognition rate (%)
			Training time (sec)	Recogniti-on time (sec)		
PCA [8]	Existing		127.23	37.89	53	98.54
	With the optimization	proposed	20.45	23.67	55	98.83
2D-PCA[9]	Existing		127.26	36.87	2×112	70.51
	With the optimization	proposed	11.04	26.93	8×2	96.71
Alt.2D-PCA[10]	Existing		125.68	39.04	3×92	70.51
	With the optimization	proposed	12.15	39.45	2×112	97.59
$2D^2$-PCA[11]	Existing		20.68	35.12	2×3	96.13
	With the optimization	proposed	10.68	25.12	2×3	96.13

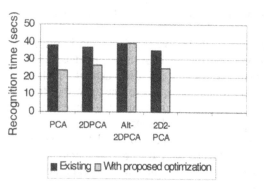

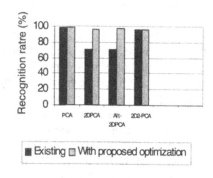

Fig. 5. Recognition time on pooled database   Fig. 6. Optimal recognition rate on pooled database

22.4 Discussions and Conclusion

Image representation also plays a crucial role in the performance of a face recognition model. Chung et al. [5], Fu et al., [1] and Belkin and Niyogi [3] have stressed upon the importance and relevance of image representation. Their works primarily revolves around the reduction of dimensionality of the image by projecting them onto a subspace. However the intrinsic dimensionality remains unaltered. As a result, the span of the feature vector dimensions remain large. Consequently when a new image is added to the training set, the heuristic to arrive at the optimal dimension of feature vectors would take considerably more time. As in this paper we have reduced the intrinsic dimensionality of the image by moment-based representation, the training and recognition times are reduced largely. The moment computation is carried out in the row direction of the original image.

We can also compute the mean and standard deviation of every column to arrive at the lower dimensional representative of the image. But the given face images have more information scatter in the row wise direction. And also through experimental results it was noted that the efficient way to represent the image was by considering the representative in the row wise direction rather than the column wise direction.

Mean and standard deviation are same for a given population irrespective of the permutation in which elements are sequenced. As a result two different images might have the same mean and standard deviation descriptor vectors. Even a small image of size 64 X 64 has 4096 pixels, that can express a large number of patterns, such a trees houses and faces, but only a few sequences of pixels form a face image [15]. But this scenario is rare where a non face image is given as a face image and it get through the system.

The optimal recognition rate obtained with the proposed scheme is much higher than the optimal recognition performance of the PCA based models. The proposed method shows superior performance especially on ORL dataset. It also achieves the optimal performance with lesser time. There is no guarantee that the proposed scheme performs better than the conventional method for any given dataset, which is also the true in case of any appearance-based methods. However the performance of the proposed method is found to be consistent for all datasets when 2DPCA and 2D^{2}PCA are used for recognition. Indeed we have not considered finer moments and have restricted to lower order moments. In future we will experiment with higher moments for better recognition.

References

1. Bo Fu, Jianzhong Zhou,.,Yuhong Li, Guojun Zhang, Cheng Wang. Image analysis by modified Legendre moments. Pattern Recognition. In press.
2. Belhumeur, P. N., Hespanha, J. P., Kreigman, D. J.,. Eigenfaces vs. fisher faces: recognition using class specific linear projection, IEEE Transactions on Pattern Analysis and Machine Intelligence. (1997) Vol 19(7), pp. 711-720.
3. Belkin, M., and Niyogi, P. Laplacian Eigenmaps and Spectral Techniques for Embedding and Clustering. Advances in Neural Information Processing Systems (2001).
4. Fukunaga, K., Introduction to Statistical Pattern Recognition, Academic Press, London, (1990).
5. Kuo-Liang Chung , Yau-Wen Liu, Wen-Ming Yan. A hybrid gray image representation using spatial-and DCT-based approach with application to moment computation. Journal of Visual Communication and Image Representation. In press.
6. Nagabhushan, P., Guru, D.S., Shekar, B.H., (2D)^2 FLD: An efficient approach for appearance based object recognition. Journal of Neurocomputing, (2006) Vol 69, pp. 934-940.
7. Pentland, A., Moghaddam, B., Starner, T.,. View based and modular eigenspaces for face recognition, in: Proceedings of the IEEE Conference on Computer Vision and Pattern Recognition, (1994) pp. 84-91.
8. Turk, M., and Pentland, A.,. Eigenfaces for Recognition. Journal of Cognitive Neuroscience. (1991) Vol 3, no.1, pp. 71-86.
9. Yang, J., Zhang, D., Frangi, A .F, Yang, J,. Two dimensional PCA: a new approach to appearance based face representation and recognition. IEEE Transactions on Pattern Analysis and Machine Intelligence. (2004) Vol 26(1), pp. 131-137.
10. Yang, J., Zhang, D., Yang, X., Yang, J,. Two-dimensional discriminant transform for face recognition. Pattern Recognition. (2005) Vol 38(7), pp. 1125-1129.
11. Zhang, D.Q., Zhou, Z.H. (2D) 2PCA: 2-directional 2-dimensional PCA for efficient face representation and recognition. Neurocomputing. (2005) Vol 69, pp. 224-231.
12. Zhang, David. Yang, Jian. Jing , Xiaoyuan.. Biometric image discrimination technologies. Idea group publishing. (2006)

13. Mitani Y and Hamomoto Y. A local mean based nonparametric classifier. Pattern Recognition Letters. (2006), Vol. 27, pp..1151-1159.
14. Stanz Li and Anil K Jain. Handboook of Face Recognition. Springer (2004).

23 Discriminating Unknown Faces using Eigen-face Approach and a Novelty Filter

Ke Shanjing, Sameer Singh and Maneesha Singh

Research School of Informatics,
Loughborough University,
Loughborough LE113TU, UK
{S.ke, S.singh, M.singh}@lboro.ac.uk

Abstract: Novelty detection is extremely important in several application areas for discriminating between known and unknown data. With the extensive use of CCTV surveillance, and the use of facial identity to allow or block access to computer networks, buildings etc., it has become important to perform facial biometrics on human subjects in these videos for identity recognition. Face detection and recognition in unconstrained environments is obviously not a trivial task. It must take into account changes in environment, illumination conditions, and changes in face size and poses for robust recognition. An automated novelty filter is intended to isolate human subjects with any pose under these difficult conditions whose information is not present in the database, assuming that a set of poses of known subjects is recorded as images in available database. In this paper we investigate whether substantial eigen-face feature based differences exist between known and unknown subjects or not. We thereafter apply a simple threshold based novelty filter on our database and show robustness results with varying face pose data.

23.1 Introduction

Face recognition has been widely studied. In particular, appearance-based approaches that construct eigen-faces have been extensively used. Seminal papers in this area by Sirovich and Kirby [1] and Turk and Pentland [2] introduced eigen-face based approach which has been used till date with minor modifications. Over the years, face recognition with different poses, and pose recognition in itself has been an important topic of research [3], and special attention has been paid to developing near real-time recognition performance in less constrained environments [4] and with video streams [5].

In the recent past, the research focus has shifted to recognizing faces in complex background, and under varying conditions such as change in poses. The face recognition problem is therefore not limited to matching a fixed pose single image of a subject's face against a database of face templates, one per person. It is now required to store multiple templates of a human subject in the database, and match these against a captured image from CCTV camera. The problem is inherently complex because first one has to detect faces in images, and then either perform an exhaustive matching with stored templates, or find pose information to perform guided search. There are two approaches to performing multi-view eigen-face recognition as pointed out by Pentland et al. [6]. Given N individuals under M views, a universal eigenspace can be computed from the combination of NM images. This is the approach we take in this paper. In this way a single "parametric eigenspace" will encode both identity as well as viewing conditions. An alternative formulation is to perform pose recognition first, and then build an eigen-space per pose. In either case, the aim is to correctly recognize a test face image, and isolate those cases as novel for which the individual observed does not exist in training data.

Novelty detection is considerably important for biometric applications to distinguish between known and unknown faces. It will never be possible to store every person's varying face pose images, and therefore any recognition system must be able to generalize from the limited amount of templates available. However, this generalization capability must be balanced against false positive detections, where unknown faces are labeled as known by the computer. The aim of this work is therefore to develop a novelty filter that specifies the boundary between what is known and should be classified, and what is unknown and needs a human observer to investigate. Interestingly, the area of novelty detection is quite mature, and has evolved separately to a two way classification approach, e.g. normal vs. abnormal. In the following, we describe a more formal definition of novelty detection and mention some key work in other application domains. It is quite surprising that novelty detection has not been explored in sufficient detail in biometric applications, especially face recognition.

Novelty detection is aimed at finding novel events or data. Nairac et al. [7] state: "For novelty detection, a description of normality is learnt by fitting a model to a set of normal examples, and previously unseen patterns are then tested by comparing their novelty score (as defined by the model) against some threshold". One of the key challenges is how to set the threshold for discriminating between outliers of known data distribution and truly unknown class data. Early novelty detection approaches suffered the following weaknesses: i) difficulty in automated threshold determination; ii) failure to specify a generic methodology that is applicable across applications without a priori knowledge of known data distributions; and iii) failure to specify an effective incremental classifier re-training procedure. Subsequent studies by Singh and Markou [8] and Markou and Singh [9] addressed these problems and demonstrated that robust novelty detectors for image analysis applications can be built.

A number of novelty detectors can be developed for single or multiple class data. Parametric models have been found to be unsuitable in a range of applications as they require extensive knowledge of the problem and do not necessarily fit real data. Several studies have discussed the relationship between rejection thresholds and classification error for Gaussian data with single classifiers [10] [11] and multiple experts [12]. Some efforts have also been made recently on setting different thresholds for different classes [13]. Non-parametric methods based on Parzen windows [14] [15], k-nearest neighbours and Gaussian mixture models [15] [16] [17] have been widely used to find outliers in test data. Some attempts have also been made using data space partitioning into self/non-self regions and using a set of rules to assign test data into these self and non-self regions [18].

Neural networks in a variety of forms have been used for novelty detection. Their key advantage is that no a priori information is needed on data distribution and no specific parameters related to data need to be set. Traditional neural network approaches to novelty detection can be categorised as: approaches based on auto-associators [19], approaches based on Kohonen Self Organising Networks [20], approaches based on multi-layer perceptrons [9], approaches based on support vectors [21], and other exotic methods.

A number of other approaches using neural networks have also been used for novelty detection. For example, fuzzy c-means clustering can be used to cluster training data into clusters and rather than thresholding the Euclidean distance of a data point from the centroid, we can threshold its fuzzy membership for each cluster. A detailed review of the topic is available in Markou and Singh [22] [23]. In this paper we focus on testing the hypothesis that face features from unknown faces can be successfully distinguished from the same measurements of known faces. If the level of separation is good, then any of the above mentioned novelty detector can be employed. For the purposes of this paper we use a straightforward threshold based novelty detector.

23.2 Methodology

In this work we have employed the popular eigen-based face recognition approach [2]. Since we take unconstrained videos of human subjects working on their desks or walking in front of the camera, we have to first detect faces, and then perform the recognition/novelty filtering as an integrated fused step of analysis. The overall approach involves the following methodology.

23.2.1 Image Sequence Capture

We record videos of people sitting in front of the webcam or walking in front of it. We have deliberately used a moderate resolution camera with a pixel resolution of 143x182 to speed up the process of novelty detection. In our experiments we find that an increase in pixel resolution with a more advanced camera significantly increases the computational complexity of the matching process without substantially improving recognition accuracy. The videos are captured at 25 frames per second, with the camera position fixed which means that we have one or more templates of the fixed background. A number of frames containing human faces are randomly selected which show an individual with different random poses.

23.2.2 Face Detection

The process of finding faces is a detailed procedure. We cannot make any assumptions on which part of the image will have a face in it. Furthermore, we also cannot rely on detecting unique landmarks for finding faces, e.g. eyes, as poses vary. The face detection process includes first robust background subtraction to find those objects that have entered the scene, followed by skin detection, and ellipse fitting. We detail these processes in brief. Robust background subtraction is the process of using multiple background images under varying lighting conditions to create a model of how the background image varies. We use the technique developed by Horpraesert et al. [24]. The variation of each pixel with varying light intensity is used to determine the average intensity of that pixel and its variance. For a given test image, all image pixels whose values lie within a certain interval of average intensity are removed as background leaving only the remaining pixels. We thereafter use a model for skin detect as described by [25]. The output of the detector is a list of pixels in the image that are most probably skin. Skin pixels are thereafter clustered to remove any regions that are less than 20 pixels as none of these regions are likely to be face. The remaining clusters are then evaluated for how elliptical they are. It is well known that faces are elliptical in nature and we perform ellipse fitting followed by some manual correction to isolate face region(s). In the present paper we assume that there is only one face in the image, however, in the future this can be extended to include more faces.

23.2.3 Facial feature extraction

For each person, we have multiple face images, each with different pose as shown in Figure 1. From such data we can build an appearance based model that can describe a generic face set and other faces as its variations. The eigen-face recognition method is based on the Principle Component Analysis first introduced in Turk and Pentland [2]. Firstly, a set of M images $(I_1, I_2...I_m)$ with the resolution of $N \times N$ is obtained for training purpose. These images $I_i (1 \le i \le M)$ are then represented as vectors $\Gamma_i^T = (x_1...x_{N^2})$, where $(1 \le i \le M)$ and x_i denotes the pixel value taken from top-down left-right of the face image. The average face vector Ψ and mean face vector Φ_i are calculated from these face images vectors as :

$$\Psi = \frac{1}{M} \sum_{i=1}^{M} \Gamma_i,$$

$$\Phi_i = \Gamma_i - \Psi \ (1 \le i \le M)$$

The covariance matrix C can consequently be constructed as follow:

$$C = \frac{1}{M} \sum_{n=1}^{M} \Phi_n^T \Phi_n = A^T A, \text{ where}$$

$$A = \left[\Phi_1, \Phi_2 ... \Phi_M\right]$$

With the covariance matrix, the first $M'(M' < M)$ significant eigenvectors, i.e. $u_k (1 \leq k \leq M')$, of the covariance matrix are chosen as those with the largest associated eigenvalues. These eigenvectors are also called eigenfaces. Thus a face image Γ can be transformed into its eigenface component (projected into "face-space") by a simple operation:

$$\omega_k = u_k^T \left(\Gamma - \Psi\right), \quad (1 \leq k \leq M')$$

The M' weights construct a weights vector $\Omega^T = \left[\omega_1, \omega_2 ... \omega_{M'}\right]$ and describe the contribution of each eigenface in representing the input face image. Hence, a eigenface component vector calculated from a face image can be used to represent this face image with the M' eigenface.

23.2.4 Face Recognition and Novelty Detection

The processes of face recognition and novelty detection are tightly inter-linked. We can develop a classifier such as neural networks, or decision trees to learn to recognize faces based on a large training data of eigen-values as described in section 2.3. A trained classifier would output the probability of a sample belonging to each of the known classes. A novelty filter would then take this probability vector and decide whether there is an outright winner, i.e. the sample can be allocated to a class, or not. Hence, novelty filtering is the process of finding whether we have a clear winner or not so that a decision can be made, and the recognition process is thereafter a simple matter of allocating sample to the winning class if it was not filtered as novel. In the present paper we have used a k nearest neighbour classifier with $k= 1$, for determining the closest training sample to a test case, and the Euclidean distance between the best match can be thresholded for novelty detection purpose.

23.3 Experimental Design and Data

We have a total of 12 subjects divided into two groups, training and testing. Sample images of individuals participating in our experiments are shown below in Figure 1.

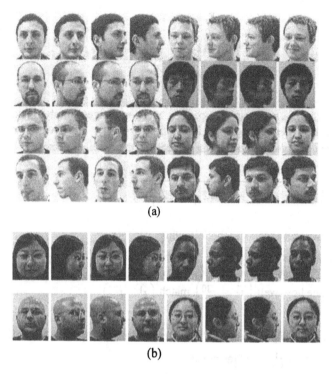

(a)

(b)

Figure 1. The subjects participating in the experiments: (a) known subjects with sample faces used in training set; (b) unknown subjects in test set.

8 subjects $(x_1, x_2, ...x_8)$ are used for training and the same 8 subjects are also present in test set but with different pose data $(\tilde{x}_1, \tilde{x}_2, ...\tilde{x}_8)$. 4 subjects that are completely unknown (y_1, y_2, y_3, y_4) are also included the test set. In training set we have 25 pose images for each individual, i.e. subject x_i, where $(1 \leq i \leq 8)$, has images $\left(I_{x_i}^1 ... I_{x_i}^{25} \right)$. Similarly, 5 test data images per individual for $(\tilde{x}_1, \tilde{x}_2, ...\tilde{x}_8)$ and 30 test data images per individual for (y_1, y_2, y_3, y_4). They can be indexed as $\left(I_{\tilde{x}_i}^1 ... I_{\tilde{x}_i}^5 \right)$ and $\left(I_{y_j}^1 ... I_{y_j}^{30} \right)$, where $(1 \leq j \leq 4)$. Now we first compute eigen-faces from the training set and use this information to project test images into their corresponding face space. We generate 12 eigen-faces $(E_1...E_{12})$ from the training set.

Hence, any image in the training or test set can be thought of as a linear combination of the 12 Eigen-faces. A weight vector unique to reconstructing an image is determined from our analysis, e.g.

$$I_{x_i}^k = \mathbf{w}.\mathbf{E}, \text{ where}$$

$$\mathbf{E} = (E_1...E_{12}),$$

$$\mathbf{w} = \left(w1_{x_i}^k ... w12_{x_i}^k \right)$$

We can now perform a similarity comparison between images simply by comparing their corresponding weight vectors. Hence, the similarity S between two images $\left(I_{x_i}, I_{x_j} \right)$ is given by the Euclidean distance between their weight vectors:

$$S = \sqrt{\left((w1_{x_i} - w1_{x_j})^2 + ...(w12_{x_i} - w12_{x_j})^2 \right)}$$

In our experimental set-up, we do the following:

1) First determine how well $\left(I_{\bar{x}_i}^1 ... I_{\bar{x}_i}^5 \right)$ match $\left(I_{x_i}^1 ... I_{x_i}^{25} \right)$.

2) Then determine how well $\left(I_{y_j}^1 ... I_{y_j}^{30} \right)$ match $\left(I_{x_i}^1 ... I_{x_i}^{25} \right)$.

On the basis of similarity values, we then determine an appropriate threshold T such that we can filter out $\left(I_{y_j}^1 ... I_{y_j}^{30} \right)$ as novel.

The next step is to perform novelty detection based on the thresholding scheme- in the next section we show the matching results and novelty filtering.

23.4 Results

As described earlier, we have a data set consisting of 8 adults with 25 pose images for training and 5 different pose images for testing. A total of 4 different individuals are used as unknown people to test the novelty filter's capability. In Table 1 we show the results of matching the 40 samples of known people with the training set comprising of 200 images of the same individuals but in different poses. The least distance value is highlighted in each row, and it can be clearly seen that all 40 samples of known individuals are correctly assigned to their correct classes (100% accurate).

In this work we have employed the popular eigen-based face recognition approach [2]. Since we take unconstrained videos of human subjects working on their desks or walking in front of the camera, we have to first detect faces, and then perform the recognition/novelty filtering as an integrated fused step of analysis. The overall approach involves the following methodology.

Table 1 : Training Data

Test Data	Training Data (25 samples per person)							
	x_1	x_2	x_3	x_4	x_5	x_6	x_7	x_8
$\tilde{x}_1(1)$	82	322	515	2730	361	375	403	1257
$\tilde{x}_1(2)$	94	307	477	2134	369	399	461	870
$\tilde{x}_1(3)$	92	331	546	2201	342	337	407	934
$\tilde{x}_1(4)$	98	332	578	2338	394	277	413	972
$\tilde{x}_1(5)$	87	296	557	2590	351	309	366	1156
$\tilde{x}_2(1)$	255	215	492	2701	319	422	244	1251
$\tilde{x}_2(2)$	296	175	460	2865	320	525	253	1368
$\tilde{x}_2(3)$	355	85	457	3027	254	631	310	1505
$\tilde{x}_2(4)$	385	60	454	3056	241	657	289	1534
$\tilde{x}_2(5)$	356	67	450	3024	220	597	272	1484
$\tilde{x}_3(1)$	412	344	57	1924	570	559	743	786
$\tilde{x}_3(2)$	541	452	154	2290	369	658	450	1089
$\tilde{x}_3(3)$	373	336	56	2268	344	538	427	845
$\tilde{x}_3(4)$	384	329	216	2274	427	496	412	783
$\tilde{x}_3(5)$	568	447	64	3064	263	729	390	1580
$\tilde{x}_4(1)$	2035	2212	2232	207	2432	1386	2680	1398
$\tilde{x}_4(2)$	1771	2153	1990	72	2350	1126	2559	1154
$\tilde{x}_4(3)$	1656	2081	1902	73	2278	1010	2493	1049
$\tilde{x}_4(4)$	2330	2361	2411	151	2596	1676	2889	1517
$\tilde{x}_4(5)$	2186	2264	2299	257	2492	1536	2764	1446
$\tilde{x}_5(1)$	376	333	334	2569	202	480	302	1255
$\tilde{x}_5(2)$	420	366	309	2746	101	521	258	1366
$\tilde{x}_5(3)$	450	344	299	2927	98	621	283	1465
$\tilde{x}_5(4)$	561	373	318	3151	170	767	240	1628
$\tilde{x}_5(5)$	581	383	245	3200	202	793	228	1674
$\tilde{x}_6(1)$	251	326	343	1918	491	180	795	544
$\tilde{x}_6(2)$	297	343	523	2135	557	157	516	602
$\tilde{x}_6(3)$	235	369	490	2255	508	70	507	743
$\tilde{x}_6(4)$	248	366	494	2316	484	96	477	808
$\tilde{x}_6(5)$	235	350	490	2308	470	142	477	780

$\tilde{x}_7(1)$	554	295	335	3185	270	748	93	1655
$\tilde{x}_7(2)$	484	256	355	3080	254	630	155	1538
$\tilde{x}_7(3)$	402	270	313	2920	226	483	67	1382
$\tilde{x}_7(4)$	370	260	307	2734	199	346	73	1185
$\tilde{x}_7(5)$	379	223	325	2582	206	352	142	1027
$\tilde{x}_8(1)$	554	857	781	1314	1027	329	1213	78
$\tilde{x}_8(2)$	624	904	874	1376	1023	454	1194	200
$\tilde{x}_8(3)$	787	912	948	1457	1107	657	1212	102
$\tilde{x}_8(4)$	726	860	901	1476	1056	592	1180	142
$\tilde{x}_8(5)$	609	756	777	1554	941	451	1094	158

We next compute the degree of similarity between 120 images of 4 unknown people $(y_1,..., y_4)$ - 30 images per person, and the training data set (which contains 25 images of known 8 people, 200 images altogether).

Table 2. The minimum, maximum and mean distance of the closest matching face image of a person $(y_1,..., y_4)$ to the images of known people $(x_1,..., x_8)$.

Test Data	Training Data (25 samples per person)							
	x_1	x_2	x_3	x_4	x_5	x_6	x_7	x_8
y_1 min	1701	1781	1845	235	2026	1028	2368	914
max	2212	2820	2598	783	3072	1611	3302	1645
μ	1920	2304	2188	445	2548	1290	2805	1267
y_2 min	984	1165	982	304	1273	510	1503	584
max	2057	2598	2362	1134	2890	1435	3310	1343
μ	1537	1832	1700	710	2033	995	2273	937
y_3 min	891	979	891	945	1070	546	1228	464
max	1035	1324	1071	1579	1506	846	1734	726
μ	966	1107	963	1352	1215	740	1398	636
y_4 min	811	976	900	677	1100	333	1281	321
max	1887	2193	1969	1334	2494	1120	2714	1028
μ	1175	1458	1377	998	1694	664	1955	550

The results are summarized in Table 2 below which shows the Euclidean distances for the best matches. It can be easily seen that these distances are far larger than the distances shown shaded in Table 1. A threshold of 250 or above can easily novelty filter the unknown faces- only one mistake is made which is shaded (error of 1 in 120 images).

In the above results, we have shown that a reliable novelty filter can be built for face recognition. In future experiments, as the number of people are increased, the decision boundaries between known and unknown people can blur, and far more advanced novelty filters will be needed.

23.6 Conclusions

There is no doubt that future biometric applications will require novelty filtering. The quality of novelty filters will depend on how well a face can be detected in the first place, and how well an eigen-face based approach generates features that are discriminatory. Based on our experiments, we have shown that there is much promise in building novelty detection based systems for detecting unknown faces. In CCTV type surveillance applications, such knowledge can be used to spot unauthorized people in secure areas, and further technologies on human dynamics can be integrated to recognize their behavior. Our further work will now focus on replicating these results on much larger database.

References

[1] L. Sirovich and M. Kirby, (1987) "Low-dimensional procedure for the characterization of human faces," *Journal of the Optical Society Of America A*, 4(3), 519-524.
[2] M. Turk and A. Pentland, (1991) "Eigenfaces for Recognition", *Journal of Cognitive Neuroscience*.
[3] R.Gross, S.Baker, I.Matthews, and T.Kanade, (2004) "Face Recognition Across Pose and Illumination", *Handbook of Face Recognition*.
[4] Cendrillon, Raphael, Lovell and Brian, (2000) "Real-time face recognition using eigenfaces", *Visual Communications and Image Processing*, vol. 4067, pp. 269-276.
[5] L. Lorente, L. Torres, (1998) "A global eigen approach for face recognition", *International Workshop on Very Low Bit-rate Video coding*, Urbana, Illinois, Octorber 8-9.
[6] A. Pentland, B. Moghaddam, T. Starner, (1994) "View-based and modular eigenspaces for face recognition", *IEEE Conf. on Computer Vision and Pattern Recognition*.
[7] A. Nairac, T. Corbett-Clark, R. Ripley, N. Townsend and L. Tarassenko, (1997) "Choosing an appropriate model for novelty detection", *Proc. 5th ICANN, UK*, pp. 227-232.
[8] S. Singh and M. Markou, (2004) "An Approach to Novelty Detection applied to the Classification of Image Regions", *IEEE Transactions on Knowledge and Data Engineering*, vol. 16, issue 4, pp. 396-406.
[9] M. Markou and S. Singh, (2006) "A Neural Network based Novelty Detector for Video Analysis", *IEEE Transactions on Pattern Analysis and Machine Intelligence*, vol. 28, no. 10, pp. 1664-1677.

[10] C.K. Chow, (1970) "On optimum rejection error and reject tradeoff", *IEEE Transactions on Information Theory*, vol. 16, no. 1, pp. 41-46.

[11] L.K. Hansen, C. Liisberg and P. Salamon, (1997) "The error-reject tradeoff", *Open Systems and Information Dynamics*, vol. 4, pp. 159-184.

[12] P. Foggia, C. Sansone, F. Tortorella, and M. Vento, (1999) "Multiclassification: reject criteria for the Bayesian combiner", *Pattern Recognition*, volume 32, pp. 1435-1447.

[13] G. Fumera, F. Roli and G. Giacinto, (2000) "Reject option with multiple thresholds", *Pattern Recognition*, volume 33, pp. 2099-2101.

[14] C. Bishop, (1994) "Novelty detection and neural network validation", *Proc. IEE Conference on Vision and Image Signal Processing*, pp. 217-222.

[15] L. Tarassenko, (1995) "Novelty detection for the identification of masses in mammograms", *Proc. 4th ICANN Conference*, vol. 4, pp. 442-447.

[16] D.M.J. Tax and R.P.W. Duin, (1999) "Support vector domain description", *Pattern Recognition Letters*, vol. 20, pp. 1191-1199.

[17] S.J. Roberts and W. Penny, (1996) "Novelty, confidence and errors in connectionist systems", *In Proc. IEE Colloquium on Intelligent Sensors and Fault Detection*, no. 1996/261.

[18] D. Dasgupta and F.A. Gonzalez, (2001) "An immunogenetic approach to intrusion detection", Dept. of Computer Science, University of Memphis, Report No. CS-01-001.

[19] S. Singh, M. Markou and J.F. Haddon, (2000) "Detection of new image objects in video sequences using neural networks", *Proc. SPIE Electronic Imaging '2000*, San Jose, pp. 204-213.

[20] J. Lamirel, M. Crehange and J. Dulcoy, (1994) "NOMAD: a documentary database interrogation system using multiple neural topographies and novelty detection", *Advances in Knowledge Organisation*, vol. 4, pp. 334-341.

[21] C. Surace, K. Worden and G. Tomlinson, (1997) "A novelty detection approach to diagnose damage in a cracked beam", *Proc. of SPIE*, vol. 3089, pp. 947-953.

[22] M. Markou, and S. Singh, (2003) "Novelty Detection- A Review: Part 1: Statistical Approaches", *Signal Processing*, vol. 83, pp. 2481-2497.

[23] M. Markou, and S. Singh, (2003) "Novelty Detection- A Review: Part 2: Neural Network Based Approaches", *Signal Processing*, vol. 83, pp. 2499-2521.

[24] T. Horprasert, D. Harwood and L.S. Davis, (1999) "A statistical approach for real-time robust background subtraction and shadow detection", *IEEE ICCV'99 frame-rate workshop*.

[25] M.J. Jones and J.M. Rehg (1999). "Statistical color models with application to skin detection", *Computer Vision and Pattern Recognition Conference*.

[26] H.A. Beveridge, and R.P. Carlyon, (1996) Effects of aspirin on human psychophysical tuning curves in forward and simultaneous masking. Hear. Res. 99, 110-118.

[27] Rajkiran, Gottumukkal and Vijayan K. Asari, (2004) "an improved face recognition technique based on modular PCA approach", *Pattern Recognition Letters*, vol. 25, issue. 4, pp 429-436.

[28] S. Srinivasan and K.L. Boyer, (2002) "Head Pose Estimation Using View Based Eigenspaces", *International Conference on Pattern Recognition*.

[29] W. Zhao, R. Chellappa, P. J. Phillips, and A. Rosenfeld. (2003) "Face recognition: A literature survey", *Source ACM computing Surveys*, vol. 12, pp. 399-458.

24 Using Timing to Detect Horror Shots in Horror Movies*

Min Xu[1], Jesse S. Jin[1], Suhuai Luo[1], and Qingming Huang[2]

[1] School of Design, Communication and IT, University of Newcastle, Australia,
 M.Xu@studentmail.newcastle.edu.au, Jesse.Jin,Suhuai.Luo@newcastle.edu.au
[2] Digital Media Lab, Institute of Computing Technology, Chinese Academy of Sciences,
 Beijing, China, qmhuang@jdl.ac.cn

Summary. Affective content directly attracts an user's attention, appreciation and memory which also provides feasible entry for video highlights. Different from the existing movie emotion detection which makes use of traditional features, we introduce timing to detect horror shots in horror movies. From movie's point of view, timing is an important feature of movies and an important part of their power to affect viewers' feelings and emotions which talks about duration and duration relationship between frames. Shot-length and motion intensity are used to represent duration and duration relationship respectively. Decision tree is used for classification. Later, post-processing reduces both the classification error and human errors in subjective labeling on experimental data. Experimental data includes 4.5 hours video from 3 horror movies. Experimental results show that timing is effective and efficient to detect horror shots.

24.1 Introduction

The increasing amount of multimedia data desiderates intelligent indexing and retrieval systems which can support the interaction between human and multimedia database. Most of the existing approaches focus on video analysis which is conducted on three aspects: 1) low-level feature analysis; 2) video structuring and 3) event detection and semantics modeling. These works try to provide feasible entries to manage and access multimedia databases. However, there is a gap between video structure or semantics and users' sensation or perception. In multimedia field, users may prefer "emotional decisions" to find affective content because emotional factors directly reflect an audience's attention and evaluation. Nowadays, multimedia affective computing attracts more and more research efforts. The existing works try to detect emotions from speech [1], textual input [2], facial expression [4], music [3] and so on.

In the emotional landscape of the modern world, the movie theater occupies a central place, as one of the predominant spaces where audiences gather to express and

* This research is partially supported by National Hi-Tech Research and Development Program (863 Program) of China under grant No. 2006AA01Z117.

experience feelings. Emotions are carefully packaged and sold with movies, but they are rarely analyzed with much specificity. Movie emotion detection occupied dominant role in multimedia affective computing. In [5], Alan et. al. utilized the features of motion, color, and audio to represent arousal and valence. Kang [6] employed HMM to mapped low level visual features to high level emotional events (i.e. fear, sadness and joy). Our previous work [7, 8] use audio and subtitle to detect emotions from films.

Those works take use of traditional features for video analysis. According to movie theory, timing is an important feature of films and an important part of their power to affect viewers' feelings and emotions. In particular, timing is the duration and durational relationships between and among parts of a film to which one is exposed when the film is presented in its canonical mode. [9]. Shot-length is an efficient representation for duration of similar images. Durational relationship talks about the relationship between or among images. In this paper, we consider to represent duration relationship by motion intensity, since from durational relationships' point of view, a sudden, explosive motion produces a startle response.

As a movie genre, horror movie packaged with strong emotions which cause audiences' strong reactions or special horrible experiences. In this paper, we try to use timing features, namely, shot-length and motion intensity to detect affective content (horror shots) in horror movie. Decision trees are used for classify movie shots into horror and plain. Through the experiments, we prove that timing which is introduced by movie theories as an important feature to affect viewers' feelings and emotions provides a feasible way for affective content detection.

Section 2 introduce the timing features in detail. Section 3 gives details of our decision tree structure and related parameters. Post-processing is described in section 4. Section 5 introduced our experiments and related results. Some conclusion and future work is discussed in section 6.

24.2 Timing Features

In the section, shot-length and motion intensity are introduced as timing features.

24.2.1 Duration: Shot-length

According to movie theory, duration do with length of time (duration) of an image. A video shot is created of a series of frames, which runs for an uninterrupted period of time. The frames from one shot have more similarity than the frames from different shots. Therefore, we use the shot-length to represent duration feature. We have the experience that the shot duration in a film can directly affect our emotional or felling responses to the film. Fast-paced montage and rapid cross-cutting often work directly to create feelings of excitement, so that an effect can be produced without requiring us to think. On the other hand, if the duration of an image is longer than one might expect, we might think about why the shot continues for so long.

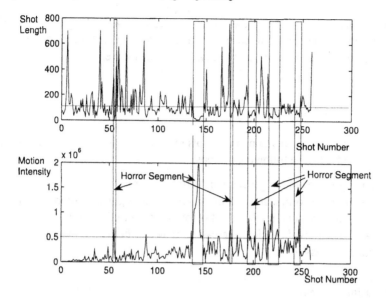

Fig. 1. The relationship between shot-length, motion intensity and horror segments.

In this paper, we use the frame number to represent shot-length, which indicates how many frames in the shot. The shot detector output the starting frame for each shot. Shot-length SL is calculated by $SL = N_i - N_{i-1}$, where N_i is the starting frame of shot i. Figure 1 shows the relationship between shot-length and horror segments. We can find that the horror segments mostly take place along with the shot changing fast i.e. short shot-length.

24.2.2 Durational Relationship: Motion Intensity

Durational relationship talks about the relationship between or among images. In this paper, we consider representing duration relationship by average motion intensity within one shot because of the following two considerations: 1) from durational relationships' point of view, a sudden, explosive motion produces a startle response; 2) motion is estimated from the difference between two frames.

Motion intensity roughly estimates the gross motion in the whole frame, including object and camera motion. Motion intensity MV is computed as the average magnitude of motion vectors in a frame:

$$MV = \frac{1}{\Phi} \sum_{\Phi} \sqrt{v_x^2 + v_y^2} \tag{1}$$

where $\Phi = \{inter - coded\ macro - blocks\}$, and $\mathbf{v} = [v_x, v_y]$ is the motion vector for each macro-block. Then the average motion intensity is calculated for the whole shot.

From Figure 1, we find that the horror segments always take place in the shots where the motion intensity are relative high because high motion intensity easily catch our intension and make us nervous while we watch the movie.

24.3 Decision Tree

Decision trees are powerful and popular tools for classification [10]. We choose decision trees considering the following reasons:

1. Decision trees are able to generate understandable rules.
2. Decision trees perform classification without requiring much computation.
3. Decision trees are good in classification problems with two class.
4. Decision trees provide a clear indication of which fields are most important for prediction or classification.

24.3.1 Decision Tree Structure

We use C4.5 to generate the decision tree (See Figure 2). The output of attributes' values for decision points are the values after normalization. To help understand the rules of decision, the original values are shown in Figure 2.

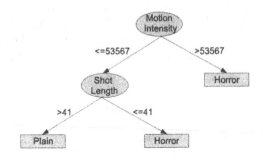

Fig. 2. The decision tree.

24.4 Post-processing

Note that video itself has a continuous existence and humans normally make decisions about emotions within a certain time video segment. Any sudden change in the shot sequences can be considered as an error. Hence, we exploit a sliding window to eliminate those sudden changes by majority-voting on the emotion type from a sequence of shot-based classification results. Alterable sliding window length w_l and step-size w_s

are defined experientially. In our case, we set $w_l = 4$ and $w_s = 1$. Algorithm 1 shows how to detect the error and correct it. The error is judged by continuous two sliding windows. An example of post-processing is shown in Figure 3. In the first sliding window, question mark label the location of a possible error. Then the window slides to justify the error. The smile face means keep the current value.

Algorithm 1 Post-processing (H_i: Horror shot number within the sliding window i; P_i: Plain shot number within the sliding window i)

---

   if $H_i > P_i$ and $H_{i+1} > P_{i+1}$ **then**
      P is changed by H;
   else if $H_i < P_i$ and $H_{i+1} < P_{i+1}$ **then**
      H is changed by P;
   end if

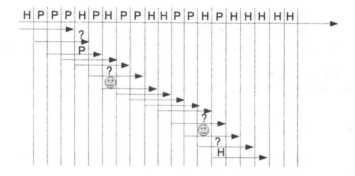

Fig. 3. The example of post-processing

24.5 Experiments

In this section, we will introduce the details of experiments including data preparation and experimental results.

24.5.1 Data Collection and Labeling

The movies from different countries more or less exhibit different cultures of those countries. As we know, the style of Hollywood movies is extremely different from Bollywood's. To eliminate subjective factors potentially, we try to select horror movies directed by different directors from different countries. Three horror movies are selected for experiments, which are "The ring (US version)", Japanese "one missed call" and Korean "face".

We ask 10 students (5 male, 5 female) from different departments to watch each movie twice. At the second time, when they are watching the segments which make them feel horrible, they will pause the video and write down the start time and end time of the horror segments. Later, according to the labeled time, we find the corresponding video shots and label them as *Horror* shots. The rest of the shots are labeled as *Plain* shots.

The total length of the horror movie is around 4.5 hours which contains 3018 shots.

24.5.2 Experimental Setting

The values of motion intensity distribute from 2046 to 6522836 while the values shot-length distribute from 4 to 762. Data normalization is a process in which data attributes within a data model are organized to increase the cohesion of entity types. In our experiments, feature dimension is normalized with respect to its mean and variance.

Three groups of experiments are designed to compare the individual contribution of each feature.

- Only motion intensity is used to construct a decision tree.
- Only shot-length is used to construct a decision tree.
- Motion intensity and shot-length are used together to construct a decision tree.

For each group, the experiments runs 10 times by randomly selecting two third for training and one third for testing. The the average of 10 times outputs is calculated.

24.5.3 Experimental Results

The experiments of three groups are listed in Table 1. Moreover, the results after post processing can be find in the last line of Table 1.

Table 1. Experimental results of different experimental groups

	Experimental groups	Correct	Incorrect	Precision	Recall
	Using motion Intensity	2069	949	87.18%	58.6%
Before Post-processing	Using shot-length	1989	1028	72.3%	40.9%
	Using both	2387	631	85.72%	69.9%
After Post-processing	Using both	2546	472	87.69%	73.3%

24.5.4 Discussion

From Table 1, we find that motion intensity plays an important role of horror shots detection. Compared to high precision motion intensity achieved, the recall is not satisfactory. It might because some of the horror effects are emphasized by fast shot changing instead of high motion within the shot. Fortunately, shot-length later be used on the second level of decision tree compensates the motion intensity for some of missed detections. However, the increase of recall costs the decrease of precision.

If we compare the results of after post-processing with the results of before post-processing, it is obvious that post-processing improves both recall and precision dramatically. Since our emotions cannot suddenly change from one state to the other state, the person who label the data probably still feel fear when the video scene become milder and milder. Post-processing improve the recall and precision by revising both the classification error and human errors in subjective labeling.

From the result of "after post-processing", we find the recall is still not as good as precision. It implies using motion intensity and shot-length can detect horror segments precisely instead of completely. In order to achieve higher recall, we have to seek the help from other features, such as brightness, audio pitch, and so on.

24.6 Conclusion

We used timing related features to train a decision tree for horror shots detection. Through experiments, timing features have been proved to be effective for horror shots detection, namely shot-length and motion intensity. Moreover, decision trees are well performed in this work. In future, we will extend the work to detect more emotional events, such as cheer, sad, etc. To achieve a higher recall rate, more features from different modalities, such as audio pitch, will be considered.

References

Lee, C.M. and Narayanan, S.S. (2005 March) Toward detecting emotions in spoken dialogs. IEEE Transactions on speech and audio proceeding. VOL. 13, No. 2, 293–303.

Zhang, Y., Li, Z., Ren, F. and Kuroiwa, S Semi-automatic emotion recognition from textual input based on the constructed emotion thesaurus. In proceeding of IEEE INternational Conference on Natural Language Processing and Knowledge Engineering 2005, 571–576.

Li, T. and Ogihara, M. (2004) Content-based music similarity search and emotion detection. In proceeding of IEEE International Conference on Acoustics, Speech, and Signal Processing 2004.

Chen, C.Y., Huang, Y.K. and Cook, P. Visual/Acoustic emotion recognition. In proceding of IEEE International Conference on Multimedia and Expo, 2005

Hanjalic, A. and Xu,L.Q. User-oriented Affective Video Content Analysis. In Proceeding of IEEE Workshop on Content-Based Access of Image and Video Libraries 2001.

Kang, H.B. Affective Content Detection using HMMs. In Proceeding of ACM Multimedia 2003.

Xu, M., Chia, L.T. and Jin, J.S. Affective content analysis in comedy and horror videos by audio emotional event detection. In proceeding of IEEE International Conference on Multimedia & Expo 2005.

Xu, M., Chia, L.T., Yi, H. and Rajan, D. Affective content detection in sitcom using subtitle and audio. In proceeding of IEEE International Conference on Multimedia Modeling 2006.

Plantinga, C. and Smith, G.M. Passionate views: film, cognition, and emotion. The Johns Hopkins University Press, Baltimore & London 1999.

Mitchell, T. M. Machine learning. WCB/McGraw, 1997.

25 Indoor/Outdoor Scene Classification using Audio and Video Features

José Lopes, and Sameer Singh

Research School Of Informatics
Loughborough University
Loughborough, UK
{J.e.f.c.Lopes,S.Singh}@lboro.ac.uk

Abstract: Indoor/Outdoor scene classification is an important field that has been addressed either as an image or audio processing problem. Combining audio and image processing for understanding video content has several benefits when compared to using each modality on their own. In this paper we describe an indoor/outdoor recognition model that explores the fusion of audio and video systems. With this purpose, we extract a range of audio and visual features, followed by feature reduction and classification. We show that combining audio with video system decision improves the quality of indoor/outdoor recognition in videos by 3% over an audio-only system and 4% over an image-only system.

25.1 Introduction

Video understanding is a significant research field that has important practical application in areas such as Biometrics, Content Based Video Retrieval, Video Security and Autonomous Robotics. The classification of visual scenes as Indoor or Outdoor is a much researched topic often serving as a basis for further sub-categorization in digital imaging understanding (Vailaya, Jain and Zhang 1998). In parallel, in the audio field, some studies have tried to address the same problem using audio samples only. There is, however, a need to investigate the benefits of combining these data modalities to take advantage of the fact that video sequences often contain them both.

The classification of images as indoor/outdoor problem has been extensively studied. It is a difficult problem due to the complexity and variability that images can present. For example, similar objects can be present both in indoors and outdoor scenes (e.g. people, plants). Also, illumination, in both cases, spans a high dynamic range and object clutter can offer further difficulty in producing a clear distinction. Solutions to indoor/outdoor discrimination often use colour, texture and shape features, typically performing a combination of features as a descriptor for classification or retrieval. High classification rates have been reported in most studies, with a small variation depending on the specific features, database and optimization of the classification scheme (Szummer and Picard, 1998).

Audio scene understanding is a growing field and so, there is a limited number of studies that address the indoor/outdoor problem from an audio perspective. Most often, audio studies concern with discriminating between music, speech and noise (Li, Sethi, Dimitrova and McGee, 2001). Nevertheless, a few studies have begun addressing the identification of natural environmental context. There is a great heterogeneity in terms of the data collected and its labeling. More often than not, authors use a database of sparsely populated categories and eventually group them in meta-classes after analysis of the results. Common features extracted from the data include mel-frequency spectral coefficients (MFCC) and LPC analysis (Peltonen, Tuomi, Klapuri, Huopaniemi and Sorsa 2002). Similarly to the image processing case, the solutions depend on the classification methodology used as much as the proposed features.

Multimodal data analysis is becoming a popular tool for a variety of applications. It has roots in Human-Computer Interaction, and fields such as Person Recognition, Video Segmentation, Robotics, Biometrics have take advantage of sophisticated fusion techniques that gather data from different data sources and combine it for enhanced results. In the last few years, it has become possible to truly develop such systems as the cost of processing data from different sensors has fallen, allowing real-time data analysis for these applications.

This integration can take many forms such as transfer, equivalence, specialization, redundancy and complementarity (Martin, Veldman and Beroule 1998). Several approaches to audio and video fusion have been suggested in the literature. These can be classified into three main groups: data fusion, feature fusion and decision fusion depending on the stage of the classification system where the integration is established (Lopes and Singh 2006).

25.2 Problem Description

This work addresses the problem of discriminating as indoor or outdoor, the environment of natural and highly unconstrained videos of day-to-day situations. As a part of a broader study in video understanding, we use a video database that covers a diverse number of situations where both audio and video cues are present. More specifically, the videos contain instances of the following:

- Car – a vehicle driving past;
- Clap – a person clapping his/hers hands;
- Door – a person opening, going through and closing a door;
- Step – a person walking;
- Talk – a person talking;
- Train – a train going past;
- Type – a person typing at a keyboard.

This video database was collected using a digital video camera. The only constraint is the fact that only one object has spatial movement in the scene. Each of these sample video clips was later reduced to 8 seconds in length. The audio signal was extracted and saved in a mono, uncompressed PCM .wav file, sampled at 44.1 kHz at 16 bits. One of the major problems with audio analysis is the presence of background noise. We decided not to perform any preprocessing to remove such noise because of the risks involved with affecting the signal of interest and the difficulty in modeling the differences between the signal of interest and other signals. The database used contained 50 samples (videos) per activity – a total of 350 samples.

Fig 1. Scene image examples. Top row – outdoor; bottom row – indoor.

The data was labeled as 'indoor' or 'outdoor'. Specifically, all 'car' and 'train' samples are 'outdoor'; all 'door' and 'type' samples are 'indoor'; 'clap' is 'indoor' except in 2 cases; 'step' contains 34 instances of 'indoor' and 16 of 'outdoor' and 'talk' is 'indoor' except for 3 cases. In total, there are 229 samples of 'indoor' and 121 of 'outdoor'.

Figure 1 shows examples of scene images from the database. A preliminary inspection of the images reveals a lot of variability in terms of lighting properties, colour distribution and shape of the objects present in the scene. There are, nevertheless some properties that may be explored, such as most outdoor images contain a region of sky and natural objects such as plants and rocks. Indoor scenes are more artificial and streamlined, presenting a higher amount of objects delimited by straight edges.

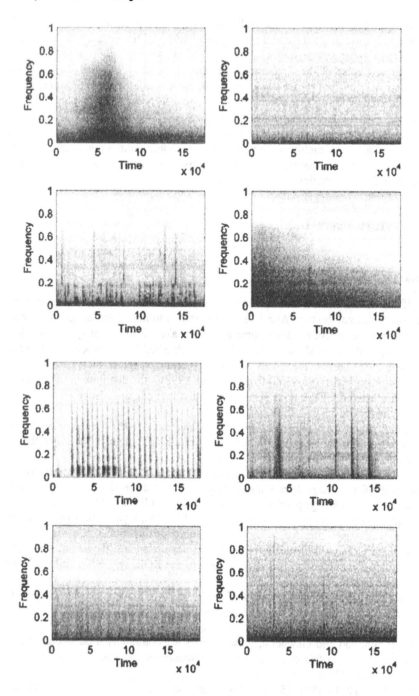

Fig 2. Scene spectrogram examples. Top 4 examples – outdoor; bottom 4 examples – indoor.

Figure 2 shows example of the audio spectrogram from the database. A preliminary visual inspection of the audio signal gives an idea of the difficulty in automatically distinguishing indoor from outdoor signals. In some cases, the simple amount of energy and noise of the signal might be enough to identify some outdoor cases where cars or trains are present. In other cases, more subtle cues are required, especially when considering that similar audio events can occur both indoors and outdoors (e.g. people talking and people walking).

As a result, the automatic description of a video scene as indoor or outdoor based on these modalities is highly challenging and can benefit from a combined strategy. In the next section we describe the audio and visual features extracted from videos and discuss their correlation.

25.3 Feature Extraction

25.3.1 Visual Features

Classifying indoor and outdoor scenes is usually done using low-level visual features based on colour and texture. Also it is quite common to divide the image in separate blocks to reduce the computation complexity and take advantage of spatial information (Vailaya et al. 1998). A number of well-established image processing features were computed to reflect the scenes' colour and texture characteristics:

Colour Histograms (v1-v320) (Vailaya et al. 1998) – the distribution of pixel colours in a clustered HSV colour space. These distributions are computed over 5 regions of the image.

Colour Coherence Vector (v321-v960) (Vailaya et al. 1998) – a colour histogram that includes information about the coherency of a pixel colour in the sense that its neighbours are of similar colour.

Edge Direction Histograms (v961-v1033) (Vailaya et al. 1998) – edges are extracted using Canny edge detection and image texture is defined as the distribution of the direction of each edge pixel with an extra dimension for non-edge pixels.

Edge Direction Coherence Vector (v1034-1178) (Vailaya et al. 1998) – again, this distribution uses information about neighbour edge direction.

Colour Spaces (v1179-v1286) – statistics (mean, standard deviation, skewness, kurtosis, entropy and energy) of each channel of the RGB, rgb, YIQ, HSI, TSL and LCH colour spaces.

Laws Masks (v1287-v1736) (Laws 1980) – the RGB channels were convoluted with 5x5 Laws masks to enhance texture structure and statistics computed.

Colour Moments (v1737-v 1741) (Mindru, Moons and Van Gool 1999) – invariant to illumination and viewpoint, these features are commonly used in characterizing object colour, in this case we use it to characterize the whole image (we used feature set G from Mindru et al. 1999).

Wavelet (v1741-v1885) (Sonka, Hlavac and Boyle 1999) – we computed the statistics on the coefficients resulting from discrete wavelet decomposition to 3 levels using Daubechies basis functions.

Canny Edge Count (v1886-v1965) – the quantity of edge pixels relative to the size of the image for different parameters of Canny edge detection.

Object Colour Models (v1967-v1972) – for each of 7 classes of objects (building, bush, car, road, rock, sky and water) we extracted an extensive collection of object images from the MIT's LabelMe database (Russell, Torralba, Murphy and Freeman 2005). A distribution of pixel colours was computed for each class as well as with a model of all objects that do not belong to it. For each model, we count the pixels in an image that are more probable to belong to the object than not.

25.3.2 Audio Features

Signal and audio processing are mature fields with several well-established, reliable techniques. Past studies propose using MFCC or LPC as good scene recognition features (Peltonen et al. 2002). We extended that set and computed several popular audio features to be included in our machine learning system. These are:

MFCC (a1-a1020) (Boersma 1993) – The Mel Frequency Cepstral Coefficients emphasize the lower frequencies which are perceptually more meaningful in speech.

LPC (a1021-a1375) (Hu and Hwant 2002) – Linear Predictive Coefficients exploit the auto-correlated characteristics of the input waveform by estimating the value of the current sample using a linear combination of the previous samples.

Gabor (a1376-a1730) (Hu and Hwant 2002) – The Gabor function is widely used as a filter and as a basis function for de-correlation. For this study, the signals were Gabor filtered and then the main LPC coefficients were used as features.

Silence and VDR (a1731, a1732) (Liu and Wang 1998) – based on Volume Contour (VC – divide the signal into overlapping frames and take the Root Mean Square of the signal magnitude in each frame). Silence reports the ratio between the period of time with low VC and the time with high VC. VDR corresponds to VC range.

HPS (a1733) (Boersma 1993) – Harmonic Product Spectrum is a methodology employed to approximate fundamental frequency f0.

FQC (a1734-a1823) (Liu and Wang 1998) – Frequency Centroid. This feature represents the clarity of the signal by evaluating the centre of each frequency domain obtained by the Fourier transform and the magnitude information.

Bandwidth Features BW (a1824 – a1913) (Liu and Wang 1998) – This includes the width between two frequency bands and over the whole signal. For the purpose of this work, it represents the width of the smallest frequency band within which a signal can fit. This uses the frequency centroid value of each time component.

FCVC4 (a1914) (Liu and Wang 1998) – Frequency Component of the Volume Contour around 4Hz.

Power (a1915-a2014) (Liu and Wang 1998) – The power spectrum is the energy present in the signal's Fourier transform.

HER features – the High Energy Region uses the spectrogram of the audio signal. It is defined by the highest energy, together with the left and right thresholds defined as a fraction of that maximum. Features are computed within this region as:

- Duration (a2015) – The duration of the HER;
- Peak value itself (a2016);

- Area (a2017) – The energy area within the HER:

$$(\forall f \in spec : energy_f = \sum_{w \in f} |A_w|, \text{ where } f \text{ is a frame, } w \text{ is frequency and } A_w$$

the corresponding Fourier coefficient);

- Average Distance (a2018) between peaks. This is achieved by finding other high energy peaks and computing their average temporal distance;

- Spectogram Moment (a2019) – is defined as $\sum_{f,w \in HER} |A_w| \times d((f,w),\mu)$,

where $\mu = \left(\underset{f \in HER}{mean(f)}, \underset{f \in HER}{mean(w)} \right)$ and $d(.)$ is the Euclidean distance.

In addition, we compute the previous features within this region (sMFCC, sLPC, sGabor, sVDR, sSilence, sHPS, sFQC, sBW, sFCVC4 and sPower) (a2019-a4033).

25.3.3 Data Analysis

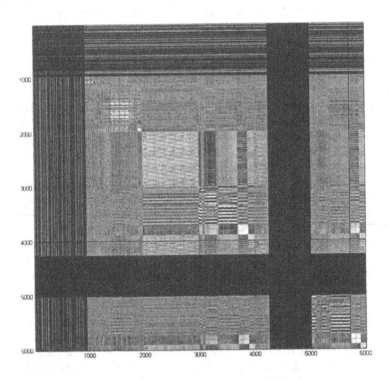

Fig. 3. Correlation matrix of video and audio features

Figure 3 shows the correlation matrix in a graphical form for the entire 6005 feature set (1972 video + 4033 audio). Each pixel represents a correlation value and rows and columns of pixels (left to right, top to bottom) index the features in ascending order. Brighter areas denote high correlation. The matrix presents a block diagonal structure, suggesting some dependency between features of each set and, more importantly, low correlation between features of different modalities. Also, some features are constant across all samples (black bands).

This figure shows that there are several regions of high image intensity confirming that there is high correlation amongst features and sufficient scope for removing redundant features. This is the property we intend to explore – that by selecting features from different sets, the recognition rate will improve.

25.4 Experimental Setup

25.4.1 Feature Selection

As seen in the previous section, there is redundancy and irrelevancy in the data. This fact allied with the fact that data dimensionality is very high, creates an argument for performing some form of feature selection. For this purpose, we use the Sequential Forward Floating Selection (SFFS) algorithm (Pudil, Navovicova and Kittler 1994). The measure of separability used for SFFS was the success rate of a leave-one-out kNN classifier using all the training data.

Feature selection is performed separately for the video and audio feature groups. The number of features selected (5) was chosen empirically such as to reach a compromise between classification rate and redundancy. Too few features are not able to describe the data and too many provide no new information.

In the case of video, features selected were from the following sets:

- v1361 – Laws mask;
- v1258 – TSL Colour Space;
- v1849 – Wavelet;
- v1068 – Edge Direction Coherence Vector;
- v1958 – Canny Edge Count.

This shows a balance between colour and texture features, which agrees with literature suggestions that solutions to indoor/outdoor require a combination of different features (Szummer et al. 1998).

In the audio case, features selected were from the following sets:

- a2017 – HER Area;
- a781 – MFCC;
- a3402 – sGabor;
- a785 – MFCC;
- a3194 – sLPC;

The first feature is directly related with the energy of the event present in the scene as hypothesized in section 2. As concluded in previous work (Peltonen et al. 2002) MFCC coefficients are good discriminant features for scene recognition.

25.4.2 Classification

All classification experiments were performed using a leave-one-out strategy, in order to maximize the confidence of the result. For each sample, we use the remainder of the database (349 samples) as training data and use the sample to test the classifier. Success rate measures the quantity of samples that were correctly classified and a confusion matrix is presented for further detail.

With the appropriate features are selected, in order to study the benefit of combining both modalities, we compare the performance of different systems using the same classification setup. A Bayesian classifier was chosen for all experiments (Domingos and Pazzani 1997). The class-conditional distributions $P_{X|Y}$ are modeled by a simple Gaussian Mixture Model and the *a priory* probabilities are estimated by the relative occurrences in the data. The *a posteriori* probability is used to discriminate between the two (Indoor and Outdoor) classes. All experiments were performed using the selected 5 features using SFFS.

The video classifier shows a 90% success rate for the confusion matrix in table 1.

	Indoor	Outdoor
Indoor	213	17
Outdoor	16	104

Table 1. Video confusion matrix.

The audio classifier shows a 91% success rate for the confusion matrix in table 2.

	Indoor	Outdoor
Indoor	226	4
Outdoor	25	95

Table 2. Audio confusion matrix.

It is apparent that although the audio classifier seems better, it makes more mistakes in the outdoor case, which the video classifier seems better at. This fact suggests that the combination of the strengths of both modalities can produce a better result yet.

With that objective, we implemented classifier fusion at the decision level. We achieve this by using the *a posteriori* likelihoods of each classifier and combining them using the sum rule as proposed in (Kittler et al.,1998). This improves the success rate to 94% for the confusion matrix in table 3.

	Indoor	Outdoor
Indoor	226	4
Outdoor	14	106

Table 3. Decision fusion confusion matrix.

This result is an indication of the strength of the use of separate modalities in video scene description, in this particular case, audio and video.

25.5 Conclusion

In this paper we have performed exhaustive experimentation to demonstrate that audio-visual information can be effectively combined for robust classification of unconstrained video sequences as indoor/outdoor. We have performed a detailed analysis on a large number of videos by extracting a large number of features. Our results demonstrate that substantial classification gains are possible using decision level fusion. This process is very important to the future of biometrics and autonomous systems (e.g. multi-modal environment analysis to analyse context and human/machine/object behaviour. Our future work will describe video context in more detail by analysing objects present and their corresponding activities in unconstrained videos.

References

Boersma, P. (1993) Accurate Short-Term Analysis of the Fundamental Frequency and the Harmonics-to-Noise Ratio of a Sampled Sound, Institute of Phonetic Sciences, University of Amsterdam, Proceedings 17.

Domingos, P. and Pazzani M. (1997) On the optimality of the simple Bayesian classifier under zero-one loss, Machine Learning, 29:103–137.

Hu, Y. H. and Hwant, J.-N. (2002) *Handbook of Neural Network Signal Processing*, CRC Press.

Kittler, J., Hatef, M., Duin R.P.W. and Matas, J. (1998) On Combining Classifiers, IEEE Transactions on Pattern Analysis and Machine Intelligence, vol. 20(3), pp. 226-239.

Laws, K.I. (1980) Textured image segmentation, Ph.D. thesis, University of Southern California.

Li, D., Sethi, I.K., Dimitrova, N. and McGee, T. (2001) Classification of general audio data for content-based retrieval, PRL(22), No. 5, pp. 533-544.

Liu, Z. and Wang, Y. (1998) Audio Feature Extraction and Analysis for Scene Segmentation and Classification, Journal of VLSI Signal Processing, pp. 61-79.

Lopes, J. and Singh, S. (2006) Audio and Video Feature Fusion for Activity Recognition in Unconstrained Videos, International Conference on Intelligent Data Engineering and Automated Learning, 2006.

Martin, J.C., Veldman, R. and Beroule, D. (1998) Developing multimodal interfaces: a theoretical framework and guided propagation networks, In Multimodal Human-Computer Communication. H. Bunt, R.J. Beun, & T. Borghuis, (Eds.).

Mindru, F., Moons T. and Van Gool L. (1999) Recognizing color patterns irrespective of viewpoint and illumination, Proc. IEEE Conf. on Computer Vision and Pattern Recognition, CVPR99, pp. 368-373.

Payne, A., Singh, S. (2005) Indoor vs. Outdoor Scene Classification in Digital Photographs, Pattern Recognition, No 6, pp. 919-934.

Peltonen, V., Tuomi, J., Klapuri, A., Huopaniemi, J. and Sorsa, T. (2002) Computational Auditory Scene Recognition, IEEE International Conference on Audio, Speech and Signal Processing, Orlando, Florida.

Pudil, P., Navovicova, J. and Kittler, J. (1994) Floating search methods in feature selection, Pattern Recognition Letters, 15, 1119-1125.

Russell, B. C., Torralba, A., Murphy, K. P. and Freeman W. T. (2005) LabelMe: a database and web-based tool for image annotation. MIT AI Lab Memo AIM-2005-025.

Sonka, M., Hlavac, V. and Boyle, R. (1999) *Image Processing, Analysis and Machine Vision,* Brooks/Cole.

Szummer, M. and Picard, R. (1998) Indoor-Outdoor Image Classification, IEEE International Workshop on Content-Based Access of Image and Video Databases, ICCV98.

Vailaya, A., Jain, A. and Zhang H. J. (1998) On Image Classification: City Images vs. Landscapes, CBAIVL98, 3-8.

Author Index